White Man's Work

White Man's Work

*Race and Middle-Class Mobility
into the Progressive Era*

Joseph O. Jewell

The University of North Carolina Press CHAPEL HILL

Set in Merope Basic by Westchester Publishing Services

Manufactured in the United States of America

Library of Congress Cataloging-in-Publication Data

Names: Jewell, Joseph O., 1969– author.

Title: White man's work : race and middle-class mobility into the
   progressive era / Joseph O. Jewell.

Description: Chapel Hill : The University of North Carolina Press, 2023. |
   Includes bibliographical references and index.

Identifiers: LCCN 2023034106 | ISBN 9781469673486 (cloth ; alk. paper) |
   ISBN 9781469673493 (paperback ; alk. paper) | ISBN 9781469673509 (ebook)

Subjects: LCSH: Middle class—United States. | Social mobility—United
   States. | Minorities—United States—Social conditions. | White supremacy
   (Social structure) | United States—Race relations—History—
   20th century. | United States—Race relations—History—
   19th century. | BISAC: SOCIAL SCIENCE / Race & Ethnic
   Relations | POLITICAL SCIENCE / History & Theory

Classification: LCC HN57 .J494 2023 | DDC 305.5/50973—dc23/eng/20230907

LC record available at https://lccn.loc.gov/2023034106

Cover photos (top to bottom): Lee Toy (*San Francisco Chronicle*,
January 27, 1905); B. W. Currie (Willis E. Mollison,
The Leading Afro-Americans of Vicksburg, Mississippi, 1908;
courtesy of the Library of Congress); Juan T. Cardenas
(*San Antonio Police Department Illustrated*, 1901).

Contents

Illustrations and Tables

ILLUSTRATIONS

TABLES

Acknowledgments

I owe thanks to a great many people who supported me intellectually as I developed research questions into a published book. During his tenure as director of Loyola Marymount University's American Cultures Program, Edward J. W. Park gave me the opportunity to teach a course titled Race and Middle-Class Mobility that first inspired the idea for a comparative study. France Winddance Twine encouraged me to develop this idea and finally start writing about it. Nicola K. Beisel and Albert M. Broussard were kind enough to write letters of support for my application for faculty development leave. The National Center for Faculty Development and Diversity proved to be an invaluable resource in helping me to stay productive during a challenging time. I am also grateful to the Melbern G. Glasscock Center for Humanities Research at Texas A&M University, which supported me as an internal faculty fellow when I was just beginning to research this project.

The following friends and colleagues read and provided valuable feedback on earlier drafts of this manuscript, in part or in full. They have not only encouraged my research and writing on race and middle-class mobility but also pushed me to think more deeply about it: Harris M. Berger, Eduardo Bonilla-Silva, Kimberly N. Brown, Carlos K. Blanton, Mary Campbell, Michael Calderon-Zaks, Robert F. Carley, Giovanna Del Negro, Donnalee Dox, Robert Durán, John M. Eason, Sarah N. Gatson, April L. Hatfield, Sonia Hernández, Shona N. Jackson, Walter Kamphoefner, Verna Keith, Nadia Y. Kim, Karyn Lacy, Robert Mackin, Marisela Martinez-Cola, Reuben May, Anthony Mora, Mary Pattillo, Arthur Sakamoto, Toniesha Taylor, Zulema Valdez, Cara Wallis, Melissa Weiner, Joan Wolf, and Alford Young. I am especially grateful to Philip F. Rubio, who not only took time to respond to a stranger's query about African American postal workers but also generously read parts of the manuscript and offered insightful critiques. I am also indebted to the anonymous reviewers who offered such helpful commentary on earlier drafts.

I have benefited from the friendship and emotional support of the following people as I thought about, talked about, researched, and wrote this book under sometimes challenging circumstances: Jon Alston, Ernesto Amaral, Jevon Atkinson, Ophella C. Dano, Lisa Ellis, Alex Hernandez, Judith

Hamera, L. Justine Hernandez, Allyson Hobbs, Daniel Humphrey, Antonio La Pastina, Chaitanya Lakkimsetti, Darnise C. Martin, Ngoma Moghalu, Wendy L. Moore, Stephanie M. Ortiz, Laura Lee Oviedo, Nancy Plankey-Videla, Harland Prechel, Christopher Quick, Srividya Ramasubramanian, Rowena A. Robles, Curtiss Rooks, Emilce Santana, Jane Sell, Kazuko Suzuki, and Howard Winant. I am also indebted to my former students whose help with data collection and analysis was invaluable: Sarita Bertinato, Britanny Hignight, Lina Houston, Nerissa Irizarry, Octavia Jimenez-Padilla, and Angélica Rubicalva.

At the University of North Carolina Press, I was fortunate enough to work with three great (and incredibly patient) editors, Dylan White, Brandon Proia, and Lucas Church. I am also deeply grateful to Audra J. Wolfe of The Outside Reader, who diligently read and commented on multiple drafts of this manuscript, guided it along, and finally assured me that it was indeed time to let it go into the world.

In the time since I began this book, I have experienced both joy and loss. I met and married my husband, David T. Reid, whose love and unwavering support I will always appreciate. I also lost several family members, including my mother, Barbara T. Jewell; my father, Joseph U. Jewell; and my paternal uncle Richard A. Jewell. I cannot forget to thank the circle of family members and caregivers who kept me going with words of encouragement during the hardest of days: Susan Alamudun, Susan Gaunty, Audrea J. Jewell, Barbara C. Jewell, Heather Jewell-Jenkins, Rose Jewell-Jordan, Benselina John, Margaret Oliver, and Mary E. Williams. This book is for all of you.

White Man's Work

Introduction

In turn-of-the-century Atlanta, Auburn Avenue—located east of the city's bustling central business district—was a street of modest, neatly kept dwellings where, according to US Census records for 1900, African Americans were among the white-collar and skilled manual workers who rented or owned homes. Mark Anthony Thomas, a thirty-eight-year-old postal distribution clerk, was one of the homeowners.[1] Despite Whites' oft-expressed unease with and efforts to limit Black social mobility, Thomas had secured a prestigious federal job, signaling his membership in the city's Black middle class.[2]

A similar cluster of respectable middle-class homes could be found on San Antonio's Pecos Street, a block from Washington Square on the city's near west side. Among the neighborhood's white-collar and skilled blue-collar residents—which included both Anglos and Tejanos—was Juan T. Cardenas, the assistant marshal of the city's police force.[3] Although many of the city's Anglos associated Mexican residents with violence and crime, the fifty-five-year-old Cardenas had put in almost twenty years as a police officer. He served on the force alongside a number of other Tejano men before eventually becoming San Antonio's second-highest-ranking lawman.[4]

On Prospect Place, located near the outer edges of San Francisco's Chinatown district, a handful of immigrant and American-born Chinese lived close to where White homeowners on Powell Street had protested "Chinese encroachment" into their neighborhood.[5] Here, a cluster of small business owners, white-collar workers, and professionals lived among a much larger population of wage workers and their families. In 1900 Herman Lowe, a sewing machine operator, and Robert Leong Park, a clerk and interpreter for hire, lived just doors down from each other and had come to know each other through overlapping social circles.[6] Within five years, both men— each the American-born son of Chinese immigrants—would secure middle-class jobs that allowed them and their families to move to the nearby suburb of Berkeley. While Park became a salaried interpreter for the San Francisco criminal court assisting Chinese defendants, Lowe would join the local offices of the US Immigration Service as an interpreter in the division charged with enforcing Chinese exclusion laws. Park's younger brother, Edward, would follow Lowe into the Immigration Service as an interpreter.[7]

Middle-class workers in the United States experienced tremendous change in the late nineteenth and early twentieth centuries. Rapid growth in the industrial manufacturing sector fueled national economic growth that, combined with rising wages, promoted higher standards of living and increased rates of social mobility. By the 1880s, white-collar workers (those employed in clerical, technical, and managerial occupations) and professionals gradually eclipsed the artisans and small-business owners who had dominated the US middle class in both number and influence before the Civil War. Emancipation, as well as the ongoing incorporation of both the foreign-born and those living in newly acquired territories, brought new groups of workers into the nation's expanding economy. The socioeconomic changes that altered the internal structure of the middle class produced new uncertainties. In the last three decades of the nineteenth century, the centralization of capital, the consolidation of wealth among the upper classes, violent labor strikes by the working classes, and a series of severe economic downturns unsettled those in the middle. As feelings of precarity spread, many middle-class workers began to wonder whether their long and steady rise would continue.[8]

Those in the middle class who claimed Whiteness frequently identified another threat to their continued prosperity: the increasingly visible presence of non-White workers in occupations they considered their own. At the same time that urbanization and industrialization fundamentally reshaped people's class identities and class locations, sociodemographic shifts and ongoing processes of racialization created new identities and positions in a shifting racial order. Reports on occupations for the 1890 and 1900 censuses indicated that African Americans and other "Colored" populations were among the ranks of skilled, nonmanual, and white-collar workers in the nation's largest cities.[9] Abolition and Reconstruction in the Southern states, the country's continued expansion into the US-Mexico borderlands and its ongoing efforts to suppress Indigenous populations in the West, the pursuit of wars to establish an imperial presence abroad, and new immigrant arrivals from Asia and Europe all gave rise to heterogeneous social landscapes and new hybrid identities that cut across race and class, prompting resettlings of middle-class Whiteness.[10] As White people's everyday encounters with foreign and non-White peoples became more common, they developed new racial ideologies, schemes of classification, and strategies of interaction and modified existing ones—laying the groundwork for new, "modern," institutionalized patterns of separation and exclusion. Collectively, these beliefs and practices constituted W. E. B. Du Bois's "color line."[11]

In the United States, then, the simultaneous consolidation of a new economic order and the emergence of modern forms of White supremacy meant that the American middle class of the late nineteenth century manifested as a deeply racialized class formation. Across the country, White workers employed as clerks, shopkeepers, salespeople, civil servants, and other kinds of white-collar professionals regularly deployed popular understandings of race to make sense of their particular place in the era's shifting social landscape. *White Man's Work* adopts a comparative historical approach to explore how urban middle-class Whites responded, culturally and politically, to middle-class mobility among different populations of non-Whites at the close of the nineteenth century. By looking at three different cases of middle-class racisms in this era, I aim to offer insights into the workings of the race-class nexus, highlighting the durability and malleability of the links between class and race. Because gender is equally important as a constitutive feature of social systems, I also consider how these links are expressed through ideas about manliness, manhood, and masculinity.

Middle-Class Racisms in a Changing America

Scholars looking at the interaction of race and class have long argued that the racialized processes of class formation in societies organized around White supremacy regularly draw on Whites' fears of economic competition from racial outsiders, often expressed in the form of "wage cutting and replacement by non-White labor." At the same time, Whites' understandings of race have also regularly applied to aspects of social life beyond the workplace in the form of political, cultural, and sexual anxieties.[12]

The work of many labor historians has deepened our understanding of White working-class racisms—the folk beliefs, everyday strategies, and formal practices of racial separation and exclusion that emerged among the industrial working classes in the nineteenth-century United States. This research has shown how in spaces of labor and leisure, the White working classes developed and enacted distinct understandings of race in their real (and imagined) competition with Black, Mexican, Chinese, and other non-White workers.[13] In the political realm, neither the established parties of Republicans and Democrats nor newer ones like the Populists eschewed appeals to White workers' racial prejudices against African Americans, Mexicans, and Chinese.[14]

The late nineteenth century also saw the emergence of parallel "middle-class racisms" developed, enacted, and reinforced in settings such as white-collar workplaces, the "genteel" neighborhoods where these workers lived, the schools that educated their children, the public transports they used, the public spaces they frequented, and the newspapers they read. These beliefs and practices aimed to sustain clear patterns of separation and exclusion, justifying Whites' continued monopoly on resources that sustained middle-class position and privilege. Between 1870 and 1910, White politicians, attorneys, journalists, reformers, and everyday citizens vociferously debated, peremptorily refused, and at times violently resisted attempts by non-Whites to demonstrate and secure middle-class mobility. Even as newspapers, magazines, plays, and novels acknowledged the presence of populations among racial outsiders that aspired to join the middle class, they mocked their ascent. At the same time, they warned of the physical and moral dangers they represented.[15]

The stories that people tell about how different groups of racial actors change or sustain their class position, the legitimacy of their claims to particular class identities, and the broad social implications of those claims are rich sites for understanding the intersection of race and class. They are very much an example of what sociologists Michael Omi and Howard Winant have famously termed "racial projects"—people's large- and small-scale attempts to interpret racial phenomena and distribute resources along racial lines. Their claim that racial projects do the "ideological and material work" of linking racial signification to structure is akin to the arguments made by race scholars favoring a Sewellian conception of racial structures as dual—created and sustained by applying racial *schema* (logics of racial classification, folk understandings of racial difference, and everyday strategies or rules of interaction) to various arrays of material and symbolic *resources* like jobs, physical capabilities, skills, citizenship rights, housing, or education.[16]

A series of business "trade cards" printed in 1882 titled "Our New Citizens" depicts what were by then becoming popular stereotypes of different European immigrants and their paths to wealth and status. Each of the three sets of cards features caricatures of men of a different White ethnic group—an Irish immigrant named Pat O'Rourke, a German immigrant named Hans Schloppenberger, and an eastern European Jewish immigrant called Sheeny Monowski. For each man, four illustrated cards tell a story of social mobility from the time of their arrival to their tenth year in the United States in a manner deemed typical for their group. O'Rourke moves from being a manual laborer to become a uniformed city policeman, and finally a politician captioned, "The Honorable Mr. Rourke." Schloppenberger, who starts out as a waiter in a barroom, becomes first a tavern owner and then a prosperous brewery owner, now called Herr Johannes Von Schloppen-berger. Monowski, beginning as a rag peddler, ends his journey as a banker named Mr. Benjamin Monowski, having previously been a pawnbroker.[17] While the end of the nineteenth century saw the popularity of racialized class stereotypes about a number of different European groups, this book focuses on less well-known or examined stories people told about race and class mobility—those featuring African Americans, Latines, and Asian Americans.

Evidence of social or occupational mobility among non-White populations typically prompted White workers to vigorously defend, reinforce, or in some cases even strategically alter dominant understandings of racial difference and its ties to class identity. This book shows how links between Whiteness and middle-class identity were sustained in part through regional racial projects that responded to the newly visible presence of populations of up-wardly mobile African Americans, Chinese Americans, and Mexican Amer-icans in jobs that supported claims to middle-class identities. These racial projects were variously geared toward what ethnic and racial studies schol-ars favoring a boundary-making approach to understanding race describe as the brightening, blurring, or shifting of *racial boundaries*—the conceptual distinctions people enact that manifest and support objectified forms of difference between racialized groups.[18] How majority-White journalists, politicians, and ordinary citizens in different regions of the United States responded to changing contours of the race-class nexus offers important historical insights into how people have understood, organized around, and actively defended their positions within interlocking systems of in-equality during periods of large-scale social change.

The analysis offered here also contributes to the organizational or meso-level turn in studies of race and racism. Race scholars have called for greater attention to the role of meso-level structures operating below the level of the state in sustaining racial hierarchy. These underscore how organizational settings such as schools, neighborhoods, and workplaces operate as sites where people enact new practices that reinforce, challenge, or alter domi-nant racial meanings and classifications.[19] To that end, this study particularly focuses on struggles over race and middle-class labor at the beginning of the twentieth century by considering how, in three different regional urban cen-ters with different racial contexts, public-sector workplaces where "middle-class labor" was performed operated as crucial sites where people developed new and refined existing understandings of the race-class nexus, enacted them, and communicated them to the wider public.

In the United States, one way that Whites have historically attempted to sustain economic domination over racialized minorities is by constructing and deploying narratives about class mobility and identity that reflected and reinforced dominant racial beliefs in White supremacy. Individual historical analyses of Black workers in Atlanta, Mexican-origin workers in San Antonio, and Chinese-origin workers in San Francisco have shown that while the overwhelming majorities of these groups were employed as unskilled, or semiskilled, workers, there were also men and women from these groups employed in nonmanual occupations—clerical, proprietary, and professional—making them part of a growing population of urban middle-class workers.[20] While the range of nonmanual employment opportunities available to them—and the wealth they garnered from it—tended to differ sharply from those of their native- and foreign-born White counterparts, they nevertheless used their employment to secure pathways into middle-class mobility.

In response, White politicians, the press, and everyday social actors actively created and disseminated new race-class narratives that suggested that non-White social mobility endangered middle-class workplaces and morality. Whites variously portrayed upwardly mobile Black men, Mexican men, and Chinese men as immoral, violent, and criminal, producing durable stereotypes that justified excluding them from middle-class jobs and social spaces well into the early twentieth century. These representations included narratives about who was, and who was not, "morally fit"—stories that described Black, Mexican, and Chinese men as unsuitable for middle-class employment on the basis of an alleged lack of the moral probity required for middle-class belonging.

In each of the cities discussed in this book, the majority of Whites deployed some version of these new racial narratives about social mobility. As we shall see, however, the specific ways that they marshaled these narratives varied with their specific purposes. Depending on the racial context, their enactments of middle-class racisms repositioned, brightened, or blurred the racial boundaries they constructed between themselves and these groups. In each case, middle-class Whites mobilized culturally and politically to defend their positions in overlapping and mutually constituted hierarchies of class and race.

Cities and Racial Formations

This book focuses on cities, a crucial late nineteenth-century site for both the formation of the middle class and what sociologist David Theo Goldberg has described as "modern modes of racism" like racial segregation.[21] The rapid pace of urbanization and the migratory attraction for native and foreign-born workers of various races threatened the reproduction of homogeneous identities. This prompted White middle-class city dwellers to separate themselves from those they perceived as outsiders in neighborhoods, schools, workplaces, and public spaces. While a study of racial categories and boundaries in any one city risks presenting a distorted picture of the overall groups' experiences, an examination of patterns found among regionally important urban centers can shed light on the dominant expressions of race and racism in a given historical moment. While Blacks were the most common targets of segregation nationally, in cities like New York, Chicago, Los Angeles, and San Francisco, law and custom also typically separated Chinese, Japanese, and other "Asiatics" from Whites.[22] In many parts of the southwestern and western United States, Blacks and Chinese found themselves alongside Mexicans and Indians as groups subject to physical and social separation from Whites.[23]

In Atlanta, where postbellum urban expansion was fueled by both White and Black migrations, Whites would become increasingly distressed by Blacks' attempts to secure citizenship rights, access public schooling, and establish settlements. As a result, the city and surrounding state of Georgia imposed increasingly rigid laws that ensured "the Negro" would remain "in his place."[24] In San Antonio, Mexican Americans—some of whose forebears had acted as "cultural brokers" for the earliest Anglo American settlers and subsequently fought for Texan independence—would encounter new forms of discrimination from both native-born Whites and European immigrants. Collectively decrying Mexican "backwardness," these groups sought to further consolidate Anglo American dominance in the city's political, cultural, and economic institutions.[25] In San Francisco, where the labor demands accompanying the West's economic growth had attracted large numbers of foreign-born workers, it was the presence of a significant population of Chinese that attracted attention from native-born and immigrant Whites. San Francisco's White middle class overwhelmingly supported restricting new Chinese immigration as well as curtailing the mobility of those immigrant and native-born Chinese living within the nation's borders.[26]

Within the racial context of the late nineteenth century, the visible efforts of Black, Mexican, and Chinese men to secure both middle-class jobs and middle-class lifestyles became the subject of intense public debate among White populations. Between 1880 and 1910, Atlanta's Whites increasingly expressed concern over Black men's employment as mail clerks and mail carriers with the city's expanding postal service. Journalists, politicians, and commentators described these men as "after-the-war Negroes" whose social ambitions endangered middle-class Whites by taking jobs reserved for White men and stealing from the mail to fund middle-class lifestyles—all the while violating norms about contact between the races. During the same period in San Antonio, journalists and politicians increasingly adopted a racialized crime discourse that regularly cast Mexicans as one of the "menacing" non-White populations that regularly contributed to the city's growing problems with crime and vice. Yet, new racial stereotypes about Mexicans' violent tendencies as urban criminals existed alongside Tejano men's visibility on the city's new police force, prompting public debates about their long-standing claims to White middle-class identities. In 1890s San Francisco, during a series of highly publicized bribery trials at the Immigration Service's Chinese Bureau, both prosecutors and the press called attention to the mixed-race and "Americanized" Chinese men employed at the bureau as interpreters and assistant immigration inspectors—jobs for which "deserving" White men had allegedly been passed over—describing them as the sources of corruption within the agency. In the years that followed, journalists and investigators would regularly link middle-class ambitions among Chinese Americans employed with the Immigration Service to organized crime, vice, and the seduction of White women.

In an era of deeply racialized class formations, middle-class Whites interpreted Black, Mexican, and Chinese men's efforts to secure social mobility through newer and more elite forms of labor as a kind of physical, economic, or moral danger. White men, in particular, regarded the efforts of these non-Whites to claim middle-class identities as an affront to the moral prerogatives of middle-class manhood. Middle-class White men not only found themselves sharing physical space with these and other racial outsiders but also recognized that they might lose social ground, as middle-class jobs, wages, and lifestyles went to those whom they had come to regard as their intellectual and moral inferiors. Stories in White newspapers, White politicians' speeches, and everyday expressions of "racial common sense" portrayed Black, Mexican, and Chinese claims to middle-class identities with varying degrees of legitimacy by connecting the central cultural categories of race, manhood, and crime.

As clearly non-White peoples, Blacks and Chinese remained firmly outside the bounds of middle-class respectability in the eyes of most Whites. White workers regarded their entrance into public spaces, neighborhoods, and middle-class workplaces as a new moral and sexual danger to White workers, especially given the increasing numbers of young women who worked before marriage. While "Anglo" Whites in the US-Mexico borderlands regularly described Mexicans as a criminal class, they often identified "better classes" of Mexicans in the region's cities and towns who might safely be considered "White men." It was not always clear, however, where that line might be drawn. By linking Black, Mexican, and Chinese social mobility in the public sphere to political corruption, job loss, crime, and sexual danger, White commentators positioned racial outsiders' claims to middle-class identity as both illegitimate and a symptom of social decline—a foil for Whites' own narratives of middle-class mobility.

Racial Boundaries and Class Boundaries

The "White man's work" alluded to in this book's title was understood to be work that provided clear social and economic advantages to those who performed it. These advantages included salaries that provided economic stability in a rapidly changing economy, the possibility of continued social mobility, and a material style of life that publicly signified membership in the respectable middle class. A broad range of scholarship on the articulation of the nation's racial hierarchy with its economic order has shown how under White supremacy, White racial dominance is instantiated and maintained through an evolving collection of structural arrangements, discourses, formal practices, and everyday strategies. These various formations—segregated labor markets, organizational hiring practices, occupational possibilities, and the stories people tell about non-White workers—reflect and reinforce racialized understandings of economic inequality. As a vast body of research on non-White middle classes during the late nineteenth and early twentieth centuries has shown, even in the face of these barriers, non-White populations in the United States have developed strategies for navigating and securing social mobility within a racially structured economy.

How people achieve, interpret, and defend their positions at the race-class nexus is of particular interest because of the implications for understanding how people construct and maintain racial boundaries during periods of social change.[27] Social scientists studying the properties, processes, and strategies of action associated with racial boundaries have underscored their dynamic nature. Racial boundaries can be considered *bright* in those instances where racial distinctions are widely recognized by individuals and organizations, deeply institutionalized within state and local structures, or significantly determinative of everyday patterns of interaction. However, they are described as *blurred* where racial distinctions between groups are neither widely recognized nor institutionally supported, making them less important for social distance. Racial boundaries can also *shift*, effectively moving across groups of people in ways that either expand or contract the population of racial outsiders. At the same time, individual efforts to change one's racial position by *crossing* racial boundaries (e.g., passing) result in "positional moves."[28]

In each case, scholars treat *narratives*—the "shared storylines" people use as they make sense of events, interpret their own actions, and assess their environments—as important because they make boundaries, their properties, and processes more meaningful to actors and suggest relevant strategies of action.[29] These stories can serve as a "filter" of established plotlines through which individual and collective actors make sense of novel events and preserve the status quo. However, they can also generate new explanations for these events that can bring about structural transformations.[30] The cases offered here also underscore the important role of narratives in how people experience and enact social change. They show how Whites both created new stories about race and class and refit older ones to explain the existence of non-White middle classes during a period of increased economic uncertainty and profound demographic change.

These stories effected and sustained changes in racial boundaries by rearticulating race with class under new social conditions. At the same time, they were shaped by the distinct material conditions of the "places and spaces" from which they originated. In the postslavery context of the US South, Atlanta's middle-class Whites further entrenched an already bright Black-White boundary by mobilizing new race-class narratives to describe Black men's occupational and social mobility as a threat not only to themselves but to society at large—invoking fears of financial loss, declining occupational opportunities, and sexual danger. In the US-Mexico borderlands context of converging Anglo American and Spanish settler colonialisms, San Antonio's Anglo populations alternatively shifted, blurred, and brightened the Mexican-White boundary in stories about middle-class Tejano men that sometimes portrayed them as White but increasingly linked them with the violence and crime popularly associated with a Mexican-origin criminal class. On the West Coast, where overlapping settler colonialisms were further overlaid with expansionism into Asia and the Pacific, middle-class Whites brightened the Chinese-White boundary using stories that similarly invoked fears of declining opportunities for White men, sexual danger for White women, and the growing presence of a "criminally inclined" population of Chinese immigrants.

Histories of racial formation have shown how the boundaries of racial categories have been brightened, blurred, or shifted over time through collective efforts to alter their significance or even change their position relative to different populations. An important strain in the historical research on racial boundaries in the United States has mapped changes in popular and official understandings of Whiteness relative to a growing population of "new" European immigrants from southern and eastern Europe arriving during the late nineteenth and early twentieth centuries. Many of these works have reflected on how the boundaries of Whiteness changed in response to new patterns of socioeconomic mobility among the descendants of these immigrants, particularly during the post–World War II era of mass suburbanization.[31]

While the scholarship on the experiences of White ethnics has produced insights into the workings of the racial boundaries demarcating Whiteness, this book finds more compelling a critique by scholars who have questioned the extent to which these divisions truly functioned as a racial boundary separating southern and eastern European groups from Whiteness. These scholars argue that the absence of any consistent set of institutionalized practices separating these groups from the White race indicates that, while members might have encountered racial boundaries *within* Whiteness, there was no racial boundary that had to be shifted or crossed for them to be seen as White.[32]

A vast body of scholarship has analyzed the varied contours of racialization for Black, Latine, Asian, and Indigenous populations in the continental United States and its settler-colonized territories. Comparative scholars of race in the United States have called attention not only to how these groups' experiences with racialization differed from those of native-born and immigrant Whites but also to the important parallels and divergences in their experiences with racialization as non-White people.[33] Questions remain about the workings of racial boundary processes like blurring, shifting, or brightening for these persistently non-White groups. Particularly, what effect, if any, have patterns of social mobility among these populations had on the brightness, blurriness, or positioning of the racial boundaries marking them as more or less "durably non-White" populations?

Taken together, the case studies examined in this book offer a comparison across racial categories that yields further insights into how racial boundaries have operated in historically and regionally specific contexts. They further develop our understandings of blurred racial boundaries by underscoring the importance of "long histories" of race-making and the potential for people to favor both the expansion or blurring and contraction or brightening of racial boundaries multiple times over the course of decades. These case studies also further how we think about the ways racial boundaries were defended, negotiated, and crossed in new social settings. Within different regional contexts, White populations might alternatively endorse or oppose structural moves like boundary shifting, or positional moves like boundary crossing, in response to new conditions.

An Archive of Middle-Class Racisms

In what follows, I use a range of archival materials, including newspapers, magazines, internal memos, and legal records, to analyze the emergence of middle-class racisms during the late nineteenth and early twentieth centuries. *White Man's Work* relies heavily on stories published in this era about scandals, events, or court trials involving non-White men whose employment in skilled or nonmanual public-sector jobs placed them in the era's new urban middle class. Interpretive methods from the sociology of culture and cultural history allow me to analyze these accounts with careful attention to their explicit arguments about race, class, and manhood.[34] I show how ideologies among middle- and working-class Whites about race, class identity, and mobility translated into new social practices that shaped people's lives.

I also use methods of collective biography to examine patterns of social mobility among the three groups of workers examined here: Black postal workers in Atlanta, Tejano policemen in San Antonio, and Chinese-origin federal immigration employees in San Francisco.[35] Here, I use manuscript census returns, city directories, and rosters of federal civil service employment to collectively describe the social origins and trajectories of each group.

Comparative historical approaches to the study of race can offer important insights into how people act to sustain and modify racialized class hierarchies over time. *White Man's Work* compares Whites' responses to non-White men in middle-class occupations in Atlanta, San Antonio, and San Francisco to show how these responses constrained or enabled non-White workers' strategies for social mobility at the beginning of the twentieth century. I employ what historical sociologist Victoria Bonnell describes as "illustrative" methods of comparative historical analysis, which generate theoretical explanations of social life by comparing similar historical events, processes, and social actors across cases.[36] Although the composition of the non-White populations of each of these cities was by no means homogeneous, I focus in each case on a population whose presence was regularly and prominently interpreted as threatening to local Whites — African Americans in Atlanta, Mexicans in San Antonio, and Chinese in San Francisco. In so doing, I attempt to highlight the historically and regionally specific variations in the US racial order they represent.

Outline of the Book

Four chapters trace how late nineteenth-century White populations in Atlanta, San Antonio, and San Francisco came to regard social mobility among Blacks, Mexicans, and Chinese as distinct threats to their own middle-class positions; how politicians, the press, and everyday social actors described the exact nature of these threats in stories with familiar themes of moral fitness, manhood, and criminality; and how these interpretations sustained or altered racial boundaries in ways that reinforced White supremacy during a period of far-reaching social change.

As a whole, this book has two aims. I aim to highlight the importance of race-class narratives as racial projects that can sustain or alter the properties and placement of racial boundaries, with a focus on how this happens in meso-level sites, such as middle-class occupational settings. I also want to challenge generally accepted characterizations of "middle-class racisms" as somehow generally "subtle" and "less violent" by pointing out historical changes in their form and content since their emergence in response to social mobility by racial outsiders.[37]

Chapter 1 provides a historical introduction to how the middle class became a critical site of the race-class nexus during the immense social changes of the late nineteenth and early twentieth centuries. Special attention is given here to describing the important regional contexts of racial formation in this era — the postbellum South, the US-Mexico borderlands, and the far West. I explore how, in each of these regional contexts, Whites' encounters with racial others claiming middle-class identities gave rise to new forms of separation geared toward preserving the "Whiteness" of middle-class spaces and places — including organizational settings like the workplace. In this chapter I also establish the intellectual context within which regional variations of the race-class nexus and boundary making have been understood. I show not only how racial boundaries were made meaningful and defended through the stories individual and collective actors told about race but also that these stories were the means by which racial boundaries could be shifted, blurred, or brightened.

Chapter 2 examines Black postal workers in Atlanta between 1889 and 1910, specifically how they came to be regarded by middle-class Whites as embodying the racial dangers of the New South. During the 1880s and 1890s, Black men secured socioeconomic mobility through the postal service. After documenting this phenomenon, I offer an analysis of Whites' cultural responses to that mobility in the form of new racial narratives about Black mail clerks and carriers that brightened racialized class boundaries. I analyze Whites' use of these narratives in the 1889 case of Black postal clerk Charles C. Penney, showing how his appointment was popularly described as posing both moral and economic dangers to White clerks and customers. Following the Penney incident, press coverage of alleged cases of job-related misconduct involving Black mail carriers in Atlanta and other Georgia cities between 1890 and 1906 helped to further construct them as morally unfit—dangerous to both middle-class Whites and "humble," less educated Blacks. By 1910, the figure of the socially ambitious Black mail carrier had become for Whites such a popular symbol of political corruption, criminality, and illegitimate social mobility among urban Blacks that politicians used it to mobilize both urban and rural White voters against "Negro rule."

Chapter 3 examines Tejano policemen in San Antonio between 1880 and 1910, in particular how Anglos developed narratives of conditional Whiteness to explain Tejano social mobility. A generation after US annexation, in a context of blurred but progressively brightened racial boundaries, Tejano men shored up their declining middle-class position through urban law enforcement employment. As the city expanded in the 1870s and 1880s, narratives about "Mexican crime" described Mexican-origin people and their areas of settlement as chief sources of crime, vice, and social disorder. At the same time, the press popularized understandings that these Tejano policemen were socially and racially distinct from "Mexicans." Starting with Tejano policeman Jacobo Coy's involvement in a highly publicized saloon shooting, I analyze popular and press accounts of Tejano policemen's interactions with Anglo, Black, and Mexican populations in San Antonio. I show how these accounts supported Tejano claims to Whiteness, but these claims were fragile, as witnessed by the press's later attempts to subtly link Tejano policemen accused of misconduct or moral unfitness to regionally dominant tropes of Mexican criminality.

Chapter 4 examines the case of Chinese American employees of the Immigration and Naturalization Service's San Francisco Chinese Bureau between 1896 and 1907 and how they emerged as racially dangerous figures for San Francisco's middle-class Whites. During the early Chinese exclusion era (approximately 1882 to 1910), interpreter work was an important mobility pathway for Chinese American men. I show how Whites responded to this development with new racial narratives linking Americanized Chinese men with crime, corruption, and vice. I trace the emergence of these narratives during the 1896 corruption trial of Richard S. Williams, a mixed-race Chinese American interpreter whose conviction on bribery charges was used to symbolize for the public the dangers of both Chinese employment in the Immigration Service and Chinese Americans' claims to middle-class identities. After the Williams trial, federal efforts to enforce a ban on Chinese employment in the bureau and the scarcity of qualified Whites prompted debates over the racial classification of mixed-race Chinese men like Williams. Using an analysis of criminal and corruption cases involving both mixed-race and "full-blooded" Chinese interpreters, I show how Chinese American men were described as dangerous figures who not only were "morally unfit" for middle-class employment and identities but also posed a danger to White women. By the early twentieth century, the press, the public, and politicians again mobilized modified versions of these narratives to justify downgrading the position of Chinese interpreters in the US civil service.

In the conclusion, I offer reflections on race and class mobility in the United States. Whites' efforts to variously brighten or blur racial boundaries in response to middle-class identities among Blacks, Mexicans, and Chinese stand in sharp contrast to the dominant narrative of racial boundary shifting experienced by European immigrants that is well documented in the historical literature on Whiteness. At the same time, the racial narratives about the dangers represented by social mobility among racial outsiders that emerged more than a century ago remain a part of US culture, deployed by a variety of social actors in response to large-scale demographic and economic change within the middle classes. I end with a call for more comparative work on the experiences of racialized minorities with the race-class nexus and middle-class racisms. Our use of the past to shed light on current racial situations requires a careful and systematic examination of historical cases. Used thoughtfully, it offers insight.

CHAPTER ONE

Troubling Gentility
*The Race-Class Nexus and Middle-Class
Mobility in the Gilded Age*

The rapid advance of industrial capitalism during the last decades of the nineteenth century radically transformed the nation's economy and its class structure. New machine-based labor-saving technologies dramatically increased production while advances in transportation like extension of railroad lines and the invention of the steamship revolutionized the movement of goods and people, fueling the expansion of markets.[1] Though uneven at times due to a series of severe depressions in the 1870s and 1890s—and lesser ones in the 1880s—that slowed its pace, the nation's economy continued to grow.[2] The rapid accumulation of capital during this period of expansion created a new upper class with what seemed like vast amounts of wealth. In 1890 the wealthiest 1 percent of families, with annual incomes at or above $50,000, together with the 11 percent whose annual incomes ranged between $5,000 and $50,000, owned the majority (86 percent) of the nation's wealth as measured in real and personal property. By contrast, the remaining 88 percent of families classified as poor, working class, and middle class together owned only 14 percent of the nation's wealth. The years between 1870 and the start of the twentieth century saw a transformation of class in the United States. The steady growth of industry and the accelerated accumulation of capital in the 1870s and 1880s created a new upper class with vast amounts of wealth.

These changes to the economy were especially felt by the middle classes— those workers whose modest amounts of wealth and higher-status jobs distinguished them from the working classes even as their significantly more modest incomes and lifestyles distinguished them from wealthy elites.[3] Manufacturing's rapid growth generated what seemed to be an insatiable demand for low-wage labor, but it also created new skilled trades and increased the numbers of skilled manual workers. The labor-saving technologies that increased production and fueled upper-class wealth also undermined the job security of even the most skilled of these workers, who could find their wages reduced or jobs eliminated as business owners increasingly looked for ways to reduce labor costs.[4] New modes of production and specialization also created new opportunities for white-collar employment in clerical, managerial, and professional occupations.

One of the most striking occupational changes in this era was the growing share of people employed in what were nonmanual or white-collar jobs.[5] Together with an emerging group of small entrepreneurs and business owners who mastered new mercantile techniques, these workers formed the core of a new middle class, one that by 1910 had eclipsed the independent artisans and small shopkeepers who had dominated the middle class in the first half of the nineteenth century.[6] By 1890, the annual incomes of those in the middle classes ranged anywhere between $500 and $5,000, and they possessed a combination of personal and real property that formed 13 percent of the nation's wealth.[7] Even in the face of the era's economic uncertainties, their generally higher levels of education, modest economic success, and genteel lifestyles created rising expectations of continued upward mobility and the determination to defend their social position. While native-born Whites tended to dominate the ranks of the new middle class of the late nineteenth century, the work of historians has shown that there were, as Nell Irvin Painter points out, individuals and families among nearly all ethnic and racial groups who, according to occupation, wealth, self-definition, taste, or attitude, were identified as middle class. Middle-class Whites responded to the sociodemographic changes that accompanied this mobility by readily refitting old racial ideologies that supported White supremacy at both the local and the national levels. The social transformation brought about by Emancipation and Southern Reconstruction meant that for the first time since their arrival in the United States, African Americans could (at least in theory) participate in the economy as paid workers and pursue social mobility as free people with the legal rights of citizens. Yet, in what began as a regional political movement that would have national repercussions, White Southerners of all classes — led by the middle and upper classes — organized to legally and extralegally curtail Blacks' ability to exercise these rights in the name of preserving White supremacy.[8]

The 1880s and 1890s also saw the arrival of "new" southern and eastern European immigrants who differed in culture and appearance from the earlier immigrant cohorts, in which northern and western Europeans had been the majority. These waves of newcomers sparked nativist debates among the well-to-do descendants of Anglo Protestants and older groups of immigrants about the new immigration's potential effect on the nation's future and the need to attend more carefully to the hierarchy of "races" within Whiteness.[9] However, it was the new flows of immigration from

Asia—particularly into the booming labor markets of the western states—that had long fed those White workers' anxieties about immigrant labor and the changing economy, giving rise to a popular anti-Asian racism that united both the native-born and the foreign-born as "White working men" and helped create an extensive system of immigration controls first against Chinese immigrants and later against all "Asiatics."[10] In those states and territories that had previously been Mexico's northernmost lands and were now within the nation's expanding western border, popular understandings of race were further challenged by the established presence of Spanish-speaking descendants of the region's first European settlers. Although Mexicans' own racial hierarchy had privileged Whiteness, its acknowledgment of varying degrees of racial admixture with Black and Indigenous people meant that the region's Anglo American middle classes could and did mobilize wartime-era claims about Mexicans' "mongrelized" racial origins adapted to the new era in order to justify Anglo American social dominance.[11]

The development of these new racialized middle-class identities converged with changes in the dominant gender ideologies that defined middle-class notions of manhood and womanhood. Ideologies of manliness—centered on the ability to control masculine passions and impulses—had gained popularity when most middle-class men were small-business owners or independent artisans whose success depended on evidence of moral rectitude. However, the growing numbers of clerical, technical, and professional workers in the middle class rendered notions of "manly self-control" obsolete.[12] Threats to middle-class manhood also came from the changing social position of women. Increased opportunities for women in an expanding white-collar economy sparked calls for greater social and political equality between the sexes and the emergence of a new figure—the highly educated and often economically independent "New Woman" who chose to delay (or forgo) marriage and motherhood.[13] An increasingly powerful labor movement led by White working-class men—many from immigrant backgrounds—combined with White immigrant men's successful takeovers of city governments through ethnic-based machine politics together seemed to undermine the social and political authority of White middle-class men. At the same time, the efforts of "off-White" Mexican-origin men and categorically non-White Black men and Chinese-origin men to claim middle-class manhood through assertions of their rights as citizens raised further doubts among Whites about the utility of a middle-class manliness that saw the strength of self-restraint as the source of their authority over non-Whites, immigrants, and the working classes.[14]

The rapid pace of urbanization after 1870, fueled by both domestic and international migrations of various classes of workers, made cities critical sites for the development of these new raced and gendered class identities. Between 1870 and 1900 the proportion of Americans living in cities grew from just over one-quarter (25.7 percent) to nearly half (45.6 percent).[15] With the concentration of industrial production in cities, the new middle class of white-collar and professionally employed workers figured largely among the nation's urban dwellers. These expanding urban economies generated new streams of nonmanual employment not only in business and manufacturing but also in civil service and the professions, attracting men and women seeking to either improve or secure their social position in a changing milieu.[16] As both working-class districts and wealthy residential enclaves emerged in cities across the country, middle-class neighborhoods grew out of the desires of white-collar and professional workers to settle alongside those similarly employed who shared their adherence to an increasingly accessible middle-class culture of "gentility."[17] This middle-class culture indelibly shaped the variety of new public institutions and spaces that emerged in cities—schools, museums, shopping districts—and was widely disseminated through any number of city newspapers, which, owing in part to cheaper subscription rates and political independence, emerged as a more popular form of communication in the 1870s and continued to shape public opinion well into the 1900s.[18]

The sociodemographic shifts brought about by Emancipation, Reconstruction, westward expansion, and immigration increased the populations of a variety of racial and ethnic communities in booming regional urban hubs. Most of these newcomers swelled the ranks of the new industrial laboring classes and found employment in the expanding ranks of low-wage unskilled and service workers. Also among the newcomers were those claiming middle-class identities and aspirations, whose presence increased the potential for interracial contact in public spaces. From the point of view of middle-class Whites, these groups created new threats to the homogeneity and racial purity that undergirded White supremacy. As David Theo Goldberg has noted, it was the trend toward urbanization that made racial segregation the dominant and most formalized modality of racism in the late nineteenth century. These laws and practices were geared toward precisely measuring and defining the presence of racial difference, controlling interactions among racialized groups, and preventing any unsanctioned interracial contact.[19] Major urban newspapers serving White populations also helped popularize both official and folk theories of racial difference and racial danger that supported segregationist logic with stories and reports about alleged criminal or immoral behavior among non-White groups.[20] As this book shows, these stories reflected Whites' anxieties about non-White social mobility and focused attention on the alleged wrongdoings of those who either visibly aspired to middle-class standing or had already claimed it, often identifying them as part of a de facto criminal element.

In this chapter, I explore the social science literature on racial boundaries and social mobility to explain the struggles over racialized class formations embedded in danger narratives about non-White men's social mobility during the late nineteenth and early twentieth centuries. In societies that are partially structured by race, both official and everyday articulations of race and class have played a critical role in how people conceptualized both class identity and class mobility.[21] The unequal distribution of education, employment opportunities, housing, and access to capital along racial lines, as well as the linking of racial groups to specific socioeconomic strata, has historically made it necessary for those seeking upward mobility to negotiate and navigate racial boundaries—the symbolic and material distinctions that both define and demarcate racial groups. Racialized minorities' encounters with laws, policies, and everyday practices that restrict access to the resources that facilitate class mobility produced durable patterns of institutionalized inequality. At the same time, members of dominant racial groups have mobilized claims about alleged cultural or moral distinctions between groups to justify and help sustain observed differences in social mobility. Scholars examining the intersection of race and class contend that it has primarily operated through "distancing strategies" associated with racial segregation and class segregation. However, demographic shifts, socio-legal changes, or periods of economic expansion and contraction disrupt the contours of this intersection as groups designated as racial outsiders gain access to previously withheld resources, develop new class mobility pathways, or claim new class identities. This chapter will show that a structural approach to race that highlights both the agency of social actors and the use of a varied range of boundary processes in articulating race and class at multiple levels is needed to understand the importance of danger narratives about non-White men's middle-class employment at the turn of the century.

The Race-Class Nexus

In social science literature, theorists who advocate structural approaches to race generally argue that placing people into racial categories based on real or imagined phenotypical differences has been and remains a fundamental means by which societies are politically, economically, and socially organized. Scholars like Eduardo Bonilla-Silva, Michael Omi, and Howard Winant generally see race as both fundamentally durable and malleable—characterized by dynamic institutional arrangements, mutable social relations, and variable processes of racial categorization that allow it to persist in the face of large-scale social change.[22] Recent structural analyses of race drawing on William Sewell's conceptualization of social structures offer an agency-rich explanation of how racial hierarchies emerge, persist, change, and intersect with other hierarchies like gender or class.[23] In this view, racial hierarchies are created and sustained whenever various arrays of *resources* like wealth, jobs, networks, housing, abilities, or skills are repeatedly and consistently coupled with *racial schemas*—taken-for-granted knowledge about race, logics of racial classification, folk understandings of racial difference, or rules of interaction.[24] Because racial schemas are transposable and resources can be interpreted in multiple ways, racial hierarchies experience change when actors deliberately extend or transpose racial schemas to new arrays of resources, or when resources are "racially interpreted" in new ways. Additionally, racial hierarchies can be said to intersect with class or gender wherever they share either resources or schemas as a result of the meanings, interpretations, and actions of actors.[25]

This perspective offers a useful way to think about intersections of race and class—what legal scholar john a. powell refers to as the "race-and-class nexus." Powell describes this nexus as a collection of institutional arrangements, entrenched social practices, narratives, discourses, and cultural meanings that sustain historically durable links between race and class as "mutually constitutive hierarchies."[26] A Sewellian understanding of the race-class nexus holds that racial schemas (e.g., logics of racial classification, presumptions of suitability or unsuitability for civic inclusion based on race, and presumptions of racial superiority or inferiority) systematically applied to arrays of class resources such as education, property, or employment opportunities produce patterns of interaction that are taken-for-granted aspects of social life.[27] This aligns with Omi and Winant's concept of "racial projects"—the "interpretations, representations, or explanations of racial identities and meanings" that seek to "organize and distribute resources . . . along particular racial lines." As the "building blocks" of racial hierarchies, racial projects—which can be reactionary or progressive—do the "work" of linking "signification" or racial schemas to arrays of resources in ways that establish, strengthen, or challenge patterns of racial domination.[28] The race-class nexus is actively created by actors or groups of actors developing racial projects that justify or explain class-related phenomena such as changing labor markets, competition with new populations of workers, shifting occupational structures, periods of economic scarcity and prosperity, or patterns of social mobility among different groups. Analyzing how and under what conditions people develop and mobilize new racial projects about class mobility and identity offers important insight into understanding the race-class nexus as a structural location that is subject to change and varies across time and place.

Race-class narratives, the stories people tell that articulate race and class, are a common type of racial project that offers insights into the race-class nexus. Historical sociologists like Margaret Somers, George Steinmetz, and Roberto Franzosi have shown how *narratives*—stories that place social actors in sequences of events with imputed causal connections (plots)—are crucial for understanding a wide range of sociological phenomena, including both stability and social change.[29] Where racial narratives typically feature explicitly racialized actors and invoke the supposed traits and behaviors of racial groups to explain how race matters in a given context, race-class narratives use available racial logics to explain class differences by placing explicitly racialized actors in storylines that help to explain class dynamics.[30] Developed in a variety of settings, these narratives can be deployed in ways that either support or reject the legitimacy of class identities among racialized groups or to express the desirability of interracial class coalitions.[31] Race-class narratives about class mobility—people's movements from one socioeconomic stratum to another, the conditions under which these movements happen, and the cultural strategies used to accomplish them—can offer important insights into the race-class nexus and the ways people make use of racial schemas to explain class-related phenomena. Because these stories can capture the ways that both individuals and collective actors actively link racial identities, meanings, and practices to schooling, jobs, housing, and other resources associated with class mobility, they are useful for understanding how class is lived by differently racialized actors in historically and regionally specific conditions.

Racial Boundaries and Social Mobility

Where economic resources are distributed along racial lines, questions about class mobility and identity have important implications for how people confront, negotiate, or reinforce *racial boundaries*—the social and symbolic distinctions that identify and separate differently racialized groups. In these contexts, the stories people tell about movements from one socio-economic stratum to another, the strategies they use to secure class position, and the identities they construct regularly invoke understandings of race. Cultural approaches to race rooted in the social science literature on boundaries offer a rich conceptual language for describing the mechanisms by which lines of racial demarcation are created, challenged, or reinforced alongside shifting patterns of social mobility.[32] Because racial boundaries are created in part from people's moral or cultural beliefs about race, adding or subtracting moral categories (e.g., dishonesty, truthfulness, discipline, laziness, modesty, or indecency) can shift a racial boundary's position or alter its properties.[33] In addition to being expressed as moral or symbolic criteria, racial boundaries can have properties of *brightness*, where racial distinctions are salient for social interactions and life chances, or *blurriness*, in which such distinctions are less important and have significantly less impact on the possibilities for socioeconomic mobility.[34]

In those contexts where racial boundaries are bright, members of a subordinated racialized minority may resort to individual-level *boundary crossing* in which they detach themselves from connections to their group of origin and seek membership in one with greater access to resources.[35] In *blurred* boundary contexts, by contrast, where racial distinctions are less salient or even insignificant for social interactions and individual life chances, pursuit of class mobility does not compel detachment, allowing people to sustain social ties to their group of origin while operating in what are officially recognized "zones of ambiguity" between dominant and subordinated racial groups.[36] Social mobility can also be accompanied by *boundary shifting* or repositioning in ways that can expand or contract the population of groups considered part of the majority, effectively turning outsiders into insiders or vice versa. Populations who find their position in the racial hierarchy has changed may either gain or lose access to resources that ensure class mobility and reproduce social position.

Both labor historians and sociologists have drawn on the boundary-making concept to describe and explain historical changes in the boundaries of racial categories in discussions of social mobility. Drawing on a wide range of evidence including naturalization petitions, antimiscegenation cases, labor struggles, and popular cultural representations, David Roediger, Karen Brodkin, and other historians have argued that despite their European origins, Jewish, Italian, and Slavic immigrants and their descendants variously "became White" as an older system of "racial" distinctions became less salient during the latter half of the twentieth century.[37] Sociologists like Richard Alba have drawn on this history of Whiteness to underscore the flexibility of racial boundaries, noting that the offspring of southern and eastern European immigrants experienced middle-class mobility after World War II that was accompanied by an expansion—or at the very least blurring—of the racial boundaries that demarcated and defined Whiteness. As a result, members of these groups previously identified as being of undesirable "racial stock" could now (on the condition of assimilation) lay claim to middle-class identities while gaining access to the white-collar labor market opportunities, genteel neighborhoods, and higher grades of schooling that were formally and informally denied to non-White racialized groups regardless of their level of assimilation.[38]

Works describing historical changes in the contours of Whiteness experienced by groups of European immigrants have underscored the contingent nature of racial formation while calling attention to the workings of boundary properties and processes. However, an important strain in the historical literature on Whiteness has challenged claims that these populations were ever in fact fundamentally regarded and treated as non-Whites. Looking at the experiences of the European immigrants arriving during the late nineteenth and early twentieth centuries, historians like Eric Arnesen, Ariela Gross, Nell Irvin Painter, and Thomas Guglielmo have argued that despite their frequent encounters with de facto discrimination, the White status of Irish, Jews, Italians, and Slavs was never regularly denied by the courts or state agencies, nor were the members of these groups systematically refused access to jobs, housing, schools, or public spaces on the basis of race.[39] Similarly, Cybelle Fox and Guglielmo have argued that any racial boundary that shifted or blurred for these groups is best thought of as an *intraracial* one located decidedly within the category of Whiteness and used by different groups of White people to make distinctions among themselves rather than to identify non-Whites. Importantly, they note that the historical fact of southern and eastern European immigrants' presumed Whiteness—despite their having experienced racialized forms of discrimination—tells us more about the durability of the White–non-White boundary than its flexibility.[40]

The fact of European immigrants' presumed Whiteness as they pursued social mobility suggests that efforts to understand racial boundary properties and processes in the context of social mobility could benefit from a comparative analysis of mobility patterns among those populations whose non-Whiteness was both commonly understood and legally presumed—

African Americans, Asian Americans, and Latines. The current social science literature on these groups' experiences navigating race and middle-class status in workplaces, schools, neighborhoods, and public spaces suggests that despite the demographic shift toward a more race-plural middle class in the early twenty-first century, the properties of some racial boundaries have shown a remarkable degree of persistence.[41] As sociologist Les Back notes, modern middle-class racisms have long histories. Themes of displacement (being overrun by outsiders), unfairness (the erosion of merit in workplaces or schools because of newcomers), and immorality (the dishonesty of outsiders) have long been a feature of middle-class racisms.[42] A comparative and historical analysis of middle-class Whites' cultural and political responses to social mobility among African Americans, Mexican Americans, and Asian Americans can offer greater insight into the *longue durée* of changes in the brightness or positioning of the racial boundary demarcating Whiteness. It is to the outline of such an analysis that I now turn.

Racial Boundaries and Social Mobility: Three Case Studies

Histories of social mobility in multiracial societies shed light on the variety of strategies people have used to navigate the cross-cutting boundaries of the race-class nexus and defend their social positions in it. While the literature on racial boundaries and social mobility has focused on the mid-twentieth century as a watershed era for realignments in the race-class nexus, the years spanning the end of the nineteenth century and start of the twentieth formed an equally critical period when people developed new ways of thinking about their position in a changing racial hierarchy and its relationship to an equally dynamic hierarchy of class positions. Comparative and regional analyses of race have called attention to the multiple geographic scales at which racial hierarchies exist.[43] These works, along with those of historians like Natalia Molina and critical geographers like Ruth Gilmore, have pointed out that dominant racial formations are best understood as being locally interpreted, existing in forms that emerge from "different but not unrelated" regional histories of settlement, conquest, expansion, and labor exploitation—what David Theo Goldberg calls "prior conditions . . . and modes of articulation."[44] As such, these changes in the contours of the race-class nexus were experienced both regionally—in the West, Southwest, South, Midwest, and East— and locally, in cities and towns. These varied locales developed recognizable and variously institutionalized modes of racism, all of which sought to separate a socially dominant population of Whites from subordinate populations of non-Whites in accordance with the nationally dominant racial ideology of White supremacy.

In analyzing the experiences of African Americans in the South, Mexican Americans in the Southwest, and Chinese Americans on the West Coast with racial boundaries and the race-class nexus in this period, the cases of Atlanta, San Antonio, and San Francisco are instructive.

Even as it moved steadily toward industrialization and experienced urban growth, the postbellum South continued to be shaped by the old plantation economy's rigid White-over-Black hierarchy. In the region's rural areas, labor continued to be performed by a predominantly Black population of low-wage workers under coercive conditions. In the region's fast-growing cities such as Charleston, Nashville, Richmond, and Atlanta, Black workers similarly made up the majority of unskilled or semiskilled labor, making them vulnerable to both the vagaries of a changing economy and new, modern forms of racial exclusion in urban labor markets.[45]

The populations of Black middle-class workers in these cities, whose presence has been well documented by historians, were distinguished from the masses of the Black urban poor by their higher grades of education earned in freedmen's missionary schools and colleges, their ownership of property, or their employment in a limited range of middle-class occupations, working as skilled artisans, shopkeepers, professionals serving segregated Black communities, and, beginning in the 1880s, a handful of jobs in the federal civil service.[46] But their increased visibility in the urban South prompted a further brightening of the already bright Black-White boundary in the form of an evolving Jim Crow legal system. These laws—sanctioned at a federal level by the US Supreme Court's ruling in *Plessy v. Ferguson* (1896)—cut across class lines, keeping all African Americans physically and socially separated from Whites in public spaces, as well as restricting their economic opportunities with racially tiered labor markets, segregated public schools, and physically contained Black residential spaces.[47] These new laws were accompanied by eruptions of racial violence in Southern cities and towns, signaling that the region's White residents would not so easily surrender their dominance over the Black population and were determined to "keep the Negro in his place." Each of these tools of White supremacy seemed aimed at limiting, if not altogether erasing, the newfound social mobility African Americans doggedly pursued well into the early twentieth century.[48]

Among the Southern urban centers, Atlanta was generally thought to epitomize the New South creed of economic modernization and "pragmatism" on matters of race. The city's official census population increased by more than sevenfold from 1870 to 1910, from 21,789 to 154,839. African Americans were very much a part of this new urban landscape, arriving from cities and rural towns within Georgia as well as from neighboring states.[49] Though relatively short-lived, the Reconstruction era had seen rising expectations for mobility among Atlanta's Black population, with newfound access to schooling, the growth of community institutions, and new opportunities for wage labor. As Atlanta's Black population attained greater visibility, so too did demands from Whites that the races be separated, both physically and socially. While a small Black elite of artisans, entrepreneurs, and professionals acquired wealth by serving first Whites and then their own increasingly segregated community, the majority of the city's Black workers found themselves pushed out of skilled jobs and routinely barred from competing with White workers in most areas of employment. This relegated them to the low-paying and unstable occupations as domestics and laborers that would come to be labeled "Negro jobs."[50] Yet politicians and pundits regarded Atlanta as a modern and progressive Southern city that had solved its race problem by refusing to allow old racial antipathies to interfere with economic prosperity. This view would only be challenged when the city became the site of one of the South's deadliest race riots just five years after the beginning of the twentieth century.[51]

On the West Coast, economic development and urban expansion were indelibly shaped by trade with and labor migration from Asia. The region's White residents, who had arrived through processes linked to US conquest and sectional compromises over slavery, distinguished between themselves and those they commonly referred to as "Asiatics." Asian immigrants regularly supplied the region's agricultural, mining, and transportation sectors with low-wage labor that was exploitable in ways that White labor was not.[52] An exceedingly bright, nationally recognized Chinese-White boundary that would later come to include all Asian-origin immigrants was as important for understandings of White supremacy in the West as Black-White distinctions were in the Southern states. During the exclusion era, the Chinese-White boundary also brightened visibly in the form of new segregation laws and practices targeting all classes of Chinese immigrants and their American-born children. Although mob violence against Chinese communities peaked in the mid-1880s, it remained within the repertoire of strategies Whites drew on in their defense of social position.[53]

The exclusion era also saw the emergence of a small and visibly active Chinese American middle class in the Chinese immigrant communities of West Coast cities as well as in the larger communities of the Midwest and

East. The ability of these English-speaking women and men to navigate American culture and institutions would play a crucial role in articulating Chinese American identity.[54] This exclusion-era Chinese American petite bourgeoisie consisted of entrepreneurs, artisans, and professionals who had chosen varying degrees of Americanization or assimilation into middle-class Western culture—often through the various "Chinese missions" that Protestant churches maintained in Chinese immigrant communities.[55] The limits placed on Chinese immigrants' physical mobility helped to create an immigrant broker class engaged in the business of managing Chinese immigration and settlement as labor contractors, transportation agents, and language interpreters. While the immigrant brokers profited from the legal subordination of the Chinese immigrant population, they and their children were often key figures in early struggles against the pervasive forms of racial segregation that emerged in part due to their efforts to secure access to schools, housing, and varied forms of employment.[56]

A popular destination for both foreign immigrants and native-born migrants, San Francisco was another city experiencing rapid growth during the Gilded Age, its population nearly tripling from its 1870 total of 149,473 to 416,912 in 1910.[57] San Francisco was also important as the chief port of entry for Chinese immigrants; its Chinese settlement, or Chinatown, was the largest in the United States. Two years before the passage of the 1882 Chinese Exclusion Act, the US Census reported that Chinese immigrants and their American-born children represented 9 percent of the city's population, though local estimates by city officials placed the figure at closer to 15 percent. By 1900, they would be only 4 percent.[58]

Because of its importance for Chinese immigration, settlement, and community building, San Francisco became an epicenter of White anti-Chinese protest, with politicians, labor unions, and other groups regularly enacting their anti-Chinese sentiments in the early years of the twentieth century.[59] As historian Charlotte Brooks has noted, while White San Franciscans shared dominant beliefs about Black inferiority, Chinese immigrants (and later all Asians) were seen as an "active threat to white people, their institutions, their homes, and their families."[60] Federal immigration laws targeting Chinese immigrants restricted their movement across national borders while both state and local ordinances severely limited the movements of those living in San Francisco, restricting them with few exceptions to the city's Chinatown district for housing and education. This included the small and relatively prosperous middle class of merchants, clerks, and white-collar professionals.[61] As they sought to reproduce social mobility, they, too, regularly confronted a Chinese-White racial boundary that, like the Black-White boundary, was generally bright and relatively durable, making boundary crossing an option.

In the American Southwest, a series of wars of expansion and US conquest had preceded a period of economic transformation and steady urbanization at the turn of the century. Throughout this period, the racial distinction between Whites and Mexicans remained critical if not always clearly defined. Both the blurriness and relative flexibility of the Mexican-White boundary were rooted in the convergence of European-origin settler colonialisms in the region. Even with a Spanish-derived *casta* system that privileged Whiteness, the region's Mexican-origin population had been racialized as either predominantly or categorically non-White in the years leading up to and well after the Mexican-American War, and it experienced a general decline in socioeconomic status during the late nineteenth century. The economic transformation of the region that began in the 1850s and continued through the end of the century resulted in Mexican-origin workers becoming overrepresented in a low-wage workforce tied to agricultural production, ranching, mining, or low-level service work. Racial dynamics generally reflected and reinforced a subordinate status for "Mexicans" — a label indiscriminately applied to both the US-born and the foreign-born. In the Anglo-dominated cities like Tucson, Santa Fe, and San Antonio, the majority of Mexican-origin workers could be found performing semiskilled and unskilled manual labor alongside African Americans and other non-White populations.[62]

Yet in these and other borderland urban centers, Mexican Americans could also be found among the population of turn-of-the-century middle-class workers. Before Mexico's defeats in wars of US expansion and settlement in the mid-nineteenth century, Spanish and Mexican settlers on what was Mexico's northern frontier were among the local elite of prosperous landowners, merchants, and government officials. However, as Anglo American settlers established their own legal, political, and economic institutions in the region's new states and territories, only a minority of the old elite retained their fortunes and social position, though to varying degrees by locality.[63] The Mexican American middle class encountered a Mexican-White boundary whose properties of blurriness and flexibility were subject to change. Even as popular racial ideologies cast Mexicans as non-White foreigners, overlap between Anglo American and Iberian understandings of Whiteness, coupled with the desirability of social and economic alliances among well-to-do families, blurred racial boundaries in some locales.[64] By the century's end, the growing population of Mexican immigrants entering the region would encounter a Mexican-White boundary that was becoming increasingly bright and less flexible.

San Antonio—long considered an important city for regional trade, Mexican culture, and US-Mexican politics dating back to the Texas secession era—was representative of this dynamic. It remained a prominent borderland city during the Gilded Age, with interstate railroad lines arriving in the late 1870s and early 1880s. Between 1870 and 1910, San Antonio's population grew at a rate similar to Atlanta's, from 12,256 to nearly 100,000 people. By 1890, San Antonio was the second-largest metropolis in Texas and one of the region's most ethnically diverse cities.[65] Mexican-origin San Antonians were especially aware of these changes. Formerly the city's majority, by 1880 they made up only 16 percent of its population, now outnumbered by a growing population of native-born Whites and European immigrants. By 1900, however, as political unrest in Mexico fueled migration northward into borderland cities, the Mexican-origin population had sprung back to 26 percent.[66]

San Antonio's Gilded Age Tejano elite of civil servants, small-business owners, and professionals enjoyed privileged status in the new order.[67] While some Anglo San Antonians had articulated understandings of Whiteness that included Tejano elites, others had not. The Anglo Americans of southeastern origin who settled in San Antonio during the last third of the nineteenth century frequently sought to apply some of the same racial logics of Black-White segregation to "Mexicans"—especially the immigrant laboring classes—casting them as a criminal element, limiting their access to public spaces, and even attempting disenfranchisement on racial grounds. This prompted the emergence of a newer bicultural Mexican American middle class focused on serving the needs of a growing and increasingly segregated immigrant community.[68]

Taken together, stories about the populations of African Americans, Chinese Americans, or Mexican Americans who occupied what were visibly middle-class jobs helped Whites make sense of a changing racial and economic landscape. A recent organizational turn in the study of race has shifted attention toward how people generate and extend racial meanings within inhabited institutional sites like neighborhoods, schools, and individual workplaces. Workplaces become crucial sites where individual-level understandings of race and strategies of interaction regularly confront novel situations in the context of state-level racial policies and official organizational practices.[69] The race-class narratives that people develop about different workers and workplaces as they perform assigned tasks, compete for opportunities, and enact class identities both reflect and help constitute the larger racial order. Within and through different sites of middle-class labor, Whites interpreted these new racial actors as either nonthreatening or potentially dangerous, producing varied responses from individuals and from the state. In the chapters that follow, I analyze White racial panics over non-White men's middle-class employment in these three turn-of-the-century urban centers. I do so with an eye toward understanding what these different cases can tell us about how middle-class Whites have responded culturally, politically, and legally to disruptions in their understandings of the race-class nexus. In considering the similarities and differences in how Whites understood and defended racial boundaries between themselves and African Americans, Mexican Americans, and Chinese Americans, I also consider how they mobilized beliefs about middle-class manliness to describe the dangers of occupational mobility among non-White men. I begin in the next chapter with the case of African American mail clerks and carriers in turn-of-the-century Atlanta.

CHAPTER TWO

Fit Only for a Carrier's Place

Black Postal Workers in Atlanta, 1889–1910

On May 23, 1906, city postal commissioner John Broyles decided to dismiss assault charges against Edward C. Ripley, a thirty-seven-year-old White physician, for violently assaulting Julius C. King, a twenty-four-year-old African American mail carrier. The *Atlanta Constitution* reported that King had been seated next to Ripley on a Peachtree Avenue streetcar while making deliveries on his mail route, when two White passengers boarded the car—an elderly, blind man led by a woman. Ripley offered the woman his seat and ordered King to do the same. When King refused, pointing to an already vacant seat behind him and the bundles of undelivered mail in his charge, Ripley struck him in the face with a closed fist, producing serious injuries. Although assaulting a mail carrier was a federal offense punishable by either a one-hundred-dollar fine or up to three years in prison, Broyles stated that while King was entitled to his seat on the streetcar, he had failed to show the "politeness which was once proverbial with the old-time southern negro." Two weeks later, a grand jury also failed to charge Ripley for assaulting King, giving the opinion that "the uniform of government service does not protect its wearer from all circumstances."[1]

The decision of both the local postal commissioner and the grand jury to dismiss the charges against Ripley would prove remarkably prescient. Only three months after the verdict, Atlanta—heralded as the capital of the forward-looking New South—would make international headlines as the scene of one of the nation's bloodiest race riots to date, instigated by sensationalized and largely fabricated newspaper reports claiming an "epidemic" of sexual assaults against White women by Black men in the city and its surrounding areas. For five days beginning on Saturday, September 22, mobs comprising White men and boys from a variety of classes, including those rumored to be from some of the city's "best families," attacked Black men and women on the streets with boards, bricks, guns, and knives, pulling them from streetcars, assaulting them in their places of work, and destroying Black-owned business and homes.[2] George Washington White, one of the city's forty-four Black mail carriers, had been out delivering mail on his route

NEGROES SHOW NO POLITENESS

So Says Recorder While Dismissing the Case Against Dr. Ripley.

Dr. E. C. Ripley was arraigned in the recorder's court yesterday morning for striking Julius King, a negro mail carrier, on a Peachtree street trolley car several days ago.

The evidence was that King declined to give up his seat to a crippled white woman when asked to do so by Dr. Ripley, and an altercation led to the doctor striking the negro.

King contended that there was a vacant seat in the car which the lady could have taken and did take.

Recorder Broyles dismissed the case against Dr. Ripley, as he has been bound over by the United States commissioner for "striking a mail carrier who was in uniform," and because he could be prosecuted in the state courts for an assault.

In rendering his decision the recorder took occasion to say that he deplored the fact that the old-time negro of the south was fast passing away.

"While King had a right to his seat in the car," said the recorder, "he did not show that politeness which was once proverbial with the old-time southern negro. I have often seen negro men sitting in cars while white women with babies in their arms were standing up. So long as such things occur, so long will there be a probability of such affairs occurring as that which took place between Dr. Ripley and King."

Newspaper headline from the *Atlanta Constitution*, May 23, 1906, 5, reporting on the assault against mail carrier Julius C. King by Edward C. Ripley.

accompanied by his thirteen-year-old son, future NAACP executive secretary Walter Francis White, when the rioting began. After using their wagon to carry other Blacks to safety, the two managed to escape to their two-story home on Houston Street in the city's Black Fourth Ward, where the rest of the family sheltered in place. Writing about the incident in his memoirs, Walter later recalled that as he and his father—armed with guns to defend themselves—watched the mob make its way into their neighborhood, he heard one of the mob's members call out, "That's where that nigger mail carrier lives! Burn it down! It's too nice for a nigger to live in."[3]

The mob's targeting of an African American mail carrier's home was far from coincidental. Atlanta, like many turn-of-the-century Southern cities, continued to depend significantly on Black labor, much of it unskilled manual labor paid at low wages. At the same time, the emergence of a formalized system of racial segregation served to increasingly curtail Blacks' social and physical mobility.[4] As one of a limited number of skilled occupations open to educated Black men in Atlanta, employment with the postal service—facilitated both by the city's rapid physical expansion and by the Civil Service Reform Act of 1883—had become an important occupational pathway under Jim Crow. In addition to the status of a civil service job and the promise of steady wages that advanced middle-class aspirations at the city's missionary-founded colleges for Blacks, employment with the postal service also gave Black men the ability to move through the city's segregated spaces. An important body of literature on race and gender has examined how popular understandings of White middle-class manliness were regularly juxtaposed to representations of Black manhood as dangerous and requiring coercive or violent forms of control. These beliefs contributed to an emerging discourse of urban criminality that took shape in the last decades of the nineteenth century.[5] In a context where Whites actively organized to enforce racial boundaries in a rapidly expanding labor market, the visibility of literate and often highly educated Black federal workers represented for them a definitive—and especially troubling—break from the antebellum social order.

Between 1890 and 1910, newspapers in Atlanta and other Georgia cities would regularly report on both actual and alleged cases of theft involving Black men employed as mail clerks and carriers in Atlanta and other cities. In this chapter, I show how the press, politicians, and everyday citizens used these stories to construct new racial danger narratives about Blacks who aspired to join the middle class, casting them as "after-the-war negroes," a new racial type that embodied White anxieties about the urbanized New South. Press coverage of the appointment of Charles Penney to a clerk's position in the Atlanta post office, as well as subsequent stories about the criminal trials of Nelson Martin and other Black mail carriers, called the public's attention to the growing number of formally educated Black men employed in jobs traditionally held by middle-class Whites. In covering these cases, journalists crafted racial narratives claiming that Black mail carriers were representative of a younger generation of educated Blacks whose desires for middle-class lifestyles and social equality with Whites led them to engage in criminal activity and show "disrespect" for traditional racial mores. The victims in these stories included "deserving" White men who allegedly lost civil service jobs to "unqualified" Black applicants; merchants whose funds and goods were stolen from the mail; and White women whose virtue was jeopardized by regular contact with sexually predatory Black mail clerks and carriers. Ultimately, by the early twentieth century, the figure of the Black mail carrier—synonymous with criminality and illegitimate social mobility—would become a potent symbol of racial danger for Whites living in both urban and semiurban areas, capable of rallying them to violent assertions of White supremacy. These cases show how fears of rampant racial boundary crossing helped to develop the middle-class racisms that brightened racial boundaries between Blacks and Whites.

Postal Employment and Black Occupational Mobility

The 1883 Civil Service Reform Act, which established the Civil Service Commission, democratized access to federal employment, particularly for educated Blacks.[6] Sponsored by progressive elements in the Republican Party seeking to eliminate the corruption accompanying the "spoils" system in federal employment, the act created an open examination-based hiring process for federal jobs. Republicans' continued reliance on Black voters led them to stress equal opportunity for Black federal job seekers, but the persistence of racial barriers meant that political patronage and personal connections remained crucial for Blacks looking to secure federal employment, especially in the Southern states.[7] In Georgia, where Republicans actively courted the continued support of Black voters, the act's passage increased Blacks' access to federal jobs beginning in the 1880s. By the 1890s, continued "racial progressivism" in federal appointments by presidents made Georgia the leading Southern state for Black federal employment. In the state's largest urban centers—Savannah, Athens, and Atlanta—civil service reforms opened up new occupational pathways for literate Blacks, many of whom were educated in missionary-run schools.[8] Blacks in these cities were appointed to high-profile federal offices such as register of the Treasury (Athens), collector of internal revenue (Atlanta), port collector of customs (Savannah), and postmaster, while gaining access to lower- and midlevel federal jobs as messengers, porters, and janitors in federal buildings and in the US Postal Service as mail clerks and carriers.[9]

African Americans' history of employment with the postal service dates to the 1860s, when the first known Black postal workers in the United States were appointed. Before these appointments, postal work was considered the exclusive racial province of Whites, with statutes in the early nineteenth century stipulating that only "free white persons" could be employed in the carrying or conveying of mail, punishing those who might subcontract to Black workers with a fine. Exceptions prompted by labor demands allowed Blacks access to only the lowest and most physically demanding jobs, such as the moving of mailbags.[10]

Atlanta's status as an urban hub for the state and the Deep South fueled the expansion of its postal service, creating an important occupational pathway for Black men. Beginning in the 1880s, increased revenues from mail and shipping prompted the Atlanta post office's classification as a "first-class" office. With the new designation came the steady addition of clerks to process mail and monetary transactions, as well as an increased number of regular letter carriers to serve new delivery routes.[11] In 1881 Blacks were three of the city's eight regular letter carriers, but only one of the Atlanta office's five postal clerks.[12] Within four years, Black men were almost half (eight) of the seventeen carriers and had secured four of the main branch's twenty-two clerkships.[13] Records indicate that Atlanta's White postmasters maintained Blacks' access to postal clerk jobs but established a practice of assigning them duties as canceling clerks, distribution clerks, shipping clerks, or assistant paper clerks, where they had no contact with the public and carefully structured interactions with White clerks. Black letter carriers, in addition to being employed in fewer numbers than Whites, appear to have been restricted to urban routes within the city limits. Available records indicate that of the six rural carriers employed in 1911, all were White men.[14]

Civil service records between 1890 and 1910 show that Black men readily took advantage of employment opportunities as both regular and substitute letter carriers, even as racialized employment patterns within the postal service became clear. In 1891 the city's mail was being delivered by 34 full-time letter carriers, 11 of whom were Black men.[15] Of the 36 clerks working at the Atlanta post office, 4 were Black men, and they were still confined to positions that limited interaction with the public.[16] By 1901, the city had nearly doubled the number of regular mail carriers serving routes within Atlanta's city limits to 66, but Blacks were only 10 of those employed. At the same time, Black men were 5 of the 80 postal clerks at the city's main office.[17] Civil service records for 1909 show continued growth in Atlanta's postal service corresponding with the growth of the city's population. As the number of Atlanta residents swelled to nearly 150,000 (nearly one-third of them Black), the number of city carriers increased to 110 and the number of clerks grew to 158. African American men held 30 of the letter carrier positions, and only 5 of those as clerks.[18]

The National Association of Letter Carriers (NALC), the first national labor union representing letter carriers, was established in 1889. The organization had a complex and contradictory relationship with African American postal workers. African Americans were a minority of the association's members. Although the organization included Black men as members and officers nationally, local union chapters in cities and larger towns, called branches, often enforced racial segregation and sometimes organized "Jim Crow" locals. The Postal Record, the official newsletter of the NALC, published stories for its White readers like "Affairs at Coon City" that trafficked in racial stereotypes, even as it failed to report on the violence facing Black postal employees.[19] Atlanta's Gate City branch, No. 172, was started by the city's White letter carriers in 1891.[20] Newspaper reports about the activities of NALC's Atlanta chapter made no mention of Black men as members, and union events were held at segregated establishments.[21] But by the late 1890s the branch had begun to include Black men, even electing them to positions such as branch vice president and "alternate delegate" to the union's national convention. By the early 1900s, White men held only two offices in the branch, president and financial secretary, while Black men held office as vice president, secretary, and delegates to the Federation of Trades.[22]

The Black men who became postal workers between 1880 and 1910 experienced marked social mobility over the course of their lives. The majority of those who secured jobs at the postal service in the 1880s when positions for letter carriers first became available had been children at Emancipation and, owing to the efforts of both Black and White reformers, had managed to acquire formal schooling at an early age. Available records suggest that despite having gained access to education, they typically entered the urban labor market as service workers or as laborers in the city's railroad yards and foundries before managing to make the transition to white-collar work. By the 1890s, however, those Black men who became letter carriers were more likely to have secured federal employment directly after leaving school. Those who moved into postal employment from other lines of work continued to include former manual laborers, but also those who had been clerks, bookkeepers, or teachers in rural school districts. As federal employees, their salaries—which in the early 1890s ranged from $600 to $850 per year—were often the same as those paid to some White letter carriers, and they provided

"Evolution of the Negro home; Residence of a Negro railway postal clerk, South Atlanta," ca. 1908. Schomburg Center for Research in Black Culture, Jean Blackwell Hutson Research and Reference Division, New York Public Library, New York Public Library Digital Collections, https://digitalcollections.nypl.org/items/510d47df-333c-a3d9-e040-e00a18064a99.

security within an increasingly segregated labor market that had been shaken by a number of economic depressions and financial panics.[23] Of the eighty-two Black postal workers serving over this thirty-year period, twenty-three remained employed by the postal service for at least ten years.

Those who chose to leave the security offered by federal employment generally managed to remain within the Black middle class, becoming small-business owners or professionals serving an increasingly segregated African American community. After working as a letter carrier for four years beginning in 1883, former teacher Charles C. Cater opened a grocery store serving Blacks in Atlanta's Fourth Ward.[24] Artaway Tabb, who joined the postal service after graduating from Atlanta University's normal course in 1878, worked for three years as a letter carrier before securing a teaching position in Chattanooga's public schools.[25] By the beginning of the twentieth century, letter carriers would remain among the best-educated and highest-paid Black male workers in Atlanta, with annual salaries ranging from $600 for junior-level carriers to $1,200 for senior-level carriers, and the job was recognized as a viable occupational pathway.[26]

Access to postal clerkships for Black men, however, remained more severely restricted by race. Between 1885 and 1889, the highest-paid Black clerks were college-educated men like Mark Anthony Thomas who earned salaries ranging from $500 to $800 per year, well below the salaries earned by the highest-paid White clerks, which ranged from $1,000 to $2,200 per year.[27] This salary differential remained in place during the 1890s, as the demand for labor market segregation in Atlanta and other cities increased.[28] The few Blacks employed as clerks earned between $700 and $1,000 per year, while White clerks earned as much as $1,700 per year. By 1900, clerks' salaries had generally increased, but racial gaps remained. Black clerks earned between $900 and $1,100 per year. Just before 1910, even with a $100 increase, Black clerks' salaries remained below those of White clerks.[29] In what follows, I show how Black men's initial entrance into new clerkships with more visibility and the potential for higher salaries prompted White clerks to mobilize new narratives about the dangers Black social mobility posed to White men—and White women—in the workplace.

"A Negro in a White Man's Place": The Penney-Lyon Affair

In July 1889, Republican president Benjamin Harrison appointed John R. Lewis, a Union army veteran and part of Atlanta's community of Northern-born Whites, to the position of postmaster for Atlanta. A month later, Lewis's decision to employ Charles C. Penney, a twenty-three-year-old African American man, as a clerk in the post office's registry department prompted the immediate resignations of the office's two White clerks, a fifty-year-old Confederate army veteran named Nathan Lyon and his twenty-one-year-old daughter, Mary. As news of the incident became public, two prominent White businessmen withdrew their names from Lewis's $100,000 civil service bond, and White Atlantans held a bonfire protest in front of the post office where they burned effigies. In the pages of local newspapers, journalists and everyday citizens called Penney's appointment an "insult," claiming that it represented the new perils that urban White middle-class workers faced from upwardly mobile Blacks. Press reports made use of "Black rapist" narratives—popular folk stories about Black men who sexually assaulted White women—to describe the dangers posed to Mary Lyon, refitting them for the workplace as a danger that required new ways of thinking about the defense of White women's "racial honor."[30] At the same time, journalists also used Nathan Lyon's resignation and the revelation that Wilson Sturgess, a seventeen-year-old White youth who had not been placed in the registry department, to argue that Black social mobility was also endangering the occupational prospects of middle-class White men. Ultimately, journalists, politicians, and ordinary workers would draw on linked understandings of race, class, and manhood to articulate the new social and economic dangers that Blacks' movement into white-collar federal employment posed to Whites in Atlanta and other Georgia cities.

Penney's social trajectory was representative of postbellum Atlanta's Black middle class, which had managed to make significant strides since Emancipation. Penney's father, Ernest, a prosperous hotel cook, was among the many former slaves who found employment as semiskilled service workers.[31] The family's eldest son, Edgar, became an ordained minister after graduating from Atlanta University, one of the city's missionary-run Black colleges, in 1877 and subsequently joined its board of trustees. Edgar became acquainted with Lewis, a well-respected business owner, through his membership on the board. Charles followed his elder brother to Atlanta University and completed its three-year college preparatory course in 1883.[32] According to what he later told the press, Lewis encouraged Penney to seek employment at the postal service, which at that time employed two Black clerks and only three regular mail carriers. When he sat for the civil service examination that March, Penney was one of fifteen other examinees, nine of whom were Black.[33]

Historians of the US civil service note that appointments generally followed a "rule of three," in which appointing officers were allowed to select from among the three highest-scoring candidates on the civil service examination when filling vacancies.[34] As one of the two highest scorers on the exam, Penney was considered eligible for a position as a postal clerk. The other high scorer was a White seventeen-year-old bookstore clerk named Wilson N. Sturgess, whom Lewis assigned to the money order department, where he would have regular contact with post office customers, at a salary of $600 per year. Lewis, claiming to have been aware of "southern prejudices" and thinking Sturgess "too young" for monetary responsibilities, assigned Penney to the registered mail department, which entailed limited contact with the public and an identical salary. Though the majority of postal clerk positions continued to be held by White men, two other Black men already served as clerks at the Atlanta office—one as a distribution clerk charged with sorting mail and one as a letter and paper clerk. The registry department had previously been staffed only by White clerks and was supervised by Nathan Lyon, a five-year veteran of the postal service. As the supervisor of the Atlanta post office's registered letters department, Nathan Lyon earned an annual salary of $1,100 while supervising his unmarried daughter Mary, whose own $800 salary as a delivery and window clerk supplemented the Lyon family income.[35]

According to press accounts, on Monday, August 5, 1889, after Penney's swearing in, Lewis escorted him to the registry department, where Lewis introduced him to Nathan Lyon. Lyon immediately took offense at the "insult" offered him, reportedly exhibiting both anger at Penney's presence in the office and "fear" that he "would next be introduced to his daughter." Refusing to work alongside Penney, Lyon asked Lewis to delay his installment in the office, allowing him and his daughter enough time to complete their work before resigning their positions. Lewis's refusal to accommodate Lyon's request prompted Mary Lyon to offer written notice of her "immediate" resignation. As news of the incident spread, members of the press and the public called and visited the registry office to express support for the Lyons and anger at the appointment. When interviewed by a *Constitution* reporter, Nathan Lyon revealed that he intended to resign once the registered mail he was responsible for had been delivered, expressing concerns about leaving cash receipts "in the hands of a negro."[36] Lewis, when questioned by the same reporter about his decision to place a Black man in an office with a "young, unmarried White woman," replied that he had been bound by civil service laws to appoint Penney, "the highest on the list of eligibles," adding that contact between him and the window clerk would be minimal. In the following days, Lewis would be assailed by the press and the public for having leveled a "grave insult" against both Mary and Nathan Lyon, and for having "pushed aside" Sturgess, who, the press claimed, should have received the clerkship now held by Penney.[37]

Statements from the press about the Penney-Lyon affair invoked the increasingly popular beliefs about Black men as sexual predators to describe the dangers of a racially mixed white-collar workplace for White women like Mary Lyon. By the late 1880s, White working women, particularly those who were young and unmarried, had become an increasingly common sight in Atlanta. Noting their numbers in the city, an 1881 *Daily Constitution* article made careful distinctions between the "working girls" from modest backgrounds who found employment in factories and mills and the "young ladies" from "excellent families" who, like Mary Lyon, managed to secure white-collar or skilled employment as teachers, saleswomen, or office clerks.[38] Regularly stressing the belief that these women should work only

A NEGRO APPOINTEE

CREATES A DECIDED STIR IN THE POSTOFFICE.

A Negro Is Appointed to a Place in the Registry Department—This Leads to Two Resignations—Both Sides of the Story.

The first colored appointee of General Lewis the republican postmaster, reported for duty yesterday.

This new servant of the United States government is C. C. Penny. He will occupy the position left vacant by the resignation of Mr. Fred Wedemeyer in the reistered letter, department.

Early yesterday morning General Lewis took his porotege to the United States court where he was sworn in by Clerk O. C. Fuller. When this formality had been complied with, General Lewis and the negro returned to the postoffice and entered the registered letter room of which Mr. Lyons is superintendent. The only other occupant of the office at the time was Miss Lyons, who acts as delivery clerk for her father.

General Lewis began to introduce the negro as "Mister" Penny. As soon, however, as Mr. Lyons realized what was being done he turned his back on the new clerk and fearing that he would next be introduced to his daughter took General Lewis by the arm and led him into the outer room.

Mr. Lyons, thinking that a gratuitos insult had been offered himself and more particularly his daughter, was very angry. Exactly what was said neither gentleman would say. Mr. Lyons asked if the installation of the negro could not be deferred for a day or two in order to give himself and Miss Lyons an opportunity of settling up their books and leaving. General Lewis said that it would be out of the question. This made it impossible for Miss Lyons to remain and she at once wrote to General Lewis:

General J. R. Lewis.—Dear Sir: This is to tender my resignation as delivery clerk to take effect immediately. Respectfully, A. V. LYONS.

She found, however, that it would take several hours to put her work in order and she was obliged to remain until this was done.

In the meanwhile, Mr. Lyons cleared a little space at one end of a big table in the outer office for Penny and there he did his first day's work for the United States. Mr. Lyons has signed receipts for a considerable amount of registered matter and he will be forced to remain until it is delivered or leave it in charge of Penny, which he refuses to risk.

WHAT GENERAL LEWIS SAYS.

When questioned about the appointment General Lewis said:

"I had no choice under the civil service law other than to act as I have done."

Newspaper headline from the *Atlanta Constitution*, August 6, 1889, 8, reporting on the appointment of Charles Penney to a postal clerk's position and the ensuing scandal.

until marriage, clergymen, reformers, and workingmen's groups expressed concerns about the need to protect them from some of the city's more harmful influences—including the potential for interracial contact.[39] While Atlanta's employers generally maintained segregated workplaces, white-collar workplaces like the post office were considered to be among the safest and most desirable for White women—places where they could be safe from men of questionable reputation and, more importantly, from non-White men.

In the days after the story became public, *Atlanta Constitution* editor and New South apostle Henry W. Grady attacked Lewis for "placing a black negro where he would be in almost constant association with the best Anglo-Saxon blood in the south." Grady rejected claims that Lewis had considered Southern attitudes in choosing Penney's assignment, arguing that Mary Lyon could have been "surrounded . . . wholly with white men," where she would presumably be safe from sexual danger.[40] Citing what he argued was common knowledge about Black men, Grady later described the specific perils of interracial interactions in a clerical environment. "There is not a man in the country from the president down who will not agree that it was unwise to say the least, to put a negro man at the same desk with a young white woman and where she would be forced to constantly consult with him and exchange papers and data!" Had Mary Lyon not resigned, he continued, she "would have been forced into a constant exchange of papers with the negro appointee—to sit facing him at a desk for most of the day—and to have been in constant association with him."[41] Reports of the incident also appeared in large and small newspapers across Georgia, highlighting Mary Lyon's "immediate resignation" as well as the "considerable indignation" raised by Penney's "obtrusion" on what some embellished to include multiple "white ladies" in the registry department.[42]

Prominent members of the public like ex-postmaster John Renfroe and former assistant postmaster Howell Jackson amplified fears about contact between Penney and Lyon in an office environment when they told a *Constitution* reporter that, based on their knowledge of the registry clerk's duties, it was "absolutely impossible" to have prevented Penney from having contact with Lyon. The paper also printed letters from White Atlantans expressing anger at Penney's appointment, including one local businessman who registered "his protest and indignation" that "a negro" would "be allowed to become an associate, in the business of that department, of one of the most respectable and worthy young white ladies of [this] community."[43]

In describing fears about the dangers of integrated workplaces for White women, newspaper reports and public statements about the Penney-Lyon affair also revealed an awareness of a new "troubling" development—middle-class identities among Black men. Penney, who spoke to reporters only once and "remained seated" while being questioned, would only confirm that he "had graduated from the Atlanta university on the first of June and on the 25th of the same month passed the civil service examination with sixteen others, the majority whom were white."[44] In defending his choice of Penney for the registry clerkship, Lewis openly praised his ability and intellect, suggesting that he had exhibited qualities of middle-class manliness. "I had known a brother of Penny's [sic]—had served with him on the board at [Atlanta] university," he told the *Constitution*. "I knew him to be a most excellent man, and believed his brother to be the same."[45] Lewis added that he found Penney to have better handwriting than Sturgess and claimed that he was the "brightest of the two." Though it conceded that Penney was "well-educated," the *Constitution* introduced claims that his appointment was illegitimate, noting that he "refused to say what political influences had been used on his behalf."[46] While Penney's education, social connections, and dignified bearing before the press undermined the claims of Black intellectual inferiority that had traditionally been used to support White rule, Whites would respond by introducing claims about the moral inferiority of upwardly mobile Blacks and the economic dangers they posed to hardworking Whites.

Members of the press and the public responded to revelations about Penney's education by offering new explanations of Black inferiority—ones that described Black men as morally unfit for white-collar work and a risk to the city's economic standing. Responding to Lewis's appointment of Penney, two of his bond guarantors—Judge Henry Tompkins and cotton-gin manufacturer Edward Van Winkle—resigned as signatories, citing their belief that Blacks were untrustworthy and incapable of performing the work of postal clerks. "I do not think a negro responsible," Van Winkle told the *Constitution*, "and believe him fit for only a carrier's place."[47] In his letter of resignation from Lewis's bond, Tompkins stated that as a man who wished "to ensure the preservation of the white man's supremacy," he was concerned that Lewis had "seemed swift to make a selection of the negro rather than the white man, and for a very responsible place in the handling of registered letters."[48] Statements from ordinary citizens underscored the perceived dangers of employing Black men as clerks by alluding to alleged tendencies toward theft. Nathan Lyon told a reporter for the *Athens Weekly Banner* that he "would not have [stayed] a week in the office with that negro," as he had "too much money to handle."[49] The *Constitution* quoted businessmen and former postal workers who expressed similar views, including an "Alabama Street Merchant" who received "large sums of money through the registered letter department of the postoffice [sic]" and an unnamed "old postoffice [sic] employee" who pointed to what he saw as the certain financial "ruin" that a Black registry clerk would bring to registered mail customers, Lewis, and his bondsmen.[50]

As the press and public had quickly homed in on the perceived threats Penney's appointment posed to White women like Mary Lyon, they also called attention to the new challenges middle-class White men like Nathan Lyon faced from Black men's social mobility. Given the privileged place White men were presumed to occupy in the labor market—and as his family's primary breadwinner—Nathan Lyon's resignation was even more significant than his daughter's. Letters from the public lauded him for his "stand" against Penney's appointment and his defense of his daughter's honor. Newspapers outside Atlanta offered embellished accounts of his initial meeting with Penney and his exchange with Lewis. On the evening of August 8, a group of White men that included two former mail clerks organized a protest against what they described as Lewis's attempted "humiliation" of the city's Whites.[51] During the protest, which reportedly drew hundreds to the corner of Marietta and Forsyth Streets, organizers burned effigies of Lewis and a state Republican Party official while a hired brass band played "Dixie" and "The Rogue's March." Members of the crowd offered chants of "Hang them" and "Give us Penney." After being asked to disperse by Georgia's governor, John Gordon, a smaller group led the band to Lyon's home on Poplar Street, where they "serenaded" him and expressed approval of "his conduct throughout the trouble."[52] Even as Grady, concerned with how the image of a violent Atlanta would be used by Northern critics, chastised the event's organizers and called for "wise and quiet" methods of protest, fears that Black workers were displacing White tradesmen remained central. On the same day that it printed Grady's rebuke of the protests, the *Constitution* ran a column by Addison Milton Wier (writing as Southern "everyman" Sarge Plunkett) titled "Who Loves the Nigger?," in which he claimed that a preference among White "town folks" for Black labor had forced White craftsmen into idleness.[53]

Wilson Sturgess also emerged in popular depictions as a victim of Blacks' "illegitimate" social mobility, a middle-class White man whose "natural" ability to secure social position and ensure manliness through white-collar employment had been undermined. In press reports, editorials, and letters from the public, Whites in Atlanta and surrounding communities had seized on

Sturgess's performance on the civil service exam to advance claims that he had been unfairly "pushed aside" by Lewis for Penney's advancement, making no mention of the "rule of three."[54] "The report of the civil service commission shows that in examination [Sturgess] stood $87^{1/2}$, and the negro Penny [sic] stood only 85," the Athens Weekly Banner reported. "This, saying nothing of the proficiency of a white man over a negro, is sufficient to condemn Mr. Lewis for the appointment."[55] Although it had been reported that Sturgess had been terminated from his clerkship in the money order department after failing to secure a bond for federal employment due to his age, the press continued to amplify claims that, having been assured he would receive a post, he had become the victim of a corrupt process that favored Blacks.[56] After speaking with Sturgess about the affair, a reporter for the Athens paper described him as having "soured on the Atlanta postoffice [sic] managers," claiming that Lewis fired him in order to "fill the positions with negroes instead of white men."[57]

Newspaper stories about Penney, Sturgess, and the Lyons helped White Georgians to make sense of a changing social landscape in which the ability to reproduce social position was no longer certain. Claims that respectable White working women like Mary Lyon faced imminent sexual danger from educated Black workers reinforced popular stories about Black men as savage and unmanly rapists, refitting them to describe the new population of educated Blacks who managed to secure white-collar jobs. Although both Nathan Lyon and Sturgess managed to secure other white-collar employment after the incident, depictions of White men like them—and the skilled workers depicted in Wier's column—as being threatened by Black men's pursuit of middle-class jobs also resonated with the public. These new challenges to middle-class White men's manliness, which included threatening their economic livelihood and undermining their ability to protect White women, required new responses that fit the middle-class workplace. Press attention to Penney's clerkship eventually waned, but not before the Constitution ran a story about Lewis being put on "trial" at Atlanta's elite Capital City Club, where some of his fellow members had demanded that he be expelled on the grounds of "indecency" for having placed "a negro" in the same office as "a young white lady." During the hearing, in which the Lyons gave statements to an assembly of club members, Lewis—who was ultimately exonerated—maintained his innocence and stated his "unfailing support for physical separation of the races."[58]

Black newspapers within Georgia and elsewhere described Whites' public furor over Penney's hiring as politically motivated. The Savannah

Tribune reprinted an item from the *Chicago Inter-ocean* claiming that prominent White Atlanta Democrats, upset over the "dangerous" popularity of Lewis and state Republican party chairman Alfred E. Buck—a Union army veteran—with the city's moderate Whites, had used Penney's rightful placement in the registry department to "impair" their social influence while attacking Black social progress.[59] The *Washington Bee*, whose readership included many of that city's federally employed Black elites, took a similar position, claiming that the entire episode was evidence that as Blacks advanced, there were "some brave and honest white Republicans . . . as anxious for the Negro to succeed as some of our Bourbon Democrats in the South, are anxious for them to fail and be the menials of the most common type of white humanity." The *Bee* also reprinted excerpts from sympathetic columns in the *New York Press* that criticized White Southerners for their readiness "on the slightest provocation to lapse into the 'niggah-hating' rhetoric of former days" at the evidence of Black social progress. Defending Lewis's selection of Penney, whose performance on the civil service examination called attention to the "change in the condition of the colored race since the war," the paper noted the presence of Black federal employees at "important desks in the various departments in Washington," describing them as a "capable, industrious, attentive and polite" group with whom "no refined woman clerk need fear contact."[60]

Journalists and members of the public continued to use Penney's employment to underscore the view that Black men's social mobility was illegitimate as well as dangerous. The *Constitution* reported that the New York–based American Surety Company had "refused to make a bond" to secure Penney's employment as a registry clerk "on the ground [*sic*] that he has no clerical experience, and that they did not care to become his security."[61] Penney remained in his clerkship for no more than five years before leaving the postal service and turning to self-employment as the co-owner of a furniture store in Atlanta's Fourth Ward.[62] During the controversy over his appointment, the two Black men already employed as clerks, Marcus Thomas and Elijah Bass, remained absent in the press, save for in *Atlanta Constitution* editor Henry Grady's claim that the existence of Black postal clerks in other departments disproved the claim that White Atlantans were intolerant of Black social mobility. In what follows, I show how the press would build on claims about Black men's racial unsuitability for clerical work to describe the employment of Black men as letter carriers as an even more dangerous development for the city's middle- and working-class Whites.

"He Robbed the Mails": Black Mail Carriers and Narratives of "Negro Crime"

As the excitement over Penney's appointment waned, the press turned its attention to the increasing visibility of Black men's employment as mail carriers. The *Atlanta Constitution* for November 19, 1889, reported that the "colored brother" was "slowly but surely coming to the front in the Atlanta postoffice [*sic*]," noting that Black men had been appointed to clerkships on the railway mail service, the "regular force of carriers," and they were among the "substitutes in the line of promotion in case of the removal or resignation of any of the white regulars." The article, which ran in other Georgia papers, concluded with a warning that "some of the democratic employees are kicking, but they're not kicking very hard."[63] Four months after noting the increase in Black mail carriers, newspapers in Atlanta and other Georgia cities began carrying reports on the arrest, investigation, and criminal trial of a twenty-eight-year-old Black substitute mail carrier named Nelson D. Martin, who was accused of stealing cash and parcels from the mail pouch of a White letter carrier. Arresting officers and investigators claimed to reporters to have found "strong evidence" linking Martin to the theft of the packages, which contained goods, paper currency, coins, and bank drafts totaling more than $450.[64] According to investigators, Martin had already spent part of the cash—including giving his mother $25, paying a hackman $5, and giving an unidentified party $4.50.[65]

The press seized on Martin's arrest, using it to characterize Black mail carriers as devoid of middle-class manliness—lazy, dishonest, and inclined to thievery. "One of Lewis's angels! He sleeps in the station house," the *Constitution* wrote, reporting that Martin was accused of stealing from "one of the oldest, best and most reliable carrier[s] the Atlanta postoffice [*sic*] has ever had."[66] Papers outside Atlanta carried similar stories about Martin's arrest and charges, referring to him as "one of Buck's pets" or "Buck's coons," linking his alleged crime to Republican support of federal appointments going to Black men.[67] Press reports carefully tied the charges against Martin to the larger "problem" of social mobility among postbellum urban Blacks. The *Athens Weekly Banner* directly accused Buck of "wrecking" Georgia's mail service "by supplanting competent and honest white men with ignorant and thieving negroes."[68]

In addition to mail carriers, the press pointed to other figures who amplified White fears about Black occupational mobility. Three days after Martin's arrest, the *Constitution* reported his release on a $500 bond. The paper identified the bond's guarantors as Martin's father, Daniel, a carpenter employed in the central railyards, and Christopher C. Wimbish, a former mail clerk who had recently been appointed Atlanta's first African American surveyor of customs.[69] While the press offered no speculation about either man's wealth or its source, White readers would certainly have taken notice of Black men who had acquired resources associated with middle-class manhood. On April 4, the paper reported that the US postal commissioner had issued a warrant for Martin's arrest at the same time that he had been rearrested on a charge of public drunkenness. Reporting that the prosecution claimed to have an "overwhelming amount of evidence" that would prove Martin's guilt, the *Constitution* predicted his conviction, reporting that he would "probably be added to the list of unfortunates who pay high for the privilege of holding office under the present administration."[70]

The press reiterated its claims about the dangers of Black social mobility at the start of Martin's trial, using his case to link the problem to generational differences among Atlanta's postbellum Blacks. "The case is one that contrasts sharply the old and the new issue of darkeys," the *Constitution* wrote. "The defendant is a highly educated negro. He went to school twelve years, finally graduating from the Atlanta university. He was one of the civil service examiners once and afterwards a letter carrier, when something got wrong with a registered package."[71] Turning to Martin's father, the paper described him as "a typical old-fashioned negro" with "no education," who was now "footing the bill . . . for his son's defense." The paper noted, "When the trouble came the resources of the educated negro were measured by the clothes on his back." Although the *Constitution* printed a correction the following day, noting that Atlanta University officials had confirmed that Martin was not a graduate of the institution, there was likely little doubt among White Atlantans that Blacks' access to higher education and middle-class jobs posed real dangers to both individuals and institutions.[72] Although newspapers neglected to report the outcome of his criminal trial that year, Martin was apparently dismissed from the postal service and found work as a mechanic.[73] Martin's dismissal from the postal service seemed to confirm for Whites that the younger generation of educated Blacks who aspired to middle-class manhood were a problem for the city's Whites, but they also burdened older Blacks like Martin's father who earned a living without overtly violating racial norms.

In the wake of the Martin case, Georgia newspapers would continue to link mail theft with Black postal employees and substitute delivery men in both rural and urban areas, portraying them as using their federal positions to pilfer money and goods from those who used the mail. In April 1892 when Robert Harkness, a Black seventeen-year-old part-time delivery man for the Forsyth County postmaster, was arrested for stealing thirty dollars from two registered packages, the *Constitution* described him as a "young negro mail carrier" who had committed a "cunning theft."[74] Yet Black men were not the only ones to be found guilty of this crime. In July 1892, the *Constitution* reported that two young White men—eighteen-year-old Foster Blodgett and nineteen-year-old Will Gause—both from prominent Atlanta families, had been arrested for "systematically" stealing some "several hundred dollars" from a local ticket scalper's mailbox over a matter of weeks. Blodgett, whose elder brother was a superintendent at the Atlanta post office and whose family members had long included high-ranking officials in the mail service, was described by the paper as "heartbroken" after confessing his crime and showing remorse that was "pitiful in the extreme." The *Constitution* was also quick to point out that while Blodgett had secured his position in the post office through his family connections, he was "not an employ [sic] of the government at all, being only eighteen years of age." The paper added that "the young men have hundreds of friends who regret the trouble. The boys are young and they feel heartily the serious trouble in which they find themselves."[75]

In December of the following year, the *Constitution* reported on allegations against another Black mail carrier, Eugene M. Martin (no relation to Nelson Martin). Eugene Martin was emblematic of the city's emergent Black middle class. A former schoolteacher of visibly mixed racial ancestry, Martin had come to Atlanta from Tennessee. Before securing work as a substitute mail carrier, he had worked as a clerk for R. W. Wright, a Black wholesale grocer. Martin was promoted to the rank of carrier in 1891. Martin and his family, which included two small children, lived on Leach Street in Atlanta's Fourth Ward surrounded by mostly Black and some White neighbors.[76] On December 14, 1893, the *Constitution* reported Martin's arrest on charges that he had embezzled funds from two letters found in his possession.[77] The paper speculated that there might be a connection between Martin's arrest and an investigation into a series of thefts at the post office involving missing bank drafts addressed to local merchants. In fact, it used the occasion of Martin's arrest to report on physical changes in the post office building that "give absolute protection to the mails."[78]

As it had in the Nelson Martin case only two years earlier, the press used reporting of Eugene Martin's arrest and trial to strengthen dominant narratives about the dire consequences of Black men's desire for social mobility for both Whites and Blacks. In addition to linking the charges against Martin

MARTIN ARRESTED.

A Colored Mail Carrier Rests Under a Heavy Imputation.

BEFORE JUDGE BROYLES THIS MORNING

He Was Nabbed on Suspicion, and Letters Were Found on His Person—The Elevator Man Implicated.

Newspaper headline from the *Atlanta Constitution*, December 14, 1893, 10, reporting on Eugene Martin's arrest after being accused of theft.

with the ongoing investigation into financial losses by Atlanta merchants, the *Constitution* again alluded to claims that older, uneducated Black men who tended to respect racial boundaries faced personal ruin from their associations with young, educated Blacks. The paper claimed that at the time of Martin's arrest, Andrew Jones, a forty-five-year-old Black elevator operator in the Atlanta Customs House building, had "been nabbed as his accomplice." Jones became a sympathetic figure for the press, having been drawn into corruption by Martin. Describing Jones as "a harmless and inoffensive fellow" who would never have "planned or executed a fraud," the paper reported, "those who know him say that he must have been taken in."[79]

The following day at Martin's hearing, however, Postal Commissioner John Broyles dismissed the charges against Martin. Testimony revealed that Martin had been personally delivering the two letters found in his possession to Black residents who were neighbors of his and not listed in the city directory. Other papers Martin had at the time of his arrest had been given to him by Jones, which he had offered to deliver to the proper authorities at the post office. Postal delivery superintendent Edwin F. Blodgett, who supervised the letter carriers, spoke in Martin's defense about his good character, as did the White customers on Martin's route.[80] In reporting on Martin's exoneration, the paper printed what it claimed was a quote from Jones in exaggerated dialect, in which he appeared to largely shrug off his ordeal with "a smile of complacency" that "began to circulate around his face, and seemed to lift his hat above his forehead." "Well, boss, here I is . . . They had the wrong man . . . but I'se satisfied. I guess de Lord wuz tryin' my pashuns like he did Job's. He knows what's best, He knows what's best."[81]

Although the *Constitution* made no direct reference to Martin's education, its juxtaposition of him alongside the "inoffensive" Jones would serve to reinforce differences between what the paper had previously described as "old" and "new" Blacks. While efforts to link Martin to criminal activity had failed, the press nevertheless managed to convey to the public the dangers of Black social mobility. Martin's exoneration likely alarmed Whites more than his alleged crime. Immediately after his trial, the *Constitution*'s editors printed a letter it received from Martin in which he gave a fuller accounting of his arrest and exoneration. He explained how he had come by the letters and "other papers" that were in his possession at the time of his arrest. Martin wrote that Jones, who saw him "passing on the street," called him into a barroom to look at some papers, which Martin had offered to take to the "proper authorities" at the post office. "The papers were entrusted to me and I started out," Martin wrote, "when I was met at the door by Detective Bedford and others, placed under arrest and marched off to police headquarters."[82] He further noted that the hearing—at which he had appeared with his own lawyer—had resulted in his being fully exonerated, but dismissed from the postal service. "Great injustice having been done me," he concluded, "I wish at least, my friends should now know that I have been fully vindicated."[83] The day after the *Constitution* published Martin's letter, it reported that "one hundred and fifty business men," all on Martin's route, had signed a petition praising his character and asking for his reinstatement, which was effected immediately. Martin would remain with the postal service until his retirement in 1912, during which time he would be elected to a two-year term as state vice president of the NALC for Georgia.[84]

By the 1890s, Whites in Atlanta and other Georgia cities had come to accept racial narratives that cast Black letter carriers as thieves and fraudsters. Newspapers across the state regularly ran stories about cases of theft or impropriety involving Black postal workers.[85] These stories, which regularly featured educated Black men as perpetrators of crimes, helped Whites of all classes to make sense of a changing racial landscape where Blacks could now access both higher grades of schooling and white-collar jobs that supported claims to middle-class manliness. Highlighting these alleged crimes and violent incidents bolstered the popular belief in Black inferiority in the face of visible Black mobility—that despite their education, Black men remained morally incapable of true middle-class manliness. In Georgia's largest urban centers, where Black mail carriers remained a common sight, Whites continued to accuse them not only of theft but also of taking jobs from eligible White men and violating racial etiquette with illegitimate claims to middle-class identity.[86] However, as requests were made for rural mail routes serving smaller towns, Whites openly resisted any efforts to assign them to Black mail carriers, drawing on "Black rapist" narratives to link them with sexual assaults against White women.

In April 1899, the appointment of two Black men to serve as mail carriers on a newly established rural route in northeast Georgia prompted Bibb County's congressional representative Charles Bartlett and Georgia senator Augustus Bacon to request a meeting with Charles E. Smith, the US postmaster general in Washington.[87] According to the press, the postmaster in Macon, the county seat, had selected the names of two White applicants when he was informed by Smith's office that the appointments had already been given to Martin Logan and Charles Stubbs, both of whom were among the highest scorers on the exam and active among the city's Black Republicans.[88] The *Savannah Morning News* reported that in their meeting with Smith, Bartlett and Bacon had insisted that the two mail carrier positions—each paying an annual salary of $400—should go to White men, adding that "it would be unwise to put negroes in such places," given the "conditions and sentiment in Georgia."[89]

The "conditions and sentiment" the paper referred to was the mood among Black and White residents following the brutal lynching of twenty-four-year-old Black day laborer Sam Hose (or Holt) in the nearby town of Newnan that same week. Hose, after killing a White farmer in self-defense, was falsely accused of killing him in cold blood and raping his wife and child. News of the alleged assault was widely reported, with varying details but with a consistent depiction of Hose as a violent sexual predator. According to later reports, members of the White mob at Hose's lynching fought over his body parts, which were sold as souvenirs.[90] Shortly after returning from Washington, Bartlett received word from Smith's office that Bibb County's free mail service, which had been scheduled to begin on May 1, would be "indefinitely postponed" pending a decision.[91]

Three weeks later, in a widely publicized address, former Georgia governor William J. Northen called attention to Bartlett's efforts to secure White mail carriers in the context of the Hose lynching, linking Black mail carriers with White women's sexual peril. An influential Baptist minister turned politician, Northen was an avowed White supremacist who publicly supported New South ideals.[92] Speaking at Boston's Tremont Temple Baptist Church before an audience of civic leaders and parishioners who had gathered to hear him debate prominent Black clergyman Benjamin W. Arnett on the "the present situation as to the colored people of the South," Northen gave a lengthy address in which he condemned "mob law" but condoned lynching as fit punishment for rape.[93] Offering a lurid and entirely embellished account of Hose's alleged crimes, Northen contextualized Bartlett's efforts on behalf of his constituents not as a matter of prejudice but because, under the circumstances, "the farmers did not want negro carriers to deliver their mails in the absence of all but the women of the families from home."[94] Northen's use of what Jacqueline Dowd-Hall has called the "folk pornography" of the "black beast rapist" appealed to Whites in the audience who, despite his exceeding his allotted time, invited him to finish his remarks. Both Southern and Northern newspapers reprinted excerpts from Northen's speech, where it not only met fierce rebuttal by Black civic leaders and White progressives but also prompted letters of support for "shedding new light on the negro problem."[95]

While the figure of the Black rapist had been invoked a decade earlier in the Penney-Lyon affair in opposition to Black men receiving postal clerkships, mail carriers—who had previously been seen as posing no threat to White women—were now popularly described as sexual predators. By July, Georgia papers reported that Bartlett had contacted Washington to withdraw Bibb County's request for mail service. The press generally praised his efforts, placing the blame on Republican politicians seeking "negro votes."[96] In Atlanta, where the common sight of Black mail carriers inspired concerns about labor competition and theft but not sexual assault, the *Constitution* expressed support for Bartlett's efforts, attributing them to the difference between urban and rural tastes. "However unobjectionable negro carriers might be for the cities," the paper editorialized, "they would necessarily be very objectionable to the country communities."[97] The *Savannah Morning News*, however, praised Bartlett in a lengthy editorial where it repeated Northen's claim that Black mail carriers posed a danger to White women in rural areas. "Carriers would have to visit the homes of farmers when the men-folks were away in the fields or in the villages or county towns," the paper wrote, "and the women-folks of the widely separated homes would be afraid of such outrages as are often committed in the rural districts." The paper further cited the risks of employing Black men as mail carriers. "Of a dozen carriers in the rural districts eleven might turn out to be decent and well-behaved men. The twelfth, however might be a brute and commit a horrible crime in some lonely farm house if the opportunity presented itself." "As there would be no way to distinguish the one that might be bad from the good ones," the *Morning News* editorialized, "there would always be apprehension of a tragedy in the free delivery district."[98]

New narratives about Black mail carriers as sexual predators became a useful resource for White Democratic politicians in Georgia and other Southern states in the early 1900s. While stories about Black mail carriers and mail theft had spoken to White men's economic fears about Black social mobility, these new narratives played on a fear that would resonate in the rural districts—that of Black men's physical mobility as mail carriers. In May 1903, newspapers reported that White residents of Gallatin, Tennessee, threatened Black mail carrier John Allgood with death if he continued servicing the rural route. The county's congressional representative responded to claims of "southern barbarism" by Northern journalists by referencing narratives about Black mail carriers as sexual predators. Gallatin's congressional representative defended his constituents, claiming that "knowing the characteristics of the negro," Whites living in "sparsely populated and poorly policed rural sections" would be "in a state of distress when they realize that a negro, whether he is a mail carrier or not, is walking about the neighborhood."[99] Tennessee's ex-governor was quick to concur, telling a news correspondent that "when the father, husband, or son is away from home he is not anxious to have a negro official go to the home and across the threshold, either to deliver mail or for any other purpose."[100] The *Tammany Times*, a New York–based weekly aimed at Democratic loyalists, reprinted claims from a Tennessee congressman that given the "nameless crimes of the negroes," rural White men "could not but regard with apprehension the prospect of negro mail carriers coming to their homes in their absence." The paper also blamed President Theodore Roosevelt, whose administration it claimed "had encouraged many negroes to cherish hopes of social equality and miscegenation."[101] The following year, J. J. Spalding, a vice-chair of Georgia's Democratic Party, specifically pointed to Black mail carriers in Georgia's rural districts as the unavoidable outcome of Republican control in Washington. "Do the people of our state, particularly those living in the sparsely settled districts," Spalding asked rhetorically, "want negroes carrying mail to their homes when they are away at business or at work in the field? . . . We have them in the cities now, and given the republicans [*sic*] the opportunity, and they will put them in the rural districts."[102]

In Atlanta, concerns about Black mail carriers focused on their violations of racial etiquette stemming from their dangerous claims to middle-class manliness. Only three months before Spalding's warning about Black mail carriers in rural districts, the *Constitution* reported that Silas L. Chandler, a recently hired mail carrier, had been fined $3.75 for disrespecting a White policeman. Officer William Englett, who made a case against Chandler for "disorderly conduct," claimed that Chandler had "abused him when asked to move along late at night." The paper reported that once it had been announced to the courtroom that Chandler was not present because of his duties at the post office, Englett stated to the court that he "wanted the case dismissed" because Chandler had offered him an apology. According to the paper, the White city councilman Frank Hilburn, acting as the court's recorder, refused to dismiss Chandler's fine. Insisting that the city's policemen "must be respected," Hilburn upheld the fine.[103]

Press coverage of other interactions between Black letter carriers and White men in Atlanta and other Georgia cities helped to only further brighten racial boundaries by strengthening links between Whiteness and middle-class manliness. This was made clear in Edward Ripley's assault on uniformed mail carrier Julius King, mentioned at the start of this chapter. When Ripley appeared before Postal Commissioner William Colquitt for his arraignment, he was represented by his brother, attorney T. J. Ripley, and accompanied by "a number of gentlemen who witnessed the occurrence." The charge itself, that Ripley had "willfully and maliciously assaulted a mail carrier in uniform engaged in the discharge of his official duties," was undisputed and carried a penalty of a one-hundred-dollar fine or imprisonment for up to three years. King appeared at the arraignment accompanied by several witnesses, wearing "a patch of court plaster near his left eye" and carrying "a package of blood-stained envelopes which he had collected from persons to whom he had delivered them after the alleged assault."[104] Recounting Ripley's request that King give up his seat to help accommodate White passengers, the press claimed that Ripley was "met with an insolent refusal," which—for White readers—would have required a defense of Ripley's honor as a White man, in the form of the brutal blows delivered to King.

In addition to suggesting that it was King's response to Ripley that had caused the altercation, the press altered the incident's details to emphasize the idea that King's behavior had insulted vulnerable Whites, requiring a violent response. Reporting on Ripley's subsequent appearance in court, where recorder John Broyles dismissed assault charges against him, the press changed the passengers at the center of the controversy from a White woman leading a blind White man to a "crippled white woman" or a "lady" who was traveling alone. In these scenarios, King's actions were described as the source of concern and justified Ripley's attack, as acting in defense of White supremacy in public spaces. More than a decade earlier when he had served as postal commissioner, Broyles had cleared Eugene Martin of theft charges against him, describing him as a model employee and indirectly furthering his claims to middle-class manliness. Now, as a recorder for the city court, Broyles used the case of Ripley's assault of a Black mail carrier to ensure that middle-class manliness remained the province of White men. "I have often seen negro men sitting in cars while white women with babies in their arms were standing up," Broyles told the courtroom. "So long as such things occur, so long will there be a probability of such affairs occurring as that which took place between Dr. Ripley and King."[105] A month after Ripley's acquittal, the *Atlanta Georgian* reported that Edward M. Rosser, a White streetcar conductor, and J. T. Fagan, a Black mail carrier, had both been charged after Rosser assaulted Fagan in front of passengers, alleging that Fagan "had cursed him and used abusive language."[106] By the time violence broke out in September of that year, Black mail carriers were already fixed in the White imagination as symbols of Blacks' illegitimate social mobility.

Following Atlanta's lead, Black mail carriers would become targets for physical violence in other Georgia cities and rural areas as politicians and the press regularly called attention to their "troubling" displays of middle-class manhood and "defiant" attitudes toward Whites.[107] In June 1907, Savannah congressman C. G. Edwards received letters of support from Whites across the state for having refused a meeting with a delegation of the city's Black mail carriers, calling them "pets of Republicans" and "vain negroes." A month later, mail carrier Charles Deveaux, the younger brother of John Deveaux, Savannah's first Black collector of customs, was brutally assaulted by two White men while making his deliveries.[108] In the wake of the assault, a letter to the editor of the *Weekly Jeffersonian*, a Populist organ published by White supremacist Thomas E. Watson, called for an investigation of the large numbers of Black men employed in the postal service and other branches of the civil service in Georgia. The letter's author, who identified himself only as "a friend," alleged that an investigation into conditions in Atlanta, Savannah, and other cities would show that "humble" White men were regularly being passed over as mail carriers, shutting them out of opportunities for government employment. "In other words," he wrote, "a white man is denied a chance to earn a living simply because he is a white man."[109]

By 1910, narratives about Black mail carriers had brightened racial boundaries by convincing White Atlantans that Black men's access to middle-class jobs threatened even the most vulnerable Whites, underscoring the need for White men to reclaim middle-class manhood. The claims of White displacement remained a central part of White Georgians' narratives about Black postal workers. Writing in 1909, Robert L. Ballantine, a farm manager and former mail clerk in Augusta's post office, echoed these claims in response to an editorial in the *Augusta Herald* that chastised the city's "young White men" for being "indifferent" to civil service employment, resulting in the "Africanizing" of the city's post office. "Indifferent they may be," Ballantine wrote, "but it is an indifference born of the common belief . . . that a negro's chances of appointment in the post office service of this city are much better than a white man's."[110] Responding to Ballantine, the *Herald*'s editor asserted that "there should be no negro letter carriers," adding, "The reason for this is so plain that it requires no argument. . . . If we desire to have white mail carriers, young white men must make themselves eligible by passing the required civil service examination."[111]

Yet even with the increased possibility of physical danger and growing national trends toward segregating federal workplaces, African American men in Atlanta would continue to see employment in the postal service as an important and reliable pathway to middle-class mobility. Their elevation to the status of folk demon among Whites, in which they represented the dangers of not defending racialized class boundaries, justified the steady and forceful brightening of racial boundaries, particularly within Atlanta's urban middle class.

Conclusion

As early as the Reconstruction era, White Southerners had been confronted with African Americans' desires for both physical and social mobility. By the end of the nineteenth century, Whites commonly equated Black mobility with new forms of danger. In a bustling New South city like Atlanta, Whites were accustomed to seeing African Americans perform various types of low-wage, manual labor that reflected and reinforced White supremacy in the city's labor market. However, Blacks' increased access to schooling, their incremental inroads into white-collar jobs, and other manifestations of middle-class identity fueled Whites' apprehension. In particular, Atlanta's Whites had grown increasingly wary of the growing number of Black men who were securing federal employment with the postal service. Between 1889 and 1910, journalists, politicians, and members of the public responded to Black men's occupational mobility in the postal service in ways that reflected new understandings of how race operated in classed contexts as well as the importance of demarcating and defending racialized class boundaries in a shifting racial landscape.

Newspaper stories about Black postal workers' alleged criminal tendencies gave popular expression to White anxieties about reproducing social position in a changing social milieu and underscored the need to brighten racialized class boundaries. Beginning with the controversy over Charles Penney's clerkship, newspaper coverage of theft allegations or other claims of wrongdoing involving Black postal workers helped to durably link Black social mobility to new forms of racial danger for middle-class Whites. Press accounts of the Penney-Lyon affair and the concerns expressed about race, class, and manliness in the workplace provided justification for White resistance to Black men's movement into white-collar jobs traditionally held by White men. Claims that Penney's clerkship would result in financial losses for Atlanta's White merchants and taxpayers owing to theft or sheer incompetence easily drew on the postbellum popularity of what historians have described as a "negro crime narrative" that cast Black men as not only inherently dangerous but also morally deficient and incapable of middle-class manliness. As Whites' attention turned to Black mail carriers, these same storylines about the dangers of Black occupational and social mobility would remain an important resource for politicians and everyday citizens as well as journalists. Overall, Black men's movement into jobs popularly thought to be reserved for White men became emblematic of the social disorder brought on by Black claims to social equality and their support from White Republicans.

This high-profile coverage surrounding Black postal workers also popularized a new racial type in White Atlantans' narratives about urban Blacks and racial danger—the literate, highly educated, and morally inferior "after-the-war Negro." In its coverage of the Penney-Lyon affair, Nelson Martin's trial, and Eugene Martin's trial, the press described access to higher education as having had a corrupting influence on Black men and, as such, having further endangered Whites. Journalists and popular writers like Philip A. Bruce, John A. Macon, and Georgia's own Joel Chandler Harris suggested that younger generations of Blacks—urbanized and educated—appeared to show little regard for White authority, an aversion to work, a troubling desire for social mobility, and expectations of "social equality" with Whites.[112] Penney, identified in the press as a graduate of a local missionary college with a reputation for practicing social equality, now dared not only to compete for a "White man's job" but also to enter a workplace where a White man worked alongside his unmarried daughter. In Nelson Martin's trial the following year, the press underscored the dangers of Black men's access to education when it attempted to link his criminal activity to his "twelve years" of education at the hands of White abolitionist missionaries. Eugene Martin's ability to both secure a lawyer for his defense and demand in writing that the press print news of his exoneration was proof that White Atlantans were now faced with a population of Black men who not only felt entitled to fair treatment before the law but, with federal wages, might even have the means to secure it. In both these cases, much was made of the counterpoint they presented to un-lettered Black men like Jones or Martin's father—deemed "inoffensive" or "old-fashioned negroes" by Whites—who also faced negative consequences from their contact with younger Blacks.

While Atlanta's Blacks saw postal employment as a secure pathway to middle-class mobility for educated men, White Atlantans saw Black mail car-riers and postal clerks as personifying a new and dangerous type of manli-ness. Claims in the press that Penney's appointment had both derailed Wilson Sturgess's ambitions and forced Nathan Lyon into temporary unemployment drove home the dangers that Black men's occupational mobility posed to "deserving" White men. Black men's mobility meant that men like Sturgess and Lyon were being deprived of opportunities to earn a living and support families—both of which were central to understandings of middle-class manhood at the beginning of the twentieth century. Newspapers highlighted the "manly strength" of White men like Nathan Lyon, the Capital City Club members who charged Lewis with indecency, the lawmen who ferreted out mail theft, and the politicians who railed against "negro mail carriers," por-traying them as heroic figures who protected the civic order from Blacks' illegitimate claims to social mobility. These displays of White manliness, which began with Nathan Lyon's public resignation rather than accepting a Black mail clerk, gradually escalated into the use of police authority and even-tually took the form of White men's verbal and physical assaults on Black mail carriers.

Whites also saw in Black men's postal service employment the embodi-ment of the New South's dangers for White women. Speculation in the press and among members of the public about the inevitability of interactions be-tween Penney and Mary Lyon invoked newly popular narratives about Black rapists to claim that Black men's presence in white-collar workplaces posed a particular type of sexual danger for White women who worked before mar-riage. Even after newspapers in Atlanta and other Georgia cities had turned their attention to Black men's growing presence among Atlanta's mail carri-ers, the "negro crime" narrative that linked them with dishonesty, incom-petence, and theft had made no mention of sexual danger. By the end of the nineteenth century, Black men's continued occupational gains in the federal workforce under Republican administrations would spur a marked change in how politicians talked about Black mail carriers in the context of a changing raced and classed landscape. Whites residing in Atlanta and other urban centers generally tolerated Black mail carriers, while associating them with theft and disorder. In appealing to their rural constituents, politicians used stories about Black rapists to describe Black mail carriers as a threat to the safety of White women and children. Atlanta's 1906 race riot and Walter White's recollection of a call to target Black mail carriers showed how over time, by durably linking Black mail carriers to specific types of dangers, politicians and journalists helped justify increasingly violent methods of brightening racialized class boundaries.

Southern Whites' concerted efforts to develop new and extend existing practices of racial separation into new realms like the middle-class workplace further institutionalized what were already bright racial boundaries between themselves and Blacks. Beginning in the postbellum era, they responded to Black social mobility with stories that helped to heighten the importance of racial distinctions within the middle class. At the same time that Atlanta's Whites publicly embraced a New South ethos that stressed economic development and practicality on matters of race, they also developed "deep stories" about race and class mobility—ones that described Black men's occupational mobility as not only illegitimate but also tied to economic losses for White men and sexual danger for White women. These stories sustained bright racial boundaries using racial logics that were widely recognized, forcefully articulated, and violently defended in and through the middle-class workplace. The South's urban centers were not unique as sites where local racialized class hierarchies underwent important change at the century's turn. In the emerging and established cities of the US-Mexico borderlands, defining, fixing, and defending racial boundaries between Whites and Mexicans appears to have garnered levels of attention and energy that were different from the ones that characterized the policing of the boundaries between Whites and Blacks. In cities like San Antonio, the blurriness of the Mexican-White boundary meant that stories about middle-class mobility and identity among the descendants of Texas's Mexican and Spanish settlers revealed varying degrees of tolerance, fear, and anxiety among the city's Anglo population of Anglo Americans and European immigrants.

CHAPTER THREE

The Policeman Was a Mexican
Tejano Lawmen in San Antonio, 1880–1910

In the spring of 1884, the press, public officials, and Texans of diverse backgrounds had lauded a Tejano policeman—Officer Jacobo "Jake" Santos Coy of San Antonio's police force—for his bravery during a bloody shootout at San Antonio's Vaudeville Theater in which two well-known gunmen died. Hailing from an old Bexareño family of landowners with a record of military service that included both San Antonio's presidio-era army and the Confederate army, Coy was only one of the thirty-six Tejano men who worked as law enforcement officers in late nineteenth-century San Antonio.[1] Coy had received a gunshot wound to the leg while struggling with the gunman. Both the city police captain and the owner of the theater praised Coy's "quick thinking" and willingness to risk his own life, crediting his actions with preventing additional fatalities.[2] None of the articles published identified Coy as being of Mexican origin.

While both official and press accounts of the Vaudeville shooting helped blur racial boundaries by making Coy a public symbol of manly virtue, subsequent coverage would also suggest that racial boundaries between Mexicans and Whites were brightening in the borderlands. Only a few days after the Vaudeville tragedy, Coy once again found himself in the headlines. According to the *San Antonio Daily Express* and other English-language papers, two men described as "Mexican assassins" had been seen loitering near Coy's home and were arrested in what police authorities, including Coy himself, described as a plot to kill him. The men were later identified as Celestino Charo, a La Salle County sheriff's deputy, and Santiago Tijerina, an eighteen-year-old farmhand. Both men had been summoned to the city to testify as witnesses in a federal court proceeding; neither was armed at the time of their arrest.[3] Charo and Tijerina spent the night in jail before it was determined that they had only been loitering near Coy's home in hopes of meeting the hero of the Vaudeville shooting; the two were later cleared of any wrongdoing.[4] The paper's juxtaposition of Coy, who remained racially unmarked, with Charo and Tijerina, described as "Mexican assassins," placed Tejano policemen like Coy within the boundaries of Whiteness even as it emphasized the supposed moral deficiency of "Mexicans." While "Mexicans" might subvert the law and threaten policemen for personal gain, Coy embodied a middle-class manliness demonstrated through his willingness to risk life and limb to defend law and order.

The urbanization and continued settlement of the US-Mexico borderlands during the late nineteenth and early twentieth centuries gave rise to distinct patterns of racial hierarchy that often, but not always, cast Tejanos and other Mexican-origin men as racial outsiders. As legal historians have noted, the overlapping colonial projects of first Spanish and then US empire indelibly shaped regional understandings of Whiteness, leaving Mexicans somewhere between White and non-White—what legal historian Laura Gómez has called "off-White."[5] Those Mexicans who had benefited from the privileges of Whiteness under the Spanish Mexican racial order would struggle—often unsuccessfully—to preserve those privileges under Anglo American dominance, particularly as the number of Mexican immigrants increased in the years before and during Mexico's 1910 revolution. Increasingly, the racial order in operation in the United States held Mexican Americans to be more non-White than White.

Historians of the Southwest have described the various ways that the region's Mexican-origin elites attempted to retain their influence as cultural and political brokers during the era of Anglo American dominance.[6] In the case of southern Texas cities like Laredo, Corpus Christi, Brownsville, and San Antonio, where blocs of Tejano voters influenced election outcomes, the politically connected remnants of a landed Tejano elite secured city- and county-level employment.[7] These Tejanos who clung to power did so within a restive and hostile racial climate. Anglo Americans regularly justified state-sanctioned and extralegal violence against Mexicans in rural Texas by blending claims about crime with US-Mexican war narratives about Mexicans' racial otherness.[8] In San Antonio, newspaper reporting about crime increasingly cast Mexicans as part of a "lawless element" that included most of the city's Black population and a smaller but troublesome population of lower-class White residents.[9] At the same time, San Antonio's urban crime narratives often featured the city's Tejano lawmen, now depicted as new racial actors. Their off-White racial status embodied shifting understandings of Mexican Americans' position in the region's racialized economic order.

In this chapter, I show how city officials, the press, and members of the public used stories about Tejano policemen and "Mexican crime" to alternately brighten and blur racial boundaries between Whites and Mexicans. During the 1880s, Tejano men—many of Bexareño origins—leveraged work in the city's expanding police force as a reliable means of securing their position in San Antonio's urban middle class. They did so at a time when the local Anglo press was refitting racial narratives about the city's Mexican population to help explain the "new" problem of urban crime. The reports encouraged the area's Anglo newcomers to understand Tejano policemen as off-White lawmen whose adherence to middle-class manliness distinguished them from Mexican-origin crime suspects. Over the course of the following decade, as racial segregation emerged as the dominant modality of White supremacy, Anglos' nativism exploded in the US borderlands as the number of migrants from revolution-era Mexico increased. By the start of the twentieth century, as efforts to entrench White supremacy reached their height, newspapers routinely portrayed Tejano policemen as figures of brutality, corruption, and personal immorality, effectively linking them with a dangerous manliness that required control. The incidents examined in this chapter offer an example of how popular racial narratives about policing and crime helped to brighten racialized class boundaries that had previously been more blurred.

Police Employment and Tejano Mobility

The social changes that accompanied the arrival of some 800,000 Anglo Americans into the Texas-Mexico borderlands after 1850 proved distressing to many Tejanos, especially elite landowners.[10] The wars of Texas secession and US annexation, the reorganization of local economies, Anglo American political dominance, and a steady undercurrent of anti-Mexican sentiment among both US-born and immigrant non-Hispanic Whites collectively chipped away at Mexican Texans' position and influence. The middling classes of Tejano merchants and landowners in the state's urban centers experienced these changes in varying ways, depending on local economic conditions.[11] In San Antonio, many Bexareño elites who had been powerful Anglo Mexican *cultural brokers* secured city- and county-level incumbencies through political patronage and joined White Democrats in supporting the Confederacy during the US Civil War. Reconstruction, railroad expansion, new waves of Anglo American migration, and the beginning of mass migration from Mexico, however, brought further changes to their fortunes.[12]

In the postbellum era, San Antonio emerged as a thriving center for regional trade, transportation, finance, and light manufacturing. The arrival of three national railroad lines fueled the growth of the region's economy. Between 1870 and 1880, the city's population nearly doubled, increasing from 12,000 to 21,000. By century's end, some 53,000 people called the "Alamo

City" home. Postbellum newcomers of a variety of racial and national origins made San Antonio the most ethnically diverse metropolis in Texas.[13] In addition to Tejanos, the city's population included native-born Whites (many of whom were born in the former Confederacy), a diverse group of European immigrants (with a large contingent of Germans), and African American migrants. By 1890, non-Hispanic Whites were the majority of the city's population. By 1900, despite increased Mexican migration, Tejanos' share of San Antonio's population had dropped from just over half, at midcentury, to less than a quarter.[14]

This steady stream of new arrivals accelerated Tejano landowners' relative economic decline. The city's new financial elite primarily consisted of Anglo Americans and European immigrants. Historian Alwyn Barr's analysis of mobility patterns among a sample of the city's male wage earners between 1870 and 1900 reveals an urban economy largely structured along "racial" lines—with 39 percent of native-born White workers and 31 percent of European immigrants employed in nonmanual occupations, compared with 10 percent of Mexican Americans and only 4 percent of Black workers. Both native-born White and European immigrant workers demonstrated higher rates of social mobility than either Mexican-origin or Black workers.[15] Although the near absence of Spanish-surnamed business owners in an 1885 publication describing investment opportunities in the city suggests that businesses owned and operated by Anglos were considered the most profitable by those with access to capital, the presence of Tejano-owned businesses—drinking establishments, drugstores, newspapers, grocers, dry-goods merchants, and so on—in newspapers and city directories between 1870 and 1900 indicates that some Tejano entrepreneurs managed to survive the expansion of the urban markets.[16] The desires of politicians and city boosters to fashion San Antonio as a modern "American" city for tourists and investors manifested in the removal of open-air cafés and eating establishments operated by Tejanas—colloquially known as "chili queens"—from the city's public squares and plazas.[17] With a growing demand for low-wage labor that supported agricultural production, tourism, and trade, the majority of San Antonio's Mexican-origin workers found employment as either unskilled manual laborers or service workers, a situation that mirrored that of the city's African Americans.[18]

Tejanos experienced San Antonio's urban transformation within the critical context of converging Anglo and Iberian racial ideologies. In 1845, Anglo delegates to the Texas constitutional convention expressed racist views about Mexicans and advocated that voting rights be restricted to "white persons." José Antonio Navarro, a descendant of Bexareño settlers and the lone Tejano delegate, objected, calling the proposal "odious" and arguing that the "redundant" use of the word "white" might be a tactic used by "arbitrary judges" to disqualify those Tejanos who were "unquestionably entitled to vote." Although Navarro immediately expressed support for denying suffrage to African Americans, he asked that an exception be made for those of mixed ancestry who could "scarcely" be distinguished from Whites.[19] While a majority of the Anglo delegates rejected the original proposal, in little more than a decade a series of deadly attacks perpetrated by Anglo Americans against Tejano oxcart drivers traveling from San Antonio through Karnes and Goliad Counties forcefully reasserted a Mexican-White racial boundary.

Before the advent of railroads between San Antonio and the Gulf Coast, oxcart drivers were the primary means for merchants to transport and receive goods, and Tejanos dominated the trade. Anglo American residents and politicians in Goliad County—whose Tejano residents had been driven out by Anglo settlers in 1835—defended the violence of the so-called 1857 Cart War, referring to the victims as "greasers" who allegedly stole and destroyed property.[20] Aware of the economic costs to the state, Texas's Anglo American governor, Elijah M. Pease, condemned the attacks, which counted among its victims at least one veteran of the Texian army. An 1858 letter to the editor of the *Southern Intelligencer* from a Goliad County resident defended the attacks and explained that the term "greaser" was not an insult to Mexicans, as it referred "only" to the "mongrel" criminal class, racially distinct from those Mexicans who were "white men and gentlemen."[21]

Tejano elites' support of the South's proslavery cause during the Civil War helped to abate some of the anti-Mexican sentiment that had persisted after statehood and emerged during debates over secession in the state legislature.[22] But as the nineteenth century drew to a close, a growing population of Anglo newcomers—many of them Southern-born—increasingly regarded all Mexicans as "colored" racial inferiors whose presence signaled poverty, violence, and crime. In postbellum San Antonio, Black residents were the most frequent targets of an evolving net of segregationist ordinances and political disenfranchisement intended to strengthen already bright racial boundaries, but these same measures also brightened the racial boundaries Tejanos encountered.[23] Only four years before the century's end, two White political operatives—Populist attorney Thomas J. McMinn and Republican attorney Andrew Jackson Evans—mounted a legal challenge to Mexican immigrant Ricardo Rodriguez's right to naturalize, with the intent of disenfranchising the masses of Mexican American voters.[24] Tejanos might be treated as White men who descended from the "Castilian race," or they could be racialized as "Mexicans," non-White and socially inferior to the Anglo population. While the majority of Tejanos embraced the term "Mexican" to identify their national or ethnic origins, postbellum-era Anglo American journalists, politicians, and everyday citizens regularly used the term to signify Tejanos' racial otherness, regardless of the subject's nationality.

Even as the city's Mexican-origin population became a numerical and social minority, it retained political influence within the Democratic Party. Descendants of the old Bexareño elite operated as political middlemen within the state's most diverse metropolis, which they leveraged to secure city- and county-level political offices and appointments as aldermen, commissioners, constables, clerks, and assessors.[25] The expansion of San Antonio's urban police force during the late nineteenth and early twentieth centuries provided a new occupational pathway into municipal employment. During the Reconstruction era, the city's police force consisted of fewer than twenty officers commanded by an appointed city marshal, a position that had in turn been created in 1846 as an "ex-officio chief of police." San Antonio's city charter placed the "appointment and government of the police force" under the joint control of the mayor and the city council, which initially determined the size of the police force on an ad hoc basis but later decided on a permanent number of officers.[26] Beginning in 1875, then–city marshal John Dobbin launched a campaign to modernize the force. His efforts resulted in a larger staff, equipped with standard uniforms and badges, and the creation of new specialized positions like police detective. By 1880, the city marshal—now an elected position with a two-year term—was assisted by first and second assistant marshals who could perform the responsibilities of the city marshal as needed.[27] The number of city policemen grew from sixteen officers in 1885 to a corps of over fifty after 1903.[28]

In 1901 reformist mayor Marshall Hicks created a Police and Fire Commission charged with enforcing new civil service guidelines. Under advisement from the commission's Police Committee, San Antonio's city council voted to reorganize the police department and require prospective officers to be examined and recommended by the Police Committee in order to be eligible for appointment.[29] The US Census Bureau's statistical reports on cities produced in the early twentieth century indicated that after a slight decrease between 1903 and 1904, San Antonio increased its policing expenditures by more than $15,000 over the next four years.[30] After a second reorganization under Bryan V. Callaghan Jr. in 1910, San Antonio would have ninety-three patrol officers and detectives who served under a police captain with two assistant captains and three desk sergeants.[31] Recent analyses of data on urban policing provided in these reports identified San Antonio as one of the US cities, and one of seven in Texas, that had adopted military tactics in its everyday operations, including a high reliance on mounted patrolmen.[32]

Having performed a variety of law enforcement roles since the early days of Anglo rule, Tejanos now served as members of an urban police department that nominally reflected the city's ethnic diversity, even as it remained under the political control of Anglo Americans. Based on a search of manuscript census records and city directories from 1880 to 1910 for Spanish-surnamed men identified as police officers, patrolmen, or detectives, approximately forty-three Tejano men served on the San Antonio police force in one or more of these roles.[33] Many of them obtained these jobs as a reward for service to the local Democratic Party, a practice that reached its apex under the mayoral administrations of Callaghan, who held the office three different times between 1885 and 1912. Callaghan, the son of a wealthy Irish-born merchant who had married into the Bexareño landowning elite, obtained his post by mobilizing the city's immigrant and Catholic voters against the "old guard" Anglo Protestant political establishment.[34] Like other Gilded Age political bosses, Callaghan rewarded the loyalty of various ethnic voting constituencies — including Tejanos — with access to municipal employment. While reform-minded candidates accused Callaghan of employing his "favorites," he ensured that Tejanos were visibly represented among the city's police officers.[35]

Though they were fewer in number, San Antonio's African American residents also attempted to benefit from the city's urban political machine. Black voters frustrated with Republicans' declining willingness to defend Black interests had supported the bipartisan coalition that elected Callaghan's predecessor James French. French rewarded Black voters with a handful of civil service appointments as policemen or firemen, a tradition that Callaghan maintained for those Black voters who supported him.[36] Census records and city directories indicate that fewer than ten African American men served as police officers between 1880 and 1910, all assigned to foot patrol in the city's Black neighborhoods, occasionally assisting Anglo and Mexican officers in their duties if nearby. By 1910, as in 1880, there would be only two Black officers employed on the force.[37]

Although city directories indicate that the position of city marshal would be occupied exclusively by Anglo men as late as 1910, Tejano men continued to gain access to positions above the rank of officer well into the 1890s and beyond. In 1891, Andrés S. Coy, younger brother of Jacobo S. Coy, succeeded another Tejano, Juan T. Cardenas, as one of the four assistant marshals. At that point, however, only four of the force's twenty-six policemen were Tejanos. A similar pattern would obtain for the next two decades: even as Tejano men held ranking positions, including captain and assistant captain of police, they appeared to remain a numerical minority within a larger corps of police officers, usually making up between 10 and 20 percent of the force (13 percent in 1905 and 20 percent in 1910).[38]

The Tejano men who became policemen in San Antonio during the late nineteenth and early twentieth centuries largely came from the rural land-holding class. Of the thirty-seven individuals for whom I could locate information on their father's occupation, nearly half (47 percent) had fathers who were listed in county tax records or census records as farmers, with 61 percent holding considerable wealth or assets in Bexar or in neighboring counties. This group included brothers Jacobo and Andrés Coy, who came from a prosperous Bexareño farming family in nearby Karnes County, fifty miles southeast of San Antonio. In 1870 their father, rancher Trinidad de los Santos Coy, had owned land valued at $1,000 and a personal estate valued at $2,000.[39] Celedonio Cadena and Ignacio Chavez, both of whom joined the police force during the 1890s, were the sons of landowning farmers with at least $1,000 in recorded assets.[40] Rafael Martinez, who joined the police force in 1883 as a mounted officer, was the son of a "master cartman" who on the eve of the Civil War had owned $1,700 in real and personal property.[41]

In a period when San Antonio's Mexican-origin population had lower rates of upward mobility than either native-born Whites or European immigrants, police employment offered both mobility and socioeconomic parity with Anglos. Despite the economic successes their fathers had sustained in San Antonio and Bexar County during the mid-nineteenth century, mobility came less easily for the younger Tejano generation. More than half (59 percent) of the Tejano men identified as policemen had worked at other jobs before entering law enforcement, typically following similar occupations as their fathers, coming primarily from farming (six), transportation (four), or other skilled manual trades (three). Rafael Martinez, for instance, had worked as a teamster, only to face increased competition from the railroads. Available records suggest that the city did not distinguish Anglo and Tejano men when setting police officers' wages, increasing the appeal of service in the force.[42] After sharply increasing in the 1860s and 1870s, the salaries of police officers (or patrolmen, as they were sometimes designated) plateaued at around $65 to $70 per month, while the first and second assistant marshals earned between $110 and $125 per month.[43]

Tejano men found opportunities for advancement within the city police force that further positioned them within the city's middle classes. Approximately one-third of the Tejano men who entered law enforcement during these years chose to make it their primary occupation, accumulating at least five years of employment as either city or county lawmen. Jacobo Coy was promoted from city policeman to "special officer" in 1883 after three years as a city patrolman, after which he moved to county-level law enforcement as a sheriff's deputy in 1892, before finishing out his career back in city policing.[44] Andrés Coy began his career as one of the city's mounted police officers and was eventually promoted to the rank of assistant city marshal in 1891. Modesto Torres joined the city police force in 1887 and served in a variety of law enforcement roles—special policeman, city jailer, sheriff's deputy—until his retirement in 1905.[45] In 1901, assistant city marshal Juan T. Cardenas's salary of $125 per month made him one of the highest-paid workers, and certainly the highest-paid Tejano, to draw a salary from the city.[46]

Much like their Anglo counterparts on the police force, many Tejano men used police employment as a pathway to other white-collar, middle-class jobs, whether inside or outside the city's public sector.[47] While some Tejanos found opportunities for advancement within city law enforcement, nearly half used the position to step into other occupations that kept them squarely within the city's Tejano middle-class community of small-business owners, professionals, and city- or county-level civil servants. Six of the twenty-seven Tejanos employed in law enforcement between 1881 and 1910 continued working in the public sector as city or county employees after leaving policing. Juan E. Barrera, a police officer who had served in the 1870s, became a politically active deputy county clerk in the 1880s and 1890s. After Andrés Coy left the city police in the 1890s at the high rank of assistant city marshal, he enjoyed a long political career as city clerk and, later, as Bexar County commissioner.[48] Former police officer Celedonio Cadena found work as a foreman on city sanitation crews in 1910, while Officer Antonio Herrera followed Andrés Coy's route to county commissioner in 1910 after nearly ten years on the city police force.[49] For others, police employment served as a bridge to entrepreneurship. Jacobo Coy, for example, operated a saloon after leaving policing in the early 1890s, which his son later maintained.[50]

Economic change, along with new age and physical requirements for police officers instituted after 1900, slightly changed the occupational origins of Tejano lawmen. At the turn of the century, the majority came from the ranks of skilled, semiskilled manual, and unspecified manual laborers. Lucero "Luz" Robalín had worked as a butcher before becoming a police officer in 1900. After a decade of working as a police officer, he returned to his former trade and opened a butcher shop in San Antonio's public market.[51] Norberto Galán, whose father, Francisco, had been a policeman in the 1880s, had worked as a saddle maker before joining the police force in 1908.[52] Luciano Espinosa, who also joined the force in 1908, had previously worked as a bartender.[53]

Police employment provided Tejano men with middle-class occupational identities during a period when their chances for such employment lagged behind those for Anglos, but it did so at the same time that narratives about Mexicans' alleged criminality were becoming more widespread. Stories describing Tejanos and Mexicans as violent, vice ridden, and criminally inclined became ubiquitous in the US-Mexico borderlands in the late nineteenth century, a media phenomenon that reinforced Anglos' beliefs that Mexicans constituted a distinct racial element whose presence and movements had to be controlled. Yet their experience stood in contrast to the experience of the city's handful of African American police officers, who faced resistance from Whites as well as suspicion and mockery from the Anglo press, including the use of racial epithets.[54] Tejano policemen not only performed their duties alongside Anglo officers but also received identical salaries and held positions of authority within the police force. In what follows, I show how the juxtaposition of stories about the law enforcement activities of Tejano policemen and stories about Mexicans' alleged predisposition to crime helped to blur and brighten racial boundaries between Mexicans and Whites in turn-of-the-century San Antonio.

Race and Crime in San Antonio

In February 1888, the editors of the *San Antonio Express* published a special feature touting San Antonio's "numerous business advantages" for potential investors. Alongside descriptions of the city's natural resources, schools, and "solid" city government, the feature included a report on the activities of the San Antonio police department for 1887. The piece noted 2,895 arrests, of which 95 percent (2,758) had been "adjudicated in the city recorder's court," with the remaining 5 percent (137) turned over to county, state, or federal officials for trial. With respect to crime, the report tallied fifty-seven thefts, eight robberies, six offenses related to sexual assault, seven aggravated assaults, sixteen assaults with intent to kill, and three murders that year. While the article made no mention of the racial or ethnic origins of either the perpetrators or the victims, this was an anomaly—the press had long pushed the belief that the city's problems with crime were caused by the presence of non-White populations.[55]

Racialized interpretations of urban crime were common in postbellum San Antonio, a stronghold of Confederate support during the Civil War. Despite the presence of a relatively small Black population that was itself often victimized by White offenders, San Antonio's Whites readily ascribed responsibility for the city's crime to its Black residents.[56] Press reports dating to the Reconstruction era linked the presence of African Americans in the city with vagrancy, theft, assault, public disorder, and the growth of the city's newly established poverty rolls.[57] At least one *San Antonio Daily Herald* editorial claimed that the city's increased Black population—which included discharged Union soldiers—necessitated the "maintenance of a strong police force."[58]

Even as the local press was quick to identify the city's Black population as a source of urban crime, media reports reproduced White San Antonians' persistent beliefs about the racial otherness of the city's Mexican-origin population. The racist tropes that Anglos had invoked to justify their violence against Mexicans in rural areas increasingly found expression in stories about urban crime and vice. English-language reporting on crime in San Antonio during the late nineteenth century regularly pointed to the presence of people of Mexican origin among the "criminal classes," with papers referring to "Mexicans," "Aztecs," or "greasers" in connection with theft, assault, rape, murder, and poverty-related vices (i.e., drinking, gambling, and cockfighting). These stories helped popularize the idea among Whites that Mexicans, like Blacks, were to be regarded as congenital criminals.[59]

The arrival of three railroad lines in San Antonio after 1875 increased the city's resident and transient populations, underscoring Anglos' concerns about crime and vice. These concerns centered primarily on the areas to the west of San Pedro Creek where the majority of the city's Mexican-origin population traditionally resided. The area was also home to the city's vice district.[60] In two columns written for the *San Antonio Express* in 1879, correspondent Hans Mickle described the "Mexican Quarter"—which he claimed was commonly known among Whites as "Chihuahua," "Mexico," "San Pedro," or simply "across the creek"—as being more or less indistinguishable from the vice district, dominated by the presence of saloons, gambling dens, high-end brothels, and a prostitution district he described as San Antonio's "Five Points."[61] Although Mickle began by noting the presence of respectable families and neighborhoods in the area, he justified focusing on the west side as a vice district because of its large Mexican population. The Mexican-origin residents figuring in Mickle's depiction of the west side were uniformly poor working men he referred to as *pelados*. They consumed liquor, gambled their meager earnings rather than using them to feed "hungry children at home," and loitered about the district's streets playing music of "questionable" taste.[62]

By the 1880s, these ideas about Mexicans and crime began to surface more frequently in Anglo attitudes toward the "better classes" of Tejanos. In August 1883, an altercation on an outdoor dance pavilion between two Tejano youths escalated into a fistfight on the grounds of San Pedro Springs Park, a recreational spot favored by the city's middle-class residents and tourists. Frederick Kerbel, a German American entrepreneur who leased management of the park's concessions from the city, angrily ordered "all Mexicans" from the dance floor and announced that Mexicans would henceforth be barred from the pavilion.[63] Epistacio Mondragón, editor of the Spanish-language paper *El Hogar*, claimed that when he complained to Kerbel about his offensive treatment of "respectable" and "inoffensive" patrons, Kerbel replied that he "could make no distinction between the better class [of Mexicans] and prostitutes, and hence would exclude them all." Police officers Rafael Martinez and Andrés Coy also "remonstrated" Kerbel for his behavior, and Kerbel then allegedly "declared that *he* was running the [San Pedro] springs, and would do as he pleased and exclude whom he pleased."[64]

Kerbel's actions galvanized the city's Tejano leaders into action. They formed a committee, headed by assistant marshal Juan Cardenas, that produced resolutions condemning Kerbel and calling for his removal as park manager.[65] In their speeches and resolutions, Tejano leaders, accompanied by a minority of Anglo elites, mobilized a shared historical narrative that invoked Mexicans' shared descent from European settlers, calling the "Mexican race" the "first owners of the soil" and "defenders of the State." Through their language, they essentially rejected claims that San Antonio's Tejanos were anything but White men. English-language papers in San Antonio and other Texas cities echoed this language in their criticisms of Kerbel, calling attention to the presence of "many good Mexican citizens."[66] A chastised Kerbel issued a public apology to a gathering of Tejano protesters a few days after the incident.

The broader media response to the incident, however, suggested that stories about Mexican criminality had become more popular with White readers. The city's German-language press, along with both English and German papers outside Texas, defended Kerbel and challenged Tejanos' claims to Whiteness. The *Freie Press für Texas* wrote that Kerbel had "only somewhat" mocked the social position of the city's Mexican population by stating what many in the city—Mexicans included—believed about those who used the dance pavilion. The paper wrote that it was well known that those who were among the city's "first" Mexican families generally avoided it. Newspapers in other states, such as Maysville, Kentucky's *Evening Bulletin* and the New Orleans *Daily Picayune*, referred to the protesters as "excited Greasers" and "disorderly Mexicans." Another Maryland-based German paper, *Der Deutsche Correspondent*, defended Kerbel's efforts to "keep order," writing that Mexicans formed "the lowest classes" of San Antonio's population.[67]

In the decade that followed, the Anglo press published numerous reports of Mexican-origin men engaged in "depraved" acts of violence in borderland cities and towns. By the century's end, English-language stories about Mexicans' involvement in crime and vice had become a permanent feature of the city's racial landscape. Newspapers' use of racialized crime discourses to describe both the city's Mexican-origin residents and the spaces they occupied helped to brighten racial boundaries between Mexicans and Whites. At the same time, the Anglo public's willingness to accept the presence of significant numbers of Tejanos among the ranks of the city's lawmen suggested a significant degree of blurriness remained.

Race and Policing in San Antonio

While Mexican crime narratives gained ground in San Antonio in the decades leading up to the beginning of the twentieth century, Tejano policemen's visibility—both as patrolmen and as commanding officers—positioned them as central figures of Whiteness and middle-class manliness in popular stories about urban crime. News stories about the 1884 Vaudeville Theater shooting mentioned at the outset of this chapter, for instance, portrayed Jacobo S. Coy as a symbol of urban law enforcement heroism. In his own sworn statement before the judge presiding at the inquest for the death of the gunman, Ben Thompson, Coy—identifying himself as a policeman on "special" duty at the Vaudeville—described how he had warned City Marshal Philip Shardein about the possibility of "trouble" after learning that Thompson and his accomplice, William "King" Fisher, were in town. Coy's account emphasized his command of other officers on the scene and his efforts to defuse the argument between Thompson and William Foster, the Vaudeville's owner, that ultimately precipitated the shooting.[68] Shardein's own statement corroborated

Coy's important role; he remarked to the press that it was the visibly wounded Coy who had presented him with Thompson's gun after he arrived on the scene. The coroner's jury ultimately ruled that the shots that killed Thompson and Fisher came from Coy's and Foster's guns, but ruled the killings "justifiable and done in self defense [sic] in the immediate danger of life."[69] William Sims, Foster's business partner, publicly praised Coy as a "cautious, careful, and law-abiding officer, on whom reliance could be placed."[70] Coy's manliness and implied Whiteness contrasted sharply with the immediate suspicion and racial marking of Charo and Tijerina as alleged "Mexican assassins."

Juan T. Cardenas, who served as assistant city marshal and captain of police, was also regularly presented to the public as a Tejano who fulfilled the expectations of White manliness. A Confederate veteran, Cardenas had served as a city patrolman during San Antonio's 1866 cholera outbreak. After leaving his job as a printer, he became a respected sheriff's deputy and had acted as Mickle's "guide" during his 1879 tour of the west-side vice district. Even as Mickle described the area as populated by Mexican criminal classes, the journalist described his Tejano guide—who held the position of deputy assistant marshal—as "genial." He confessed to an "involuntary edging up" toward Cardenas in areas he considered especially dangerous.[71] Cardenas's support of Callaghan's initial mayoral campaign won him favor with the new administration, and a year into Callaghan's first term he was promoted to first assistant marshal—a position he held until the early twentieth century. In 1901, Cardenas was featured in the *San Antonio Police Department Illustrated*, an advertiser-sponsored publication highlighting the city's "modern" police department for potential business investors. A biographical portrait of Cardenas portrayed him as an example of middle-class manliness, noting his military service and work in a skilled trade (printing) before joining law enforcement. It described Cardenas as a "brave and fearless officer" who "took a leading part in breaking up the law defiers" who plagued the city after the Civil War.[72] In noting his Mexican origins, however, the author seemingly elided the question of Cardenas's Whiteness, referring to his parents only as "native Texans" who had been born in San Antonio nearly half a century before Anglo American settlement.[73]

Cardenas's public profile reflected the blurriness of racial boundaries between Whites and Mexicans for Tejano elites. His social and cultural ties to the city's Mexican-origin population were well known. In addition to being a twice-elected city alderman from the west side, Cardenas was also president of the Sociedad Mutualista Mexicana, a regular sponsor of the city's Mexican Independence Day celebrations.[74] At the same time, his links to the

Photograph of Juan T. Cardenas, assistant marshal and captain of police, from *San Antonio Police Department Illustrated* (1901).

local Democratic machine, largely controlled by Southern-born Anglo Americans, appeared to place him among the city's White population. Like nearly all (93 percent) of the Tejano men who joined the police force during the 1870s and 1880s, Cardenas was a Confederate army veteran, having served in a cavalry unit that fought at the Battle of Valverde in the New Mexico territory.[75] During the party conventions of 1868, Cardenas had been a founding member of Los Bexareños Demócrátas, an organization of Tejano Democrats who embraced White conservatives' opposition to Black suffrage. He had been among those landowners and merchants responding to a call in the *San Antonio Herald* for a meeting of "all who were opposed to negro supremacy" and who believed theirs to be a "white man's Government . . . established by white men, for the benefit of white men and their posterity."[76]

For most of the second half of the nineteenth century, accounts in the Texas press recognized the presence of "white men" among the Tejano population. As both official police department publications and newspaper reports regularly used a language of race, manliness, and crime to identify Mexicans as racial others, the race of Tejano policemen like Coy and Cardenas went largely unmarked in media coverage of their exploits. If anything, they were socially identified as White men. Their identification with

Whiteness was further established in accounts of their interactions with Black and Mexican crime suspects.

In postbellum Southern cities, newspaper stories about "Black rapists" who assaulted White women and girls reinforced notions of White supremacy. In San Antonio, these accounts of Black criminality often featured Tejano policemen as heroic figures who acted valiantly in defense of White racial purity. In 1881, Charles Ward, a disabled Black army veteran, was accused of assaulting Dora Ellermann, whom papers described as "a young white woman" or "a young German girl" who was, depending on the source, either seventeen or twenty-one years of age. Though Ward proclaimed his innocence, claiming that Ellermann had concocted the allegations of attempted assault after fearing that their consensual relationship had become public, the English- and German-language press described the alleged crime as "one of the most cruel and daring outrages that has ever disgraced Texas." Ward was denounced as a "fiend" who should be lynched "on sight" or "burned at the stake." Newspapers covering the story noted that Ellermann had reported her attack to Officer Rafael Martinez—one of the city's four Tejano officers. After learning of the alleged assault, the *San Antonio Express* reported, Martinez immediately "called for his horse" and "went in search of the villain," eventually arresting Ward in a saloon in the west-side vice district.[77] Papers lauded Martinez for preventing further violence by quickly arresting Ward. When interviewed, Martinez expressed his own outrage at the alleged attack, stating that the charge of attempted rape made against Ward "did not reach the nature of the negro's deed."[78]

Anglo press accounts of the 1884 capture and arrest of Jack Langdon, an African American man accused of sexually assaulting a five-year-old White girl, portrayed Tejano officers in similar "heroic" roles. According to media reports, city marshal Philip Shardein sent mounted officers Martinez, Andrés Coy, and another to search for Langdon, who had reportedly fled along the San Antonio River. Although Langdon denied the charge and two examining physicians expressed doubts about the claims of an assault, newspapers called Langdon a "fiend" and a "negro brute," describing the alleged crime as "perhaps the most outrageous . . . ever perpetrated within the limits of the fair Alamo City." The papers called for Langdon's death.[79] According to the *San Antonio Daily Express*, Martinez was the first to spot Langdon emerging from the riverbank, while Coy was among the officers who escorted Langdon to the victim's home to be identified. Both men "performed their sworn duty nobly" by ensuring that Langdon made it to the city jail. The paper credited their "adroit persuasion and remarks" with maintaining civic order when a lynch mob assembled in front of the city jail.[80] Press coverage of Tejano lawmen's roles in the capture and arrest of both Ward and Langdon cast them as heroic, implicitly White figures in stories about alleged Black rapists, fighting valiantly in defense of White racial purity and the rule of law.

While Tejano policemen appeared as figures of White manliness in narratives about Black criminality, they also appeared in urban crime stories involving Mexican-origin men. These accounts typically portrayed the accused as having inclinations toward theft and physical violence that endangered lawmen and civilians. These stories, however, contain an interesting narrative omission: while the alleged perpetrators are identified as "Mexicans," the ethnic origins of the Tejano lawmen remain unsaid. On October 10, 1883, only two months after the San Pedro Park incident in which the city's English-language press condemned Kerbel's comments against Mexicans, papers in San Antonio and Galveston reported on a successful city police raid in the San Pedro Creek district on a thieves' safehouse, which they referred to as a "Mexican den."[81] According to reports, Officers Martinez and Coy participated in the raid, which resulted in the arrest of five men suspected of being involved in a rash of local robberies of downtown businesses of goods worth "several hundreds of dollars." Papers emphasized the racial distinctiveness of those arrested, noting that "all" of the suspects were "Mexicans" who were part of a gang that was "still at large." At the same time, the newspaper stories singled out Martinez for his bravery and "resourcefulness" in defending himself when one of the suspects reportedly "drew a big knife" on him while attempting to escape. "A prompt presentation of the officer's pistol where it would do the most good," the *Express* reported, "soon quelled the one-handed riot."[82]

In 1888, English-language papers reporting on the shooting death of a barber named Alfredo Valdez by deputy sheriff Esteban "Stephen" Sandoval drew on Mexican crime narratives to distinguish Mexican-origin crime suspects from Tejano lawmen. Witness statements and press accounts of the events leading to Valdez's death indicated that, earlier on the night of the shooting, Officer Coy had repeatedly ejected him from Villanueva's west-side saloon and gambling house for drunk and disorderly behavior. Sandoval testified that he had been patronizing the same saloon while off duty. He was escorting Valdez home at Coy's request when Valdez began "verbally abusing" him and eventually rushed at Sandoval with an "open razor." Sandoval shot him in what was later ruled as self-defense.[83] Accounts of Valdez's death reinforced earlier claims about Mexicans, crime, and the west-side neighborhoods, even while adding a new component of uncontrollable violence. Valdez, a respectable business owner and a family man, had failed to exhibit the manly middle-class virtue of self-control and become a threat to public safety. Newspaper reporting on the incident followed the by-now-familiar pattern of identifying Valdez, whose intemperance and violent outbursts resulted in his own death, as a "Mexican," without commenting on Coy's or Sandoval's background. These and similar crime stories cultivated a sense of difference between law-defending Tejano policemen and "violent Mexicans" like Valdez.

In *El Regidor*, the city's Spanish-language newspaper, reporting on crime and policing focused on Anglo Americans' racist treatment of the masses of Tejanos. Owned and edited by Pablo Cruz, the son of middle-class Mexican immigrants, the paper took a leading role in addressing anti-Mexican discrimination.[84] One of a group of Tejano leaders in Callaghan's circle, Cruz penned editorials praising the mayor's civic improvement projects and defending him against charges of political bossism. Yet as Cruz was a supporter of progressive municipal reform, the paper also contained letters and editorials that revealed tensions between the city's Mexican-origin community and the police.[85] Even with Tejano officers on the force, both the editorials and letters written by readers reported that Callaghan's policemen ignored the needs of the city's Mexican residents; the Anglo officers occasionally harassed them. In 1890, Francisco Martinez, a local barber, wrote to *El Regidor*'s editor to share his experience of being told by an Anglo police officer working special duty at a local cantina that he and his companions "were not admitted there" because they were "Mexicans."[86] Yet only four months later, a brief editorial comment called attention to the absence of police officers on "the blocks between the Military Plaza, Dolorosa, East and Commerce streets" on the city's west side. "When the guardians of public order . . . have been most needed," the item read, "they [could not be found] with a flashlight."[87]

As anti-Mexican sentiment grew during the 1890s, newspaper stories about Mexican crime in the Anglo press increasingly brightened racial boundaries between Mexicans and Whites, even as they acknowledged the presence of Tejano lawmen. In 1893, prominent San Antonio physician Frank Fanning was arrested for murdering Juan Salas, a day laborer, in the east-side Anglo American suburb of Government Hill. Coverage in the English- and German-language press drew on Mexican crime narratives while noting the involvement of Officers Jacobo Coy and Juan Garza. On the night of October 28, Fanning shot and wounded Salas while walking home from a patient visit. Salas had been walking in the same direction, and Fanning claimed that he believed he was being followed. As the first officer to arrive on the scene, Coy took Fanning's statement and determined that Salas had been unarmed. Garza, who had recently been promoted to the rank of second assistant marshal, soon arrived by streetcar with a detective who confirmed that Salas had died from wounds received by Fanning's pistol. According to the newspapers, Coy then arrested Fanning and took him to the police station, where he was jailed overnight and then released on $5,000 bond.[88] Both English- and German-language papers identified Salas as "a Mexican" who had been known to police as a "habitual drinker" who went on "occasional drunken sprees" and whose erratic behavior on a darkened street had led Fanning to shoot him in "self-defense." Relying solely on Fanning's statement, reporters described the doctor as having behaved "calmly" during the incident, only firing his pistol after giving a warning that Salas allegedly ignored while making a "hip pocket motion."[89]

In this and other racialized incidents, San Antonio's Tejano elites and *El Regidor* pushed back against the increased demonization of the city's Mexican population by Anglos. The evening after news of Salas's murder and Fanning's release became public, protesters gathered to denounce Fanning and Judge Henry Noonan's decision to accept bail. Prominent Tejanos, including former policeman and deputy city clerk Juan E. Barrera, addressed the crowd, calling the situation "unwarranted and unprecedented."[90] Heeding the advice of one protester, a young law student named Antonio D. Flores, to let the law take its course, the assembled group produced resolutions that challenged the Anglo press's characterization of Salas, describing him as "a peaceable Mexican citizen," and called Fanning a "murderer" who had killed Salas "on one of the best lighted public thoroughfares" in Government Hill using a pistol that violated laws against carrying concealed weapons.[91] The *San Antonio Daily Express* covered the protests, but mainly to describe Tejanos' anger at Fanning and to praise the "conservatism" of Flores's comments. *El Regidor* put the news of Salas's death and the protests that followed on its front page, with its ire focused squarely on Fanning and Noonan.[92]

While Tejano policemen remained racially unmarked in Anglos' responses to the Fanning-Salas affair, they were altogether absent from the statements of Tejano leaders and protesters. First at the murder inquest and later at trial, Coy gave testimony that supported Fanning's version of the events. During the inquest, Coy informed the presiding judge that Fanning had not only calmly cooperated with police during questioning but even expressed remorse, stating that "he would feel very sorry" if the man he shot "was a good man and a man of family."[93] The day after the inquest, Cruz published an editorial in *El Regidor* that referred to Salas as "an honest Mexican worker" whom Fanning had "murdered." Calling the shooting "one of the most cowardly crimes" to take place in San Antonio "according to public opinion," Cruz insisted that the doctor's cooperation with police stemmed from his regret at "having made such a cowardly [shot]."[94] The editorial did not mention Coy's name.

Fanning's murder trial in April 1894 ended in his acquittal after three minutes of deliberation by an all-Anglo jury consisting of five German immigrants and seven native-born Whites.[95] While no surviving copies of *El Regidor* from 1894 remain to document how San Antonio's Tejanos responded to the verdict, it is likely that Cruz, whose scathing editorial had ended with the hope that Salas's murder would "not go unpunished," would have expressed anger at Fanning's acquittal. The verdict may have influenced Cruz's decision to support Callaghan's progressive independent challenger alderman Marshall Hicks during the 1899 mayoral election.[96] The trial's outcome suggested that, even with Tejano policemen on the force—and in positions of authority—racial boundaries between Whites and Mexicans were continuing to brighten through perceptions of crime and criminality.

Only six months after the trial's end, Antonio Flores, now a practicing lawyer, publicly confronted this brightening trend in a letter he wrote to the editor of *Collier's Once a Week*, a nationally circulated magazine with a largely White, middle-class readership. Flores's letter, on the topic of Mexican Americans' character and capacity for citizenship, responded to an article by Hector A. McEachin, a White, Alabama-born Texan who was the chief clerk at the state capitol, titled "Our Mexican Citizens." McEachin's article claimed to present a portrait of the "average Mexican citizen" of Texas, whom he described as "below ordinary in matters of citizenship," dishonest, and with a tendency to be "law-abiding when it suits their convenience, and law disregarding when it is to their interest."[97] Calling McEachin "either totally ignorant of or entirely biased on a subject he knows nothing about," Flores noted the long and distinguished record of public service exhibited by the state's Mexican citizens. Identifying himself as a "Mexican-Texan," Flores wrote of Tejanos, "No one serves their country better than they."[98]

For Flores and other elite Tejanos, their inclusion in the apparatus of government, whether in the form of military service, civil service, or elected office, provided more than ample evidence of Mexican Americans' capacity for citizenship. His Anglo American readers appear to have heard the message—though perhaps not in the way Flores had intended it. Just two years later, McMinn—Fanning's former defense attorney—would help spearhead an effort to invalidate the naturalization claim of Mexican immigrant Ricardo Rodriguez on the grounds that Mexicans were neither "White" nor "Black," part of a broader campaign to disenfranchise Mexican American voters. In a brief submitted to the presiding judge, McMinn included a notable exception for those who were described as the "sons [and] descendants of [Texas] patriots" or "Spanish, Caucasian Mexican citizens."[99] McMinn's exceptions acknowledged the blurriness of the Mexican-White racial boundary, even as he and Evans worked to strategically brighten it. Although the courts upheld Rodriguez's right to naturalize, the belief that Mexicans were racial outsiders remained in place. As the century drew to a close, stories about crime and criminality involving Tejano policemen helped to brighten racial boundaries by conveying the idea that theirs too was a troubling non-White manliness that endangered the civic order.

Gamblers, Brutes, and Thieves: Tejano Policemen and Middle-Class Manhood

Even as reporting on Mexican-origin crime suspects continued to implicitly position Tejano policemen within the city's population of White lawmen, press coverage of their personal affairs suggested that the media harbored increasing doubts about their respectability. Only months before the *San Antonio Express* published its 1888 article touting the work of the city police department, members of the Bexar County grand jury submitted a report charging that a culture of moral laxity among the city's "peace officers" was contributing to a decline of the city's "moral sentiment." In deliberating on some two hundred felony and misdemeanor cases that showed "a lamentable disregard for public morals and decency," jurors claimed to have encountered witnesses reluctant to testify and police officers who "refused to acknowledge there were any disorderly persons or places" in the city despite evidence that they were "more numerous than the grand jury had reason to believe."[100]

The report's charges against San Antonio's lawmen elicited comment from other Texas newspapers covering its release, calling them "typical" of "cities of any size in the state." In a widely reprinted editorial, the *Brenham Daily Banner* called it "truly a deplorable state of affairs where the . . . authorities appointed for the preservation of peace and the enforcement of the laws form a league with the lawless element." Stating that "sheriffs, constables and police are under a pledge to enforce the laws, [and] to them almost exclusively does the duty belong," the editorial also noted that those who violated public trust in law enforcement "should be summarily dealt with, and convicted and deposed from office for malfeasance."[101] Though no particular classes or groups of officers had been named in the report, Tejano lawmen were highly visible as alleged perpetrators in cases of corruption and official misconduct. As the racial boundaries brightened in the US borderlands during the 1890s, San Antonio's newspapers ran stories suggesting that Tejano lawmen's relationship to White middle-class manliness was troubled at best. The same men depicted as heroes in the fight against San Antonio's criminal classes encountered skepticism when they were accused of crimes or illicit behaviors.

On July 23, 1886, the *San Antonio Express* printed a letter to the editor describing a case of alleged police brutality that took place in one of the city's plazas. Writing under the name "A Witness," the writer claimed that what began as an exchange of words between a local man and an unnamed on-duty policeman over an unleashed dog resulted in the man's violent arrest and "brutal" assault at the police station. The writer claimed that, after apprehending the man, "the policeman, who was a Mexican . . . commenced to handle him very roughly in bringing him to the station house," where he was placed in a cell by two other officers. At that point, the letter writer claimed, the first policeman "attacked the man savagely," striking him "repeatedly in the face making the blood flow freely." Protests from "several persons" against the unnamed officer's actions only seemed to increase his anger, as he "drew his pistol . . . shoving it into the faces of those nearest to him repeatedly, until he drove all the witnesses of his cowardly brutality out." Ending his letter by questioning the legitimacy of the man's arrest, "Witness" asked whether "brutes under the shield of a policeman's badge" were allowed to "so abuse a citizen when he is a prisoner in the station house." "If this is to continue," he added, "no man shall dare open his mouth within hearing of a policeman. Such brutes should not be on the force."[102] While the identity of the letter writer is unknown, the letter itself is unusual in that it commented on the lawman's Mexican origin — which press coverage of Tejano policemen appears to never have done — and linked it to a declining respect for police authority. Though regarded as defenders of law and order, Tejano policemen could also encounter a brightening Mexican-White racial boundary that described theirs as a troubling and occasionally criminal manhood.

Newspapers reported Tejano lawmen's personal scandals in ways that revealed an ambivalence about their claims to White middle-class manliness. In the years following his public celebrity as a police officer, press reports of Jacobo Coy's legal and personal troubles portrayed him as a failed example of middle-class propriety. In 1887, the *San Antonio Daily Express* reported Coy's complaints of unfair treatment by a grand jury in the matter of his frequent indictments on gambling charges. Having earned a reputation as a "sportsman" who frequented gambling dens and theaters in the west-side vice district, Coy claimed that he was among only a few men who were indicted by the grand jury with "persistent regularity," while others were "allowed to go scott [sic] free."[103] That same year, the press linked Coy with both violence and immorality, reporting on a confrontation between his wife, Presciliana, and a "variety actress" named Lillie Wilson, with whom he was rumored to be romantically involved. Papers reported that Wilson had threatened Presciliana Coy—described as "a comely young Mexican wom[a]n"—with a pistol that she "would no doubt have fired into her lady visitor" had not Coy's mother "interfered to prevent a murder." Papers in Austin and Fort Worth also covered the event and its aftermath, which included Wilson's subsequent arrest on a charge of assault and charges of adultery made against Jacobo Coy by his wife.[104] Though he managed to keep his position as a policeman, Coy's public involvement in moral scandals would have encouraged Anglo readers to see his complaints about the grand jury in new light.

Rafael Martinez had used his law enforcement credentials to win election to the position of constable. He, too, was portrayed by politicians and the press as a man of questionable moral judgment, particularly when it came to money. Constables were legally entitled to collect fees on any arrests they made and were paid by presenting arrest records to the city commissioner's court. In November 1891, Bexar County district attorney George Paschal charged Martinez with defrauding the city government by collecting nearly $400 for arrests he had not made.[105] Martinez's lawyer, M. G. Anderson, told grand jurors that his client acted in good faith when he collected the fees, having submitted records kept by his deputy constable, Adolph Pubokowski, and sheriff's deputy Warren Druse. Martinez further claimed that it had been custom for constables to collect fees on arrests made by police and sheriffs' officers when affidavits were made in justice courts to which they were assigned.[106] His attorney produced character witnesses who described Martinez as trustworthy. Paschal countered with his own witnesses—including Pubokowski and Druse—who claimed that Martinez not only had knowingly committed fraud but was also in personal debt to a number of unnamed city officials. Paschal declared that Martinez had turned his office into a "money mill" and demonstrated "a disposition to rob the state."[107] When the grand jury voted to uphold the charges against Martinez and remove him from office, his immediate resignation allowed him to secure a position as a jailor at the Bexar County Courthouse. Though Martinez was ultimately cleared of wrongdoing in his 1893 criminal trial, the public spectacle of his arrest, his indictment, and the revelations of his personal debts contributed to a public narrative of Tejano lawmen as failed exemplars of middle-class manliness.

Scandals and charges of corruption involving law enforcement during the 1890s contributed to the growing calls for political reform that fueled the 1899 mayoral campaign of reformist Marshall Hicks, who went on to defeat Callaghan. In 1901, the Police Committee of Hicks's newly formed Police and Fire Commission began screening all applicants for the police force and instituted new requirements, including the ability to read and write English and evidence of "good moral character."[108] In their 1901 public statement on the police department's activities, City Marshal James Van Riper and Police Captain Juan T. Cardenas listed new physical standards: "All members of the force should be . . . not less than five feet eight inches in height, not under twenty-one years of age or over fifty years, and should not weigh less than one hundred and sixty pounds nor over two hundred and fifty pounds." After the committee's examinations had been completed, they noted, only sixty-five of the "over two hundred applicants" were recommended as eligible. Of the forty new officers appointed by the commission that year, only four were Tejano and only two were African American.[109] While the stricter hiring requirements suggested a modernizing of the police force, officers complained about low salaries. That same year, mounted officers Antonio Herrera and Rafael Quintana petitioned the city council along with sixteen other officers claiming that having to provide and feed their own horses in addition to providing for their families "cut deeply" into the eighty dollars per month they received.

By the early twentieth century, the idea that even middle-class Tejanos, including those in positions of authority, shared the supposedly Mexican trait of "lawlessness" had taken root among many of San Antonio's Anglo Americans. During the city's 1905 mayoral race, conservative and largely Anglo American Democratic Party officials drew on Mexican crime narratives in criticizing Callaghan, who was seeking reelection on the third-party People's Party ticket. At a rally for Democrats' favored candidate, El Regidor editor Pablo Cruz quoted William J. Aubrey, a White Alabama-born lawyer presiding over the evening's events, as having said of Callaghan, "The law out of the mouth of a Mexican mayor can not [sic] have a place in San Antonio."[110]

Callaghan's efforts to circumvent the Police and Fire Commission's role in appointing new police officers and firefighters had prompted his critics to describe these city employees as a "private army" of political loyalists supported by taxpayers.[111] Stories in the Anglo press about the city's Tejano lawmen frequently connected them with behaviors demonstrating a lack of "manly self-control." In December 1906, papers reported that police detective José Cassiano Jr., the son of a high-ranking civil servant, had been cleared of conduct unbecoming an officer after firing his pistol in a hotel barroom during an argument. By February 1907, Cassiano had resigned after being charged with affray and fined ten dollars for fighting in yet another barroom.[112]

Cases of public violence involving Tejano lawmen were also linked to political rivalries. Later that same year, both English- and Spanish-language newspapers reported on an incident of assault involving police officer José "Joe" Quintana and Feliciano Flores Jr., the son of a Bexar County deputy sheriff. Papers reported that Quintana had attempted to arrest Flores for "irreverent" remarks he had allegedly made about Callaghan's administration while debating with a companion. After a fight between the two men in which Flores struck Quintana with a chair, police arrested Flores on assault and battery charges. Days later, district attorney Leonardo Garza reversed the charges, charging Quintana, rather than Flores, with aggravated assault and battery.[113] The incident did not go unnoticed in the Spanish-language press. *El Regidor* reported only that Quintana had been fined for assaulting Flores during his arrest for comments made against Callaghan, but made no mention of the additional accusations against Quintana or of Flores's arrest. By contrast, reports in the *Express* hinted that the original charges might have involved a cover-up and questioned why Quintana remained on duty.[114]

In the first decade of the twentieth century, the meanings assigned to law enforcement as a Tejano path to middle-class Whiteness changed. Press accounts of policing in San Antonio during the early twentieth century depicted police officers—many of them Tejanos—as unreliable civil servants whose political loyalties interfered with their assigned duties. *El Regidor* editor Cruz, one of the city's leading Tejano voices, agreed. Only two years after endorsing Callaghan against the racist appeals of conservative Democrats, Cruz publicly withdrew his support in the face of mounting evidence of what he saw as corruption and political bossism. In an editorial published only three months after the Quintana-Flores case, Cruz accused Callaghan of limiting opportunities for Tejanos to serve in the higher ranks of his administration, calling him an "enemy" of the city's Mexican-origin population. "Callaghan is one of those who are opposed to any Mexican occupying any important public position, because he will overtake him later," Cruz wrote. "[He] only grants Mexicans the position of policeman, dogcatcher, street sweeper, or other humble positions."[115] While Tejano men joining the police force between 1900 and 1910 continued to come from the classes of skilled manual laborers or farmers, Cruz accused Callaghan of insulting the city's "good" and "honest Mexicans" by offering them only the "worst positions" while he protected the interests of "laborers and vagrants."[116] These new uncertainties about police employment as a viable pathway to middle-class mobility suggested that what earlier generations of Tejanos had seen as an opportunity for secure middle-class employment was now significantly less desirable.

Conclusion

From the time that it began in the 1850s, Anglo settlement of the US-Mexico borderlands altered the social position of the descendants of Spanish- and Mexican-era settlers. While the speed and extent of the decline of their economic and political influence varied by state, Whites' fluctuating anxieties about Mexicans manifested as renewed concerns about their racial position and fitness for citizenship. In San Antonio, one of the borderlands' major urban centers, Anglo newcomers with access to large amounts of capital gradually dominated the city's skilled and white-collar labor markets, leaving most Tejano workers relegated to semiskilled or unskilled labor alongside African Americans and poorer Whites. However, Tejano elites' social connections and political alignments with the city's Democrat-controlled machine helped them to preserve a position within the middle class through public-sector employment. In particular, Tejanos maintained a visible presence in San Antonio's police force, which became a crucial site for negotiating White middle-class identities.

During the 1870s and 1880s, city officials and journalists writing about crime positioned Tejano police officers alongside Anglos in a corps of "White" lawmen who protected the citizenry from a largely non-White criminal class that included "Mexicans." But just two decades later, stories about Tejano policemen in the Anglo press regularly linked them with behavior that contradicted codes of middle-class manliness and threatened the civic order. Before the 1880s, the social structures of the borderlands that reinforced racial boundaries between Mexicans and Whites seemed to move from bright to blurred, with alleged "racial" differences between the two groups infrequently recognized, rarely institutionalized, and only sometimes significant for interactions with individuals and institutions.[117] By the century's turn, these boundaries again became brighter, with Anglo journalists, political figures, and members of the public portraying Tejano lawmen in ways that reflected renewed ambiguities about Mexican Americans' claims to Whiteness.

Much of this discourse focused on crime and criminality. San Antonio's English-language newspapers repeatedly ran stories depicting the city's Mexican population and Mexican neighborhoods as bastions of crime. Even as new narratives of "Mexican crime" regularly portrayed Mexican-origin men as violent, intemperate, and criminally inclined, Anglos' reliance on Tejano lawmen, such as assistant city marshal Juan Cardenas, tempered the local media's fixation on racial identity. Though Anglo men, whether born in the United States or abroad, made up the overwhelming majority of San Antonio's expanding corps of policemen, Tejanos remained a highly visible presence. In the context of popular narratives about Mexicans' alleged tendencies toward violence and crime, press accounts of "heroic" Tejano policemen contributed to popular understandings of them as White lawmen with the authority to apprehend any of the city's diverse range of crime suspects. Moreover, the trajectories of men like Rafael Martinez, Andrés Coy, and Juan Barrera suggest that policing allowed men who came from a rural landholding class to transition into the emerging urban middle class. These occupational gains shored up Tejanos' claims to Whiteness in the face of isolated efforts to segregate them alongside other non-Whites in a demographically shifting city.

In the years following the end of Reconstruction, Southern Whites' efforts to formally and legally segregate Black populations in the region's growing cities and towns overlapped with Anglo American migration into the US-Mexico borderlands. Shaped by the culture of the slaveholding South from which the majority of Texas's Anglo American postbellum settlers came, the 1880s and 1890s saw the beginnings of Whites' efforts to formally segregate Tejanos as non-Whites in urban settings like San Antonio.[118] By the late 1880s, the city's Anglo population seemed less willing to see their Tejano policemen as unmarked figures of middle-class manliness. News reports increasingly called attention to behaviors that appeared to threaten, rather than safeguard, law and order. In the early 1880s, press accounts of the exploits of Tejano lawmen like Jacobo and Andrés Coy, Rafael Martinez, and Stephen Sandoval emphasized their bravery in protecting the public from criminal activity and helped to bolster earlier claims that there were "Mexicans who were white men and gentlemen." Many of these accounts omitted commentary on the lawmen's racial status altogether, focusing instead on the "Mexican criminals" they apprehended. But by the 1890s and 1900s, the renewed anti-Mexican sentiment that accompanied a new wave of Mexican migration into the urban centers of the Texas borderlands gave Anglo narratives about and representations of Mexican criminality a new urgency. Accounts in the Anglo press now suggested that the racially inferior manliness of Tejano policemen posed threats to public order. The city's Spanish-language press, meanwhile, ran coverage expressing concerns about police interactions with the city's Mexican-origin population but minimized reports on scandals or misconduct involving Tejano policemen.

By the early twentieth century, reports of public and violent confrontations between lawmen and civilians, such as those involving Cassiano and Quintana, linked Tejano lawmen to the threat of public violence. The public failures of these men to exemplify the discipline and self-control characteristic of "civilized" middle-class manliness would have been unsettling to those readers who expected policemen to be both moral exemplars and guardians of the law. Even as Tejano lawmen continued to seek and hold middle-class jobs as public servants, they found their claims to middle-class Whiteness increasingly challenged in the Anglo press. Their long tenure in the region proved no match for a growing population of Anglos who understood legitimate middle-class identities to be durably linked to Whiteness, making them—and them alone—entitled to its rights and privileges.

In the US-Mexico borderlands, Tejano elites' status as "off-White" reflected their position relative to a blurred racial boundary that shifted to alternatively include or exclude them from Whiteness. Rapid urbanization and a shifting demographic context, including the arrival of migrants from inside and outside the United States, changed the status of San Antonio's Tejanos, making them a visible, racialized minority. Between 1880 and 1910, these struggles over the contours of the race-class nexus played out in various spheres of interaction, including the press. This brightening of racial boundaries took place against the hardening of Black-White racial boundaries across the United States, but especially in the Jim Crow South. By the 1910s and 1920s, Texas's Anglo population had expanded the logic of racial segregation to more fully include those of Mexican origin, developing laws, practices, and customs that many borderlands historians have called "Juan Crow."[119] In the developing cities of the West Coast, Whites would use both legal and extralegal means to sustain racial boundaries against another group they saw as a threat to their middle-class status: Chinese-origin cultural brokers.

CHAPTER FOUR

Chinese Blood in the Bureau

Chinese American Immigration Interpreters in San Francisco, 1896–1907

During the spring and summer of 1896, a high-profile bribery and corruption scandal at the US Customs Service's Chinese Bureau in San Francisco dominated local news coverage. The scandal involved Richard S. "Dick" Williams, a thirty-two-year-old Chinese American who was employed as a language interpreter and customs enforcement inspector. The state's attorney, William F. Fitzgerald, had charged Williams with four counts of extortion related to enforcement of the Chinese Exclusion Act. During the monthlong trial, special state prosecutor Barclay Henley unsuccessfully attempted to enter Williams's bank statements into evidence, arguing that the "large sums" deposited in the account far exceeded that of a civil servant—clear proof, in Henley's telling, that Williams had accepted bribes. The press supported Henley's claims, reporting that Williams, who claimed to have been a successful businessman before coming into a large family inheritance, lived an extravagant lifestyle. His circle of wealthy friends included the son of immigration commissioner John H. Wise, his superior at the bureau. The prosecution and the press also emphasized Williams's Chinese ancestry, portraying him as a racial impostor whose racial boundary crossing threatened the city's racial order. Within two months of Williams's conviction, US Secretary of the Treasury John G. Carlisle, under whose office immigration and customs duties fell, banned the agency from employing anyone known to have Chinese ancestry as an interpreter or customs inspector.[1]

Despite the local press's claims that there were scores of "good white interpreters" who could fill the vacancy left by Williams's dismissal, the scarcity of either native-born or immigrant Whites with a knowledge of Chinese posed a problem in filling his position. Only a month after issuing the ban, Carlisle supported the application of John Endicott Gardner Jr., the son of a White father and mixed-race Chinese mother, for the interpreter's position with the bureau. Wise, embarrassed by the Williams scandal and rumored to be annoyed by ongoing interference from the Treasury secretary in the bureau's workings, reportedly wrote to Carlisle claiming that Gardner "would not meet the requirements" for employment because he "had Chinese blood in his veins." In its reporting on the controversy, however, the *San Francisco Chronicle* downplayed Gardner's Chinese ancestry, instead stressing his father's connections to pre-Revolutionary New England and referring to him as a suitable choice in securing a "white interpreter for the Custom-house."[2]

Gardner kept his appointment, but the ban remained unofficially in place for more than a decade. In the wake of a 1904 Chinese smuggling scandal involving Hippolytus Eça da Silva, an interpreter of mixed-race Chinese background, the press put renewed public attention on the ban, citing it in opposing the appointment of Herman Lowe, a full-blooded Chinese American, to a salaried interpreter's position with the bureau. In addition to claiming that there were "many white men on the list waiting appointment," the *Chronicle* described Lowe's appointment as "directly contrary" to established policy in the agency and repeated the claim of a previous immigration commissioner that Chinese employment at the bureau "would inevitably result in corruption and malfeasance."[3]

With the United States' exclusion laws increasingly limiting the arrival of new immigrants from China in the late nineteenth and early twentieth centuries, Whites' fears about the presence of Chinese immigrants in the nation's cities fixated on a new racial actor—the "Americanized" Chinese man. An important body of recent scholarship on Chinese immigrant communities has pointed out that enclaves of Chinese settlement in cities like San Francisco, New York, and Chicago were neither racially nor economically homogeneous. While commonly understood to be thoroughly foreign spaces primarily populated by recent immigrants, Chinatowns in these cities functioned as sites where widely recognized boundaries between "Whites" and "Asiatics" were regularly contested, negotiated, and even crossed in everyday interactions with those who lived, worked, did business, or "slummed" within their borders.[4] Relatedly, Asian American historians have described how during the exclusion era, Chinese immigrants and their American-born children—whether residing in Chinatowns or just beyond their borders—increasingly asserted Americanized identities as grounds for their equal inclusion in public spaces. In San Francisco, home to nearly half of California's Chinese population, Chinese residents had made such claims as early as the 1880s.[5] The majority of Whites, however, viewed Americanized Chinese with perhaps even greater suspicion than those who had yet to adopt American ways, seeing their outward appearance as a mere concealment of their "natural" links to crime and vice.[6]

Some of this hostility undoubtedly related to the emergence of a Chinese American middle-class comprising prosperous merchants, small-business owners, and white-collar professionals. San Francisco's large Chinese community, and the city's continuing importance as a hub for Asian labor and trade, supported an emerging class of Chinese American immigrant brokers. In fact, the scarcity of Whites who could speak or read Chinese created an important labor market opportunity for bilingual and bicultural Chinese San Franciscans as court translators, transportation agents, and labor contractors.[7] At the US Customs Service's Chinese Bureau, charged with carrying out the evolving and unclear policies of Chinese exclusion, men from the interpreter class found work assisting White immigration officials and customs inspectors with incoming passengers and freight from China. At the same time that federal employment advanced interpreters' pursuit of middle-class mobility, however, their social position remained predicated on the subordinate position of Chinese immigrants as aliens ineligible for citizenship in the United States. For some, this meant lucrative opportunities for exploiting Chinese immigrants' desire to evade racist immigration laws that targeted them for special scrutiny and harsh punishment.

As historian Erika Lee has pointed out, San Francisco's local newspapers helped to further fuel anti-Chinese sentiment by regularly reporting on the work of Chinese inspectors and other immigration officials and the numbers of Chinese arrivals at the city's port.[8] Like the accounts of crime in the Chinatown district that were regular news features, sensationalized stories about cases of immigrant smuggling and the culture of corruption among immigration officials supported the public's erroneous belief that immigration laws had done little to solve the "Chinese problem." In fact, there were now new dangers for the city's White population. Between 1894 and 1910, the San Francisco press would report on a series of bribery and corruption scandals at the Chinese Bureau in which both Americanized and mixed-race Chinese American men figured as central suspects. In this chapter, I show how prosecutors and the press used the "Chinese problem" at the Customs Service to construct new racial narratives that described social mobility among Chinese immigrants and their American-born children as a source of social and economic peril for the city's Whites. Press coverage of the Williams corruption trial, the Gardner appointment, and other controversies over Chinese interpreters that followed all called attention to a new racial phenomenon—Chinese American men working alongside White men in white-collar occupations. While the press and immigration officials initially responded by calling for restricting interpreter jobs to White men, a continuing shortage of White interpreters highlighted ongoing ambiguities in the Customs Service, and later the Immigration Bureau, about the racial classification of mixed-race

Chinese men. By the early twentieth century, federal efforts to address charges of inefficiency and corruption within the Chinese Bureau continued to draw on these narratives, focusing their attention on the personal lives of Chinese American interpreters and their social networks within the nascent Chinese American middle class. These cases underscore the development of middle-class racisms geared toward not only preventing racial boundary crossing but also specifically brightening and fixing the location of racial boundaries.

Territories of Race in Gilded Age San Francisco

San Francisco was an important site for immigration and settlement in the United States during and after the Gold Rush era (1848–70). In the 1850s economic opportunities in California and the western territories attracted domestic migrants from the eastern and Southern states, as well as immigrants from Europe, Latin America, and Asia. Between 1870 and 1900, the city's population doubled from 149,473 to nearly 300,000 people, the majority of them foreign-born.[9] Continued demands for cheap labor, coupled with economic and political upheavals in China, fueled successive waves of Chinese immigrant settlement in California, where by 1870 Chinese workers represented 16.3 percent of the state's manufacturing labor force.[10] As an important site for transpacific trade, San Francisco became home to the nation's largest Chinese settlement. Scholars estimate that between 1860 and 1870, the city's Chinese population, which included women and children, increased from 2,719 to 12,022 people.[11]

Although Chinese labor had played a crucial role in San Francisco's growth and in California's economic expansion, the anti-Chinese movement that had first emerged in the 1850s gained momentum in the unstable economic environment of the 1870s, with Chinese immigrants blamed for economic depressions and high unemployment among White workers. Politicians, everyday citizens, and social reformers joined White labor organizations in calls to end Chinese immigration, citing alleged economic, physical, sexual, and moral dangers that Chinese men and women posed to the nation.[12] The growth of Chinese immigrant communities in East Coast cities prompted increased national support for anti-Chinese agitation that had emerged in the western states. By 1875 Congress had enacted the Page Law, described by the California congressman who authored it as a measure against forced contract labor from Asia and the importation of women for "lewd and immoral purposes," purposes that were popularly associated with Chinese immigrant women.[13]

Less than a decade later in 1882, Congress adopted a law that more fully embraced the exclusion of Chinese immigrants. The Chinese Exclusion Act, signed into law by President Grover Cleveland, prohibited immigration of Chinese laborers for a ten-year period and barred all Chinese immigrants living in the United States from naturalization.[14] While the act identified teachers, merchants, students, diplomats, and casual travelers of means as exempt from exclusion, they were required to present certification for travel from the Chinese government. In addition to being designated as "aliens ineligible for citizenship," Chinese immigrants living in the United States had to obtain certification to reenter the country if they traveled abroad. The act's provisions would be renewed and further tightened in the 1892 Geary Act, and again in 1902 along with new provisions governing the tracking and deportation of Chinese living in San Francisco and other US cities.[15]

Exclusion-era San Francisco's transnational Chinese community figured prominently in an urban racial landscape chiefly populated by native-born and foreign-born Whites, a relatively small Black population, and even smaller groups of other Asian immigrants.[16] Dominant nineteenth-century understandings of Chinatowns and other Chinese spaces as culturally, morally, and physically dangerous to Whites were central to the ongoing racialization of immigrant and native-born Chinese.[17] The fear that "Chinese vices" would corrupt Whites formed the core of the case for excluding Chinese from the city's residential areas and public spaces. With the exception of a few "pioneering" families or those who worked in White homes as domestic servants, Chinese residents were generally confined to Chinatown—a twelve-block area near the city's central business district that Chinese immigrants called Dabu or "First City."[18] Both the local press and official reports reinforced commonly held beliefs about the Chinese as a violent and immoral foreign element residing in a diseased and vice-filled slum.[19] An 1885 report produced for the city's board of supervisors claimed that Chinatown's residents were responsible for various public health ills, including alleged cases of venereal disease among White youth.[20] Popular accounts by writers and journalists of Chinese immigrant settlements as racially homogeneous, immutably foreign, and predominantly male often ignored the documented presence of immigrant and native-born Chinese families living alongside small but varied populations of both Whites and non-Whites.[21] Those Whites who were known to live in or near Chinese districts were commonly identified as a criminal element unfit for association with "respectable" classes, with the exception of Protestant missionaries who socialized with Chinese converts in mission homes and churches.[22]

"The Opportunities of Exclusion": Immigrant Brokering and Chinese Immigration

During the 1880s, industrialization and the growth of trade facilitated high rates of social mobility for the city's White middle class of small-business owners, professionals, and clerical workers, many of whom were from immigrant backgrounds.[23] Unlike in other turn-of-the-century cities, in San Francisco immigrant Whites were widely distributed in both its occupational hierarchy and its urban political establishment.[24] Chinese, like other non-Whites in San Francisco, remained durably excluded. In the years following the exclusion act, those who had supported its passage now expressed support for restricting both native-born and foreign-born Chinese residents' access to employment, housing, and public education. While patterns of occupational segregation kept most Chinese residents employed in semi-skilled or unskilled manual labor, a small class of merchants, professionals, and "cultural brokers" formed the core of an emergent Chinese American middle class distinct from both the masses of the city's Chinese wage earners and the mercantile elite.[25] Interpreters and translators were part of this group. Historian Mae Ngai identifies interpreters as part of an all-important community of immigrant brokers within the nascent Chinese American middle class. As early as the 1870s, she notes, bilingual Chinese workers had managed to find full-time employment with both Chinese- and some White-owned businesses, as well as with civic institutions like the post office, the police department, or the criminal courts. After the passage of the Exclusion Act, interpreting for federal immigration authorities—assisting with immigration hearings and the landing of Chinese steamship passengers at ports of entry—emerged as a new employment pathway. By the beginning of the twentieth century, professional interpreters would emerge as a highly visible and influential group in San Francisco and other cities with large Chinese populations like New York, Boston, and Chicago.[26]

Efforts to administer the Chinese Exclusion Act's complex provisions and policies were carried out through a new and evolving bureaucratic structure aimed at managing Chinese immigration. What began as the Chinese Bureau within the US Customs Service and later became the Chinese Division under the Bureau of Immigration was variously staffed by officials, inspectors, and agents—all of whom were authorized to enforce immigration laws on behalf of the federal government. The 1882 act created the position of "Chinese inspector"—an official who was responsible for administering its provisions at ports of entry or departure for Chinese laborers. Sometimes acting with a deputy, the inspector reviewed passenger lists and gave final approval to any Chinese-origin travelers claiming the right to lawfully enter the United States. Collectors of customs in these districts were also authorized by the act to issue return certificates to Chinese laborers and maintain records on departing travelers, sometimes assisted by the Chinese inspector assigned to their district.[27]

The number of Chinese inspectors employed in San Francisco's Customs Office increased gradually after Chinese exclusion became official, responding to the need to process the claims of departing Chinese laborers and entering travelers. While the number of Chinese immigrants seeking entry at San Francisco's port dropped dramatically in the years immediately following passage of the act, the numbers of departing Chinese laborers processed by the Chinese Bureau numbered 11,434 in the first year after the act's passage. Yet three years later San Francisco's Customs Office employed only one Chinese inspector, paid four dollars per day when working. Between 1888 and 1889, when the number of departures was 8,838 and the number of arrivals was 115, a second inspector had been added and each man was paid five dollars per day. In 1893, just after the decade-long renewal and strengthening of Chinese exclusion under the Geary Act, San Francisco's Customs Office had five inspectors earning between five and six dollars per day.[28] Beginning in 1899, the San Francisco offices of the Customs Service employed eight Chinese inspectors, with salaries ranging from three dollars to eight dollars. A few had been promoted from the ranks of Chinese interpreters, presumably for their language skills.[29] The majority of these inspectors were White men. Owing their employment in significant part to political patronage from pro-exclusion politicians and labor leaders, inspectors were far from impartial. The only San Francisco inspector of Chinese origin was John Endicott Gardner Jr., who in 1899 was among the highest paid at that location. Writing in 1909, sociologist Mary Roberts Coolidge described the inspectors at San Francisco's Immigration Bureau as primarily political appointees, "largely recruited" from men of European origin whom she described as prone to exhibitions of racial prejudice toward all Chinese.[30]

After its reorganization under the Bureau of Immigration in 1900, the San Francisco Chinese Bureau employed anywhere from two to four Chinese interpreters to assist the Chinese inspectors and other immigration officials. An examination of civil service records and manuscript census returns between 1882 and 1910 indicates that a few mixed-race Chinese men managed to secure work as Chinese interpreters with the Customs Service beginning in the 1890s. Coolidge's criticism of the Chinese Bureau extended to interpreters as well, as she claimed that the position of interpreter at the bureau had regularly been filled by "half-breed Chinese-Anglo-Saxons" whose incompetence at their jobs worked against the fair treatment of immigrants.[31] However, for most bilingual Chinese workers, employment with the Chinese Bureau first surfaced as a pathway to middle-class mobility in the 1900s and expanded incrementally during the first decade of the twentieth century. Racial barriers in hiring persisted; of the fifteen Chinese interpreters employed between 1901 and 1911, only three were of Chinese ancestry. In what would be an important shift after 1904, however, two of the three employed in this capacity were full-blooded, American-born Chinese.[32]

Though their numbers were small, the class trajectories of San Francisco's Chinese American interpreters suggest a picture of movement into and within a middle class characterized by white-collar employment, property ownership, and generational mobility. Of the five interpreters of Chinese descent employed at the San Francisco Chinese Bureau between 1894 and 1910, three came from families headed by low-wage workers. The remaining two came from families headed by merchants or professionals. For those from wage-worker backgrounds, the stability of federal employment and the social capital it generated allowed them to secure a foothold in the middle class, in the form of homeownership and university education for their children. Interpreting work allowed those who had been mercantile or white-collar workers to sustain their socioeconomic position. Herman Lowe and Edward Park, both of whom had been born into modest Chinatown families, managed to secure themselves in the petite bourgeoisie with a lifestyle similar to that of their White counterparts. Lowe became a middle-class homeowner in Portland, Oregon, after accepting his transfer there in 1910. Gardner, already firmly settled in the city's Anglo American elite, remained prominent both as a federal interpreter and as a sought-after expert on Chinese affairs.[33] Even those who left the immigration service under suspicion of corruption managed to continue securing work as privately paid interpreters, labor agents, and travel agents, or occasionally with White-owned businesses.[34] It would be during this same period that anti-Chinese racism would become deeply embedded at the Immigration Bureau. In what follows, I show how the criminal trials of Chinese American interpreters constituted a discursive racial project about class mobility and middle-class manhood that brightened both racial boundaries and class boundaries.

The Threat of Chinese Social Mobility:
Corruption at the Customs House

The 1896 Williams corruption trial emerged from an attempt by Treasury agents to uncover evidence of a culture of corruption among customs agents in the Chinese Bureau. Based on the testimony of several Chinese witnesses, agents supervised by US Treasury special agent Harrison A. Moore had charged Richard S. Williams, a Chinese Inspector and adviser to collector of customs John H. Wise, with accepting bribes for assisting in the illegal landing of Chinese immigrants as well as extorting money. During the trial, both the press and the prosecution attempted to characterize Williams, revealed to be the son of a Chinese father and an Irish mother, as a criminal figure whose rapid social mobility had been facilitated by his ties to Chinese criminals and his willingness to subvert Chinese exclusion laws. While both the prosecution and the press focused on Williams's sudden wealth as proof of his crimes, press reports drew on an interlocking discourse of class and race to describe the dangers of Chinese social mobility for the public: they used his racial ambiguity to underscore the dangerous illegitimacy of his claims to middle-class manhood.

Before the charges filed against him, Williams claimed a White public identity. Available public records about his background show a family that reflected the complexity of racial and ethnic identities among urban Chinese in San Francisco. Census records indicate that Williams settled in the city sometime around 1880. The manuscript census for San Francisco for that year lists him living at 835 Hayes Street with his widowed sister, Mary E. Smith, and her five-year-old son Henry. Their neighborhood was populated exclusively by first- and second-generation European immigrants, identified as part of the city's White population. Both Richard and Mary, who had come to San Francisco from their home state of New York, are listed as White, with their father's birthplace listed as China and their mother's as Ireland. Mary's son Henry was identified by the census taker as "Mulatto."[35] Over the next decade, city directories show that Williams continued to reside in White neighborhoods populated by skilled craftsmen, small-business owners, and clerical workers. A San Francisco city directory for 1891 lists Williams as a partner in a restaurant with Theodore Medovic, an Austrian immigrant who was also his brother-in-law. By then, Williams had started a family of his own and was living on Fell Street with his wife, Isabelle (née Feldman), and their daughter, Isabella. According to what Williams would later tell the press about his employment history, he also operated several other businesses during this time, one of which involved shepherding White tourists through entertainments in San Francisco's Chinatown district.[36]

The traits that likely contributed to Williams's success in selling what was probably an exoticized version of Chinese culture to Whites—his White-looking appearance and his knowledge of Chinese customs—also appear to have helped him secure work as a Chinese interpreter with the US Customs Service in 1894. As an interpreter, Williams worked under three Chinese inspectors, all of them White men.[37] Wise, a Southerner from Virginia who described himself as a "zealous opponent" of Chinese immigration, took a liking to Williams; within a year of his hire, Wise named Williams his "special advisor on Chinese matters" and the 1895 Register of federal employees listed him as a Chinese Inspector.[38] Williams, who socialized regularly with Wise, now lived with his wife and daughter on Scott Street in the city's affluent Lower Pacific Heights district.[39]

Soon enough, Williams's rapid rise in the Customs Service—and his successful navigation of racial boundaries—attracted attention from other agents and more-senior officials in the Chinese Bureau. That same year, his involvement in a failed deportation case brought increased scrutiny from senior immigration officials. In the course of the trial, the attorney for the defendant—a Chinese woman named Wong Yick Ying—argued that his client had been targeted for deportation based on Williams misidentifying her as Wong Li Hor, a woman imported for "immoral purposes." Wong claimed that when she landed in San Francisco, Williams had demanded payment from her and other Chinese passengers for securing their entry, threatening to have them deported if they refused. Williams denied the charges when questioned on the stand, but when the immigration court commissioner presiding over the hearing dismissed charges against Wong, Williams loudly protested. He blamed the case's failure on the district attorney, who he claimed bungled the prosecution by relying on "tainted witnesses" who had managed to fool both him and the commissioner. Both the district attorney and the court commissioner, the *Chronicle* reported, were incensed by Williams's "insulting" accusations. The district attorney publicly reproached him, telling Williams that he was "nothing but an interpreter."[40]

The allegations of extortion against Williams prompted other employees to raise new concerns about his relationship with Wise, with one unnamed source in the Customs Service telling the *Chronicle* that he was being "badly advised" by the racially suspect Williams. "His father was a Chinese, I understand," the source said of Williams, "but it seems he did not inherit the language of the pater familias," adding that despite "his birth and surroundings," Williams knew "comparatively nothing about the language." Wise, apparently unfazed by the rumors about Williams, kept him on and within a year had promoted him to the position of Chinese inspector at a salary of $150 per month.[41]

The following year, a federal investigation into the disappearance of some 250 Chinese workers admitted on temporary visas for the 1895 Atlanta Exposition uncovered claims of bribes, extortion, and corruption linked to Williams. A Chinese shoe factory proprietor and racketeer named Fung Jing Toy, known colloquially as Little Pete, was accused of helping the fair workers avoid their scheduled deportations from San Francisco and remain in the country illegally with the cooperation of federal customs agents. Federal investigators led by Agent Moore secured statements from several Chinese witnesses who claimed they had been forced to make payments ranging from eighty-five to one hundred dollars to Williams or Loui Quong, one of the bureau's part-time Chinese interpreters who acted as Williams's assistant, to secure legal entry into the country.[42]

Prompted by Moore's complaints to his superiors in Washington about Williams, Commissioner Wise opened and quickly closed an internal investigation, reporting to Treasury Secretary Carlisle that Moore had failed to produce satisfactory evidence to support the charges, "except the irresponsible evidence of Chinese highbinders."[43] Undeterred, Moore convened a special closed-door meeting of a federal grand jury, where jurors reviewed additional evidence that had been withheld from Wise. Wong Sam (Huang San), a well-known Chinese interpreter and smuggler who had once worked for Wells, Fargo, and Company, testified to the grand jury that he had cooperated with Williams to prevent the deportations.[44]

During the grand jury trial, Moore's agents also raised questions about Williams's personal finances and his lavish lifestyle. Wise defended Williams in the press, claiming to have previously investigated his wealth and found it to come from honest sources, including his restaurant, various business enterprises, and his Chinatown entertainment bookings. "Being a saving boy, he banked his money," Wise stated, claiming that Williams "had $5000 in the bank" when he entered the Customs Service and had received another $4,000 from the estate of a recently deceased aunt in the Arizona Territory. "During the two years he has been in the service he has saved the balance, and has about $11,000 in bank."[45] Wise offered similarly unremarkable explanations for Williams's real estate holdings across the city.[46] Despite Wise's efforts to defend him, Williams was subsequently indicted by the grand jury on four counts of extortion. With federal agents beginning a broader investigation into both his record as a government interpreter and his personal finances, Williams was suspended from the Customs Service.[47]

In covering the Williams scandal, the prosecution and the press immediately linked Williams's rapid social mobility with his dangerous cultural and racial associations with the city's Chinese population. In reporting on his indictment by the grand jury, for example, the *San Francisco Call* offered a telling explanation of Williams's rapid rise within the ranks of the civil service: "He was only a customs inspector," the paper noted, "but he conversed with the Chinese in their native tongue. Being otherwise smooth of speech and thrifty of step, he was especially prized by the Collector of the Port." The *Call* further suggested that Williams's ambition to move into the middle class had led him not only to break the laws he had been sworn to enforce but also to endanger the city's Whites by encouraging illegal Chinese immigration. "In an absent-minded hour, it is said of him, [Williams] allowed the shifty Mongolian to drop a few yellow coins into his hand, and, presto, change. Some native sons and daughters of the Chinese empire were unlawfully landed at this port."[48] As his corruption trial began, the story fashioned by the prosecution and the press about Williams and his crimes cast further doubt on his claims to middle-class propriety and emphasized the dangerous racial implications of his desire for social mobility.

At the start of the trial, the state's special prosecutor Barclay Henley attempted to prove Williams's corruption by focusing on his finances. Williams's bankbooks, properties, and even furniture once again came under scrutiny.[49] The *Call* directly linked Williams's wealth to criminal activities, reporting he had been "a financial wreck" at the time he entered the Customs Service, to the point of borrowing fifty dollars that "he immediately placed on his back in the shape of a suit of clothes." Within months, however, Williams had allegedly taken to flaunting his wealth, wearing "a diamond stud" alleged to be a gift from Little Pete that "out-glittered anything before displayed in Federal circles." When Wise took the stand, he repeated his earlier defenses of his trusted colleague: Williams had come by his wealth "honestly," from "his father or his grandparents."[50]

Williams's account of his wealth—conveyed to the public through Wise—not only denied charges of financial impropriety but also linked him symbolically with the city's native-born and immigrant White middle classes, eliding both his father's Chinese identity and his work in the Chinese American interpreter class. As the trial progressed, however, press accounts of Williams and his family would suggest that he had willingly violated both immigration laws and racial boundaries to secure his family's place among middle-class Whites. When Williams took the stand on August 31, the prosecutor directly invoked Williams's ancestry as a reason to doubt his innocence. After a "clamorous objection" from Williams's attorney to questions about specific bank transactions, the *Call* reported, Henley asked Williams "if he were not a half-Chinese—that is, if his father was not a Celestial and his mother a white woman," to which, the paper noted, Williams "reluctantly . . . replied in the affirmative." According to the *Call*, the matter had previously been raised during the closed-door hearings with the grand jury, at which time Williams had denied the claim "with a great show of resentment." However, the paper noted, "the prosecution had the necessary evidence well in hand, and there was no attempt to evade the truth."[51]

Though only hinted at in earlier coverage of the Chinese Bureau scandal, Henley's questioning made the "truth" of Williams's race clear to the public. Not only had he falsely presented himself as a well-to-do middle-class patriarch, but he had also falsely presented himself as a White man. "It was brought out in the trial," the *Call* reported, "that Williams was very closely related to the class of persons from whom he is alleged to have extorted money."[52]

Press descriptions of Williams and his family worked to further underscore the illegitimacy of his claims to White middle-class manhood, while also describing the danger of his mobility in racial terms. Reporters noted that Williams's wife, Isabelle, whose divorce case against him was pending, made a point of appearing in court only when summoned and with her attorney. Aside from a "bevy of Williams' friends," his eight-year-old daughter, Isabella, and his mother, Mary Williams Monferran, were the only family members regularly present in the courtroom. Newspaper illustrators regularly depicted Mary Monferran as a respectable-looking middle-class matron in widow's attire, but she sat under a cloud of disrepute. Not only had she violated racial boundaries by birthing mixed-race children, but her second husband had committed suicide, and Williams's real-estate holdings were connected to his death. Newspaper illustrations of Williams and his daughter emphasized their racial ambiguity, depicting them as fashionably dressed but occasionally displaying what were popularly regarded as "Chinese" facial features.

Isabelle Williams initially emerged in the press as a sympathetic figure—a White woman who had been forced into illegal activities by her husband, a racial impostor. The press reported that her pending divorce suit, in which she charged Williams with "cruelty" and "driving her from the family home," provided investigators with a "strong line of evidence" against her husband.

Illustration of Richard S. Williams from an article announcing the start of his corruption trial, from the *San Francisco Chronicle*, September 4, 1896, 9.

EX-INSPECTOR DICK WILLIAMS, WHOSE HEAVY BANK ACCOUNTS
FIGURE EXTENSIVELY IN HIS TRIAL.
(Drawn from a photograph.)

At the same time, newspaper accounts of Isabelle Williams's interactions with her daughter seemed to confirm the dangers of her failure to maintain racial purity. Little Isabella Williams, described by the press as a "pretty child" who charmed the courtroom, reportedly "clung to her father" while directing "defiant" looks at her mother that at one point caused the latter to leave the courtroom in tears.[53] The *Chronicle* reported that Isabelle Williams testified that Richard Williams had "instructed" her to deposit money "in a certain bank in her own name," telling her, "It's none of your business how I get the money."[54] Although charges were never brought against her, she remained a "person of interest" in the case, accused by federal investigators of having knowingly and willingly been the custodian of the accounts where Williams hid his illegal earnings. This, combined with the apparent ease with which she had crossed racial boundaries in her personal life, cast her as having questionable morals and racial loyalties, rendering her unfit for middle-class White womanhood.

On September 4, after deliberating for "scarcely twenty minutes," the jury found Williams guilty on two of the original four counts of extortion. Nearly three weeks later, the district judge sentenced him to serve six years at

Illustration of attendees at Williams's corruption trial, including his daughter, Isabella, and his mother, from the *San Francisco Chronicle*, August 22, 1896, 9.

SOME INTERESTING PERSONAGES IN ATTENDANCE AT THE WILLIAMS' TRIAL.

San Quentin and pay a $10,000 fine.[55] Williams continued to assert his innocence to the press, claiming to have secured evidence in the form of affidavits from several Chinese witnesses that would not only exonerate him but also reveal widespread corruption among high-ranking officers in the Customs Service. When the evidence failed to materialize, he was transported to San Quentin to serve his sentence.[56] The *Call* used the occasion of his failed defense to reassert the durability of the racial boundary between Whites and Chinese, noting that the only evidence he could produce "would be in the shape of affidavits from people of his own kind, Chinese."[57] Three months later, Williams would be released on a $3,000 bail after his lawyers submitted a successful appeal based on a "lengthy list of errors" presented to the Supreme Court, including the prosecution's "improper" use of his personal finances as evidence. After securing a new trial, he ultimately served a one-year sentence on reduced charges.[58]

Even with the later reduction in charges, journalists and attorneys used the trial to reinforce racialized understandings of class. Their treatment of the case brightened racial boundaries by articulating the upwardly mobile Americanized Chinese man as a new dangerous racial actor. Among Whites, the ex-inspector's conviction added to a core racial narrative about race and class—that Chinese American social mobility threatened not only middle-class Whites but the city's entire racial order. Loui Quong, identified by the press as Williams's "right hand" and "lieutenant," was fired from the Customs Service and subsequently indicted on perjury charges. Though he was less racially ambiguous than Williams, the press made it clear that his presence in the Customs Service also posed the danger of corrupting White employees. According to the *Call*, Quong "enjoyed a unique position in customs circles": "He is regarded as a tricky, shifty sort of fellow, with the faculty of gaining complete mastery over those with whom he comes in close touch. It is said that some months ago he loaned a prominent Federal officer $2000, and that he still holds the gentleman's 'promise to pay.'"[59]

Williams's rapid advancement in the Customs Service, despite what the press and other customs agents described as his untrustworthiness and limited facility with the Chinese language, reinforced Whites' belief that legitimate pathways to social mobility for "qualified" White men were being endangered by "undeserving" non-Whites like Williams. As for the brightness or blurriness of racial boundaries where mixed-race Chinese were concerned, although Williams had identified both personally and publicly as a White man, the acknowledged fact of his ancestry—underscored by his criminal connections to Chinese smugglers and willingness to defraud "his own kind"—appear to have cemented his Chineseness in the public mind.

The brightening of racialized class boundaries spurred by the Williams case would have been most alarming for the Chinese American middle classes. For those comfortably settled into or aspiring to middle-class mobility, assisting poorer or more recent immigrants in criminal courts and immigration hearings was a stable and respectable occupational path. Williams's trial revealed the darker side to how some in this broker class attained social mobility, and accentuated their liminal position as Chinese American elites in the city's White-dominated racial order. His cooperation with immigrant smugglers who also contributed to sex trafficking was especially troubling for those middle-class Chinese families linked to the Chinese missions that led efforts to rescue Chinese women from prostitution.[60]

The repercussions for Chinese men working as interpreters followed swiftly after Williams's conviction, as the press amplified links between Chinese employment in white-collar jobs and corruption. Williams's name would continue to be associated with corruption at the bureau, and he was regularly blamed for the bureau's failure under Wise to stop Chinese immigration into the state.[61] In the aftermath of the Williams trial, Immigration Bureau officials gradually moved to fix racial boundaries by using racial criteria to determine eligibility for employment at the Chinese Bureau. The continued shortage of Whites qualified to serve as Chinese interpreters, however, meant that struggles over these boundaries' placement and permeability would continue.

Brightened and Blurred: Racial Boundaries in the Customs House

Two months after Williams's conviction, the *Chronicle* reported that the US Treasury Department had issued an order providing "that no Chinese persons may be employed in or about the Chinese bureau of the Custom-house" and "that no interpreter at all may be employed until the special agent shall have been given opportunity to look up his record, and shall indorse him for the position." Local officials had been unable to immediately corroborate the existence of such an order, but the *Chronicle* reported that its Washington correspondent had been "assured that such an order had been issued." Describing the order as a "distinct victory" for federal authorities over the corruption in the Chinese Bureau, the *Chronicle* reported that Wise would now have to submit "the name of a white man for the position" and would have to offer a salary to match. Wise indicated that such a policy would constitute a "welcome relief."[62]

The press's reporting on the order invoked a familiar narrative about the dangers of Chinese mobility for White men—reinforcing understandings about the links between Whiteness and legitimate middle-class identity. Papers noted that Harry S. Huff, a White interpreter whom the US district attorney had dismissed less than a year before the allegations against Williams had first surfaced, would be "perfectly satisfactory to Collector Wise."[63] Huff had been working as an interpreter under Williams before being dismissed for what papers reported as no apparent cause. His dismissal reportedly prompted consternation among judges and attorneys who described him as "efficient" and "honorable," with an expert knowledge of Chinese. Although the *Chronicle* suggested that an unnamed past legal incident (later determined to be a murder for which he was cleared) might have been the cause, papers reported that neither Wise nor the new district attorney could give a reason for his dismissal. Huff requested an investigation into his dismissal, but because interpreters were not considered civil servants, officials took no action until after Williams's conviction, when a new district attorney looked into Huff's case. In January 1897, under headlines announcing Huff's "vindication," papers reported that the investigation revealed that Williams had fabricated bribery charges against Huff to secure his dismissal. Under orders from the district attorney, Wise appointed Huff to temporarily replace Williams and he remained a paid interpreter for the Customs Service.[64] However, while the press had initially lauded Huff as an innocent victim of Williams's ambitions, by 1898 he would be thoroughly enmeshed in the agency's culture of corruption, accused by prominent missionary worker Donaldina Cameron and several Chinese women of helping a known trafficker evade capture and of "owning" a Chinese "slave girl." This turn of events prompted papers to report that it had in fact been Huff's closeness to Williams's "boodling schemes" that had led to his initial firing.[65]

The Chinese ban at the Customs Service was intended to shore up racial boundaries between Whites and Chinese by establishing Chinese interpreter work as a "White man's job." But where, exactly, would Wise find White interpreters? Unable to identify a suitable replacement for Williams, Wise's agents began employing Chinese men on an ad hoc basis to serve as interpreters—a practice that was roundly criticized in the press as a willful violation of federal orders. In light of this situation, Treasury special agent Moore indicated that he personally had "been instructed to see that no more Chinese are employed in the Chinese Bureau."[66] Yet, one month later, Moore suggested that John Endicott Gardner Jr., the half-Chinese son of an English missionary, would be an ideal permanent replacement for Williams. Gardner was fluent in Chinese, highly educated, and from a family widely respected in missionary circles. Before applying for the position, he had worked as a government interpreter for the British Crown in Canada and subsequently led a Chinese mission church in British Columbia. The Treasury Department's investigation of Gardner confirmed his reputation as a highly competent interpreter.[67]

With the backing of Moore, federal authorities, and White missionaries who lobbied for better treatment of Chinese immigrants at the hands of "overzealous" customs agents, Gardner was virtually assured the position. In considering his application, the US Treasury Department consulted with the Department of State and confirmed that both he and his brother had

DR. GARDNER'S HANDS UNTIED AT LAST

Illustration of John Endicott Gardner Jr. from an article announcing his promotion to Chinese inspector, from the *San Francisco Call*, November 16, 1898, 7.

There was consternation in the ranks of the Society for the Importation of Chinese Women when the news was received from Washington yesterday that the Secretary of the Treasury had promoted Chinese Interpreter Rev. Dr. John Endicott Gardner to the position of Chinese Inspector. It came with the suddenness of a bombshell, and before the coolie brokers and their friends in the Federal building could realize that the impossible had happened, Dr. Gardner had called upon Customs Collector Jackson and had taken the oath of office.

The doctor was not promoted at the request of Chief Meredith

been granted citizenship after being adopted by their stepfather, Reverend Daniel Vrooman.[68] The *Chronicle* dismissed questions about Gardner's eligibility by reporting that there were prominent members of the Chinese missionary community who would "vouch for his citizenship" and that when "availing himself of his citizenship rights at the polls," they had "never been questioned."[69]

Where only a month before, journalists had defended the Chinese ban as a necessary precaution against Chinese corruption, press coverage of

Gardner's employment now suggested a willingness to blur racial boundaries, with the *Chronicle* expressing its enthusiastic support for a "white interpreter for the Custom-house." Attributing continuing problems with Chinese immigration to Wise's delay in appointing Gardner as a replacement for Williams, the *Call* diminished both the amount and the significance of Gardner's Chinese ancestry, which it also claimed was of elite origins.[70] Unlike Williams, who had aimed to conceal his Chinese ancestry in favor of his Irish immigrant mother's roots, Gardner enjoyed support from White elites that quelled suspicions about his racial loyalties when it came to enforcing immigration laws. Gardner was hired to the Customs Service as an interpreter over Wise's objections, appearing in the civil service record for 1897 as a salaried employee at the rate of $180 per month. By the following year, he had been promoted to the rank of Chinese inspector, which empowered him to investigate immigration cases while retaining the title of interpreter.[71] To process the numbers of Chinese passengers landing at San Francisco, the bureau relied on Gardner and a handful of interpreters hired on an ad hoc basis to provide translations.[72]

The perception of Gardner as White, however, turned out to be short-lived. In 1899 John P. Jackson, Wise's successor as collector of customs, invoked stereotypes about Chinese "shiftiness" to oppose Gardner's promotion. In a memo to his superiors, Jackson wrote that for all of his intelligence, being half-Chinese, Gardner possessed "racial characteristics in [his] temperament" that "seriously impair[ed] his efficiency as an impartial and unbiased interpreter."[73] As the only Chinese inspector of Chinese ancestry employed at the San Francisco offices of the bureau, White inspectors, and often the Chinese merchants they cooperated with, seemingly bristled at Gardner's authority. A stenographer later found guilty of aiding attorneys profiting from smuggling made disparaging remarks about Gardner's race to Jackson. After federal investigators reprimanded B. E. Meredith, a White senior inspector, for "offensive statements" he had made against Gardner, Jackson wrote the Treasury secretary that his having "the authority of inspector" had proved a disruption to the bureau's daily business.[74] Although Gardner managed to keep his position and titles, he would continue to be dogged by accusations of corruption.[75] As the exclusion era progressed, he and other men of Chinese descent employed at the Customs Service would navigate an increasingly brightened racial boundary, expressed in popular stories about the dangers posed by their Chineseness and their presence in middle-class workplaces.

Mixing Race and Class: Da Silva, Lee Toy, and the Chinese Ring

At the beginning of the twentieth century, San Francisco's Chinese Bureau found itself operating under intense and somewhat contradictory pressures. On the one hand, politicians, labor leaders, and the public demanded that a fully staffed Chinese Bureau enforce exclusion laws; on the other, the federal Whites-only employment policy prohibited the bureau from hiring those most likely to be qualified for the job. This combination of pressures contributed to ambiguity about the racial status of mixed-race Chinese interpreters.

One person who benefited from this policy was Hippolytus Leosola Amador Eça da Silva—a mixed-race Chinese immigrant from Macao—who secured employment as an assistant interpreter in 1901 without public comment. But when federal authorities later accused Da Silva of trafficking Chinese women, attorneys, politicians, and the press quickly moved to brighten racial boundaries by mobilizing familiar themes about upwardly mobile Chinese men in new ways. Journalists amplified these concerns by describing them as exemplars of new types of actors who engaged in racial boundary crossing: the Americanized Chinese man and the "half-breed" Chinese man.

Da Silva, who had been born in China to a wealthy family of Macanese merchants, had worked as a musician and interpreter for hire before taking a position at the Customs Service in 1901.[76] Under colonial Macao's "Iberian" notions of race, Da Silva's wealth, mixed racial background, and "passable" features would have marked him as White or near White.[77] After immigrating to Hawaii with his wife, Yamei Kin, and son, Alexander, Da Silva moved his family to San Francisco in 1896. Kin, the adopted Chinese daughter of American missionaries raised in Japan, was well known in missionary circles as the first Chinese woman to earn a degree from a medical college in the United States.[78] City directories and US Census records for 1900 list Da Silva's occupation as "interpreter," and he appears in the civil service register for 1901 as an interpreter, receiving a salary of $120 month. Two years after Da Silva began his employment at the Chinese Bureau, the US Bureau of Immigration assumed responsibility for administering and enforcing Chinese exclusion laws. This bureaucratic shift placed all interpreters under the supervision of San Francisco's commissioner of immigration—a position held by H. H. North. Like Gardner, Da Silva's racially ambiguous appearance, elite background, and Western education seem to have outweighed his Chinese connections.[79]

At least at first, Commissioner North considered him an asset to his team of agents at the bureau. Beginning in 1903, however, complaints began to surface that Da Silva was trading on his influence in the shipping business. Although he was ultimately cleared, questions about Da Silva's involvement in illegal activities persisted, and he was formally dismissed from government service the following year.[80]

After leaving the Customs Service, Da Silva secured employment as a foreign labor recruiter with the San Francisco–based Hong Tai company, charged with securing workers for the Chinese-themed "village" at the 1904 St. Louis World's Fair. The Chinese village was a fairground concession offered by fair organizers, run by associations of Chinese American merchants in larger cities who saw it as a way to encourage White economic tourism while challenging negative stereotypes of Chinese culture. This year's concession would be run by the Philadelphia-based Yee Ging Company, which sent its representative, Lee Toy, a prosperous and well-connected Philadelphia merchant whose uncle was known as the "mayor" of New York's Chinatown, to San Francisco in the spring of 1904. Lee and Da Silva then sailed to China together to recruit fairground workers.[81] The two men returned from China aboard the *Doric* on August 8 with some 215 Chinese workers, among them twelve women who were to be employed as waitresses at the fair's Chinese-themed café. When questioned by immigration officials upon arrival, however, four of the women reported that, while at sea, Lee and Da Silva had informed them that they "all were to be prostitutes." Immigration officials also identified one of the other eight women as Dong Moy, a "well-known procuress" who had previously been deported by US officials and was traveling under a false name. According to later reports, Commissioner North nevertheless cleared Lee and Da Silva's labor recruits—including Dong Moy—for travel to St. Louis. He made an exception for the four women, ordering that they remain at the Presbyterian Women's Rescue Mission to await deportation.[82]

Upon Da Silva's arrival in St. Louis with the workers, St. Louis immigration commissioner Frank Dunn noticed a discrepancy between the number of workers promised and those who had arrived on the train.[83] None of the remaining eight women arrived in St. Louis. Dunn opened an internal investigation that revealed not only that workers had left the group before their destination but that *all* of the women accompanying Da Silva had in fact been brought to work as prostitutes. Lee Toy and Da Silva were arrested by federal authorities and charged with illegally importing the women for purposes of prostitution.

For federal agents, the evidence that Lee and Da Silva had been trafficking immigrants suggested that their suspicions of Chinese Americans had been warranted. In September 1904, the *Chronicle* reported that Treasury Secretary Carlisle had dispatched federal investigators to look into the workings of an alleged "Chinese ring" gripping San Francisco. According to the press, investigators had uncovered a "culture of secrecy" at the bureau, one that encouraged agents and interpreters to supplement their incomes by assisting a group of Chinese American businessmen—the "Chinese ring"—who profited from immigrant smuggling. Da Silva's alleged crimes and his willingness to profit financially from violating Chinese exclusion laws he had been sworn to enforce while an interpreter fit perfectly with these claims. Newspapers reported that the four women detained at the Chinese mission had been "purchased" by Lee Toy and Da Silva in Canton at prices ranging from "$500 to $700 each."[84] According to the *Chronicle's* account, Da Silva had earlier told friends that he planned to approach fairground managers about a "proposition of employing two or three hundred Chinese." "This would indicate," the paper continued, "that the exhibition of St. Louis was seized upon as a good opportunity of evading the laws." Papers also reported that investigators had identified Da Silva, Lee Toy, and a third man, a gambler named Wong Fook, as "advance agents" of men who sought to make "between $100,000 and $200,000" by "landing bands of coolies and slave women" under the pretense of hiring them as fair workers.[85] The press identified the three Chinese men at the center of the scandal by name, calling them "slave traders" who, along with any number of other Chinese merchants and interpreters, profited from immigrant smuggling.

The newspapers' coverage of the scandal suggests that new ways of thinking about assimilated Chinese men were emerging that brightened, rather than blurred, racial distinctions. The reports on Lee Toy's arrest by federal agents, for example, described him as "a wealthy Chinese" or "an Americanized Chinese," which, the *Chronicle* explained, meant that he "wears the clothes of an American citizen to mask the wiles of the unscrupulous and acute celestial."[86] A photograph of Lee taken around the time of his arrest shows him dressed conservatively in a high-collared white shirt, neatly patterned tie, and dark coat—all suggesting his familiarity with a westernized middle-class lifestyle. Journalists writing about Lee's background elaborated on the hidden dangers that he represented as an Americanized Chinese, with the *Chronicle* calling him the "head of the Eastern Chinese ring" and "the go-between" tasked with collecting "the tributes paid by the gambling houses, lotteries, and brothels in the Chinatown of the Quaker City." At the same time, the press variously referred to Da Silva as "a half-breed Portuguese and Chinese," a "Chinese Portuguese," a "mixed blood," and a "Eurasian."[87]

Press accounts of Lee Toy's and Da Silva's travels to China underscored the illegitimacy of Chinese social mobility, showing how profits from criminal activity facilitated their entrance into middle-class spaces reserved for Whites. "Toy and Da Silva traveled first cabin," the *Chronicle* reported, adding that Lee "had the finest wardrobe on the ship and was given to displaying the creations of his American tailor." Reports of Lee and Da Silva's interactions with White passengers while on board the ship only underlined the social dangers that mobility among Americanized Chinese posed to middle-class Whites. The paper claimed that a US Secret Service agent who boarded the ship at Canton "spent most of his time playing cards with Da Silva, and is said to have won some money from the agent of the Chinese ring," adding, "Whether this fact was included in the secret service agent's report to his supervisors in Washington has not been made public."[88] Just as associating with Williams had jeopardized Wise's reputation, the press suggested that exposing Whites to the corrupting influences of people like Da Silva, Lee, and Wong Fook threatened to undermine racial distinctions.

While Da Silva's mixed racial background and elite social origins had previously challenged dominant understandings of Chineseness, press coverage of his indictment and arrest seemed to sharpen racial boundaries and remove any doubt in the public mind about his racial identity. When questioned by reporters about the charges made against him, Da Silva denied any wrongdoing, claiming he had only acted as an interpreter and had neither signed nor made any contracts with the women claiming to have been trafficked. Da Silva was particularly emphatic about his racial identification, demanding that journalists "correct the report" that he was of Chinese Portuguese descent and stating, "I am pure Spanish and I was born in China."[89] Journalists consistently rejected Da Silva's self-characterization of himself as White. The *Chronicle*'s reporter highlighted what he saw as both physical and emotional traits marking Da Silva as non-White, claiming that when asked for a statement, he responded by "thrusting his queer, Asiatic face" against the bars of his cell and refusing. "Da Silva's pride has been greatly hurt, it is learned," the *Chronicle* wrote, "through the allegations that he is a Macao Eurasian, part Portuguese and part Chinese. Several times yesterday he averred with heat that he was a full-blooded Spaniard, a contention not at all borne out by his peculiar face, sparsely bearded and marked with the unmistakable signs of his mixed race."[90] The *Call* described Da Silva as "very indignant" about "the published statement that he was of mixed blood."[91]

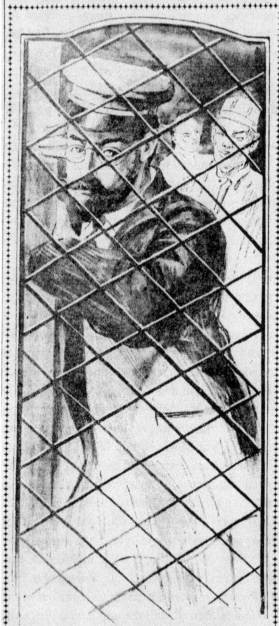

DA SILVA IN COUNTY JAIL DECLARES HE IS INNOCENT

H. L. A. ECA DA SILVA, CHINESE INTERPRETER, NOW IN COUNTY JAIL, INDICTED BY GRAND JURY ON CHARGE OF IMPORTING CHINESE WOMEN TO THIS COUNTRY FOR SLAVERY.

Illustration of Hippolytus Eça da Silva in custody, from the *San Francisco Examiner*, September 27, 1904, 4.

Both Lee and Da Silva represented troubling new racial types: they were non-White men whose wealth or ability to socialize across the color line threatened to undermine crucial social divisions. Press coverage made it clear that despite their westernized ways and—in the case of Lee—their wealth, both men's claims to middle-class identities posed dangers to Whites. This was particularly the case for Da Silva, whose ties to corruption and women of various races suggested that he lacked both manly virtue and respect for racial boundaries. Both the trial and its accompanying press coverage drew particular attention to Da Silva's romantic relationship with an Immigration Bureau stenographer named Agnes Burbank, suggesting that there was something unsettling and sexually threatening about the presence of non-White men in the workplace.

On September 30, shortly after reporting Da Silva's arrest, journalists focused their attention on Da Silva's romantic relationships with women of three different "races." Newspapers reported that Da Silva, only recently divorced from his Americanized Chinese wife, Yamei Kin, was now simultaneously engaged to two different women—a seventeen-year-old Mexican American shopgirl named Carmen Navarrete and the native-born White stenographer Burbank. Newspapers reported that, when arrested, Da Silva had on his person letters written to him from Burbank, who had become his fiancée while they were both employed at the bureau. According to investigators and the press, Burbank's letters to Da Silva incriminated them both, suggesting that she had not only known about Da Silva's smuggling but also helped him evade detection by federal investigators in North's office. Navarrete, meanwhile, produced letters from Da Silva and an engagement ring she had received from him two years prior, after meeting him at a reception given by a Mexican American social club. When asked by reporters about his two fiancées, Da Silva was quoted as saying, "If they say I am engaged to them, then it must be so."[92]

Press reports also fixated on the circumstances of his divorce. The *Call* reported that the divorce decree, granted in August shortly after Da Silva's return from China, had been requested by his "Mongolian wife." Describing his wife as an "Americanized Chinese" who had adopted "the New Woman cult" and "deserted her spouse," press coverage of Da Silva's divorce reinforced his inability to sustain claims to middle-class manliness, evinced by his failure as a provider and by the ambitions of a wife who desired self-definition outside marriage and motherhood. Newspapers also reported that Da Silva had in fact pursued Navarrete, and then Burbank, while still married. A reporter for the *San Francisco Examiner* wrote that Da Silva had "divided his attention between them for more than a year" and had neglected to send Kin "remittances he had promised" for her and their son, for which she "appealed to the officials in the Department of Commerce and Labor in Washington, D.C."[93]

The newspaper stories about Da Silva's divorce and his simultaneous engagements to Navarrete and Burbank helped underscore his position as a dangerous racial actor—one whose cultural fluidity gave him entry into respectable spaces on either side of the color line. Turn-of-the-century sexual narratives about Asian men and White women helped to convey the dangers of interracial sex in a changing social landscape. They also worked to preserve racial and sexual boundaries during a period when more White women entered the workplace as a precursor to marriage. The *Examiner's* reporting was clear about the racial implications of Da Silva's romantic affairs, alluding to the enduring popular belief that Asian men "seduced" unsuspecting White women with alcohol or opiates.[94] Under a headline reading, "Da Silva's Master Role Hypnotizing of Women," the paper reported, "A trio of women—Mongolian, Mexican and American by birth—have reason to regret that they ever came within hypnotic range of the alphabetical heartbreaker," a reference to Da Silva's multiple surnames. The story described Da Silva as having "a wizard's control of piano and violin" and cited those familiar with him for the claim that "the theory of hypnotism is . . . the secret of his success in capturing hearts." Yet despite his apparent appeal to women of various races, the paper was careful to emphasize Da Silva's non-whiteness, pointing to his "mysterious-sounding name," his "dark . . . Chinese-Portuguese complexion," and his connections to the city's Chinese population.[95]

During the trial, prosecutors tried to portray Da Silva and Lee as immoral slave traders whose behavior invalidated their claims to middle-class manhood. Federal prosecutors placed each of the four women from the *Doric* on the witness stand, and they all testified that they had signed contracts agreeing to be fairground waitresses, only to have Da Silva and Lee tell them the "true purpose" of their being transported to the United States once they were at sea—with Da Silva reportedly even striking one of the women when she protested. Da Silva and Lee's defense attorneys, who included a former US attorney from the Williams trial, argued that neither of their clients was responsible, as they had only recruited women for waitressing work and never spoke of prostitution. Da Silva admitted striking the woman only in response to her becoming disorderly and calling him "foul names."[96] Jurors voted to acquit both men of all charges almost immediately. Afterward, the

US attorney claimed that North's office had mishandled key pieces of evidence, bolstering claims in the press that North's office had willingly enabled the corrupt actions of Da Silva, Lee, and the Chinese ring.[97]

The press's changing depictions of Burbank over the course of the trial reflected new understandings of the specific dangers White women faced from Americanized Chinese men. The popular belief that no respectable White woman would ever willingly pursue a relationship with a Chinese man (even one of mixed blood) allowed newspapers, at least at first, to portray Burbank as Da Silva's victim. In this account, she might have redeemed herself by cooperating with the investigators. By the end of Da Silva's trial, however, it had become clear that her loyalties lay with Da Silva, not the prosecutors. The press shifted its portrayal of her, now casting Burbank as a White woman of dubious morality who willingly crossed racial boundaries and aided criminal activity. Newspapers reported that the letters exchanged between Da Silva and Burbank revealed that she not only communicated sensitive information about the ongoing federal investigation but also criticized North directly, calling him "arrogant" and referring to him by the name "bak-fong"—Chinese for "North Wind." After the content of these letters became public, the *Examiner* reported, Commissioner General of Immigration Frank P. Sargent ordered North to take steps to have Burbank dismissed from the civil service. North followed through with the termination a week after Da Silva's acquittal, charging Burbank with "conduct unbecoming a Government employe [*sic*]—citing her public displays of affection toward Da Silva—and of betraying secrets of the Chinese Bureau to persons not employed by the Government."[98]

Press coverage of the "Chinese ring" scandal helped the press and the public make sense of the city's changing racial landscape. The reports further articulated the idea of westernized or mixed-race Chinese men as dangerous racial actors whose claims to middle-class identities imperiled middle-class Whites. Lee and Da Silva, both non-White men who displayed White middle-class identities, not only allegedly profited from illegal activities that increased the Chinese immigrant population, but did so while undermining social divisions between the races. Press accounts of Da Silva's involvement with Burbank provided the city's White middle classes with a perfect cautionary tale about the perils Whites faced if they associated with Americanized or mixed-race Chinese people. In addition to losing her job and her reputation, press announcements later that year that Burbank had married Da Silva pointed to the dangers to racial boundaries from mixed-race or

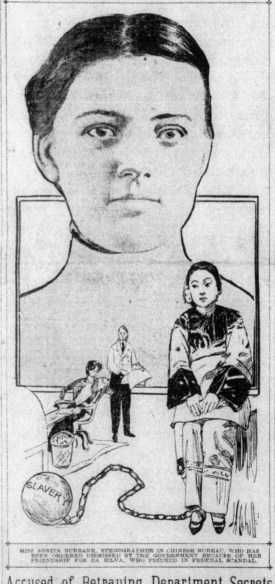

MISS BURBANK IS DROPPED FROM THE SERVICE.

Miss Agnita J. Burbank was dismissed from the Government service yesterday. She is supposed to have been carrying secrets of the Chinese Bureau to her fiance, Hippolyttus da Silva, who figured recently in a scandal concerning the importation of Chinese women. Miss Burbank stoutly denies the accusation made against her.

SLAVERY

MISS AGNITA BURBANK, STENOGRAPHER IN CHINESE BUREAU, WHO HAS BEEN ORDERED DISMISSED BY THE GOVERNMENT BECAUSE OF HER FRIENDSHIP FOR DA SILVA, WHO FIGURED IN FEDERAL SCANDAL.

Accused of Betraying Department Secrets

Illustration of Agnes Burbank (identified as Agnita J. Burbank) announcing her dismissal from the civil service, from the *San Francisco Call*, March 16, 1905, 1.

Americanized Chinese men—particularly those who might defy immediate racial classification.[99]

Cases involving mixed-race Chinese men like Williams, Gardner, and Da Silva had attracted attention in part because of the men's ability to cross racial boundaries, but middle-class Whites found the existence of Americanized "full-blooded" Chinese like Lee equally concerning. In the wake of the Da Silva and Lee verdicts, Commissioner North's decision to appoint Herman Lowe, a full-blooded Chinese American, to an interpreter's position sparked renewed controversy about Chinese mobility in the civil service.

Necessity Rules: Chinese Blood in the Bureau

Lowe, the son of Chinese immigrants, grew up in the city's Chinatown district. Having completed only eight years of formal schooling at the Chinese mission school in Chinatown, Lowe continued his education with private instruction provided by teachers at the Baptist-run Chinese Mission Home, who also found him employment performing odd jobs and domestic service in White households.[100] The 1900 census lists Lowe, his wife, and his son as residing in the rear cottage of a house on Prospect Place, just beyond the borders of the Chinatown district. Census records indicate that Lowe supported his family as a sewing machine operator before securing employment as a clerk with the Hong Tai Company's offices at the St. Louis Exposition. Lowe confirmed his recent employment with the Hong Tai Company as the "acting secretary" for its St. Louis Exposition concession to reporters, indicating that he was "a native-born Chinese." "I was sworn in on Saturday by United States Commissioner North," Lowe told the *Chronicle*, "who thought very highly of my recommendations."[101]

The local press understood Lowe's rather ordinary account of securing a civil service job as a dangerous development. Newspapers interpreted Lowe's appointment through the lens of by-now-familiar stories about Chinese interpreters willingly subverting immigration laws. His employment with the Immigration Bureau, and the subsequent inroads made by other American-born Chinese, also called attention to what middle-class Whites regarded as a separate problem—the agency's role in supporting an emergent Chinese American middle class. By the end of the first decade of the twentieth century, the policies that the Chinese Bureau adopted to address allegations of inefficiency in the Chinese Division had brightened racialized class boundaries by normalizing links between Chinese employment and corruption.

Lowe's appointment allowed the press to mobilize what had become a familiar racial narrative about Chinese American men, social mobility, and crime. The *Chronicle* reported the news under a series of sensational headlines: "NORTH GIVES CHINESE A JOB—Chooses Full-Blooded Celestial as an Interpreter, Though White Men Are on the List—SECRETARY OF TOUGH GANG TAKES OFFICE—Man Employed by Slave Importers during the St. Louis Exposition Is Presented with a Good Federal Position." The paper described North's decision to hire Lowe as "directly contrary" to the Chinese hiring ban that had been in place ever since the Williams trial and repeated claims by former immigration commissioner James R. Dunn that employing "persons of Chinese blood" in the Chinese Bureau "would inevitably result in corruption and malfeasance" in the office. The *Morning Call* also opposed Lowe's appointment, claiming that North had "undone" prior efforts to preserve the spirit if not the letter of the ban by reclassifying Chinese interpreters as "extra civil service"—receiving annual salaries but without civil service job protections.[102] The *Chronicle* stressed the theme of Chinese criminality in its reporting on Lowe's appointment, reminding readers of his former employer's association with the St. Louis exhibition scandal.[103]

Stories about Lowe's appointment and his social connections within the Chinese immigrant community also focused renewed attention on the threats the Chinese American middle class supposedly posed to Whites. Both the *Chronicle* and the *Call* noted Lowe's kinship to Joseph Tape, a prosperous and respected immigrant broker. Lowe was married to Tape's eldest daughter, Mamie, who at eight years old had been at the center of the case *Tape v. Hurley* (1885), a state supreme court case that challenged the segregation of Chinese children in San Francisco's public schools.[104] The press described Tape, who worked as a part-time translator and "expressman" transporting Chinese passengers and goods for steamships and hotels, as a "wealthy Chinese" who had "long been involved in immigration schemes." Both the *Call* and the *Chronicle* amplified the claim that Americanized Chinese had become a problem in the Immigration Bureau's Chinese Division by reporting that Dunn's reclassification of Chinese interpreters had been an effort to avoid appointing a Chinese American applicant who had earned the highest score on the civil service exam.[105] The *Chronicle* further stoked suspicions about the nature of Lowe's appointment by reporting that North had been pressured to hire him by Lee Toy and Tom Yung, the treasurer of the Hong Tai Company, who the paper alleged had "skipped the country" to avoid the legal entanglements of the Da Silva case. Pointing to North's "constant" appointments of Chinese Americans to interpreter jobs, the paper ended its article by reiterating that there were "many white men on the list waiting appointment."[106]

Despite the public controversy over Lowe's appointment, the Immigration Bureau's continued need for Chinese interpreters and the shortage of White Chinese speakers made a complete ban on Chinese employment unfeasible. As of 1907, Lowe was one of two Chinese American interpreters at the Immigration Bureau's San Francisco offices, the other being Edward Leon Park—a former successful grocer and the younger brother of the editor for the Chinese American newspaper the *Daily Chinese World*.[107] They were among the handful of salaried Chinese interpreters employed by the bureau in San Francisco after 1905, each receiving a salary of $1,200 per year.[108] John Endicott Gardner Jr. remained the highest-ranked Chinese American at the Immigration Bureau. For the remainder of North's tenure as San Francisco's immigration commissioner, the press and government officials continued to treat the Chinese Division as a "troubled" branch of the Immigration Bureau, in part because of the presence of Chinese American interpreters. North's reputation for being "just and fair-minded" toward immigrants, as well as his willingness to employ Chinese Americans as interpreters, gained him support from Chinese immigrants but also raised suspicions among supporters of Chinese exclusion about his commitment to upholding the law.[109]

In the years following Lowe's appointment, Immigration Bureau officials in Washington initiated a series of anticorruption and efficiency measures in the Chinese Division that normalized popularly understood links between Chinese American social mobility and criminality. In June 1907, Secretary of Commerce and Labor Oscar Straus stated that all Chinese interpreters in the San Francisco bureau offices would be transferred to posts in new cities. The local press described the transfers as a "violent shakeup" and a "disturbance" of the bureau's operations, noting that North and other officers were unable to offer details about why the changes were being made. Relying on reports from their Washington correspondents, both the *Call* and the *Chronicle* initially suggested that the order was in response to a problem with the bureau's employees, reporting that "many complaints have been made of inefficiencies and in some instances unreliability of the Chinese interpreters at the various immigration stations." The papers reported that the order had caused "great consternation" among the city's five federally employed Chinese interpreters, which included Gardner, Park, and Lowe. "As the majority of them have families and have settled homes here," the *Call* reported, "the order to remove to some other part of the United States is regarded as working a great hardship."[110] A few days later, however, the paper reported that "only interpreters of Chinese blood" would be transferred, causing "much comment in federal circles as to the reasons for this apparent discrimination."[111]

Under Secretary Straus's orders, Commissioner General of Immigration Frank P. Sargent oversaw and implemented changes in the Chinese Bureau that treated the issue of Chinese American employment as a matter of security, predicated on beliefs about Chinese men's "innate" criminal tendencies. Looking beyond the bureau itself, Sargent additionally issued rules forbidding Chinese interpreters (of any race) to have "outside business associations" with either Chinese mercantile firms or insurance agencies. The *Call* reported that the order resulted from the findings of an investigation into business dealings between "certain Chinese interpreters" and Chinatown insurance firms, which found a "thriving business in insurance policies in Chinatown."[112] Sargent also instructed Gardner and Thomas W. G. Wallace, a White, Scottish-born Chinese interpreter based in New York, to visit and assess each of the Chinese interpreters employed at immigration offices nationwide.[113] Sargent requested reports that assessed not only the interpreters' ability to translate commonly used Chinese dialects but also a list of character traits that suited them for middle-class employment, including their "general bearing" as well as their "personal character, conduct, and habits." Sargent emphasized that Gardner and Wallace had authorization to investigate the interpreters' personal conduct, "i.e., the class of associations they maintain outside of office hours and if they are addicted to the use of intoxicants or drugs or engage in other practices inimical to the integrity of an officer occupying a position of trust."[114]

If Sargent's intent had been to uncover evidence of widespread corruption and incompetence, he was to be disappointed. Over a period of six months, Gardner visited and interviewed twenty-nine Chinese interpreters, among them Edward L. Park, Herman Lowe, and Frank Tape, Joseph Tape's son, who had been stationed in St. Louis since the world's fair. While Gardner's report found plenty to criticize, he resisted officials' efforts to link Chinese American interpreters with crime and moral corruption. He wrote, "Taken as a whole they form an inferior body of officers," Gardner continued, "not so much as regards their conduct or character which I have found in almost every instance to be excellent, as their ability to perform the duties proper to their office." Gardner identified a lack of clarity in the job duties of the men he had interviewed, arguing that most of the men were acting as translators rather than interpreters. He argued for systematic advanced training for the men as interpreters, noting their importance to the immigration service, and even offered to personally oversee such a training program at the San Francisco office. "Inferior as most of these interpreters are," he wrote, "they are the best that can be secured on this side of the Pacific."[115]

Sargent accepted Gardner's report and forwarded it to Secretary Straus. Sargent cautioned his superior against dismissing long-serving interpreters whose skills were lacking, instead recommending that the new supervising Chinese interpreter make extended visits to those interpreters whose skills were identified as "below the average." The problem, Sargent indicated, was a continuing shortage of White applicants. "The bureau has in its files a considerable number of applications . . . , but these applicants are, without exception, persons of the Chinese race, and the engagement of any one of them is necessarily an experimental matter so far as their integrity (i.e., their ability to withstand the temptations that attach to the position) is concerned."[116]

The policy of transferring interpreters out of their home states also continued. By 1910, Lowe, now the father of two children, found himself transferred to the Immigration Bureau's offices in Portland, Oregon, while Park, now married to a bridesmaid from his brother's wedding to Emily Tape, was transferred to Port Townsend, Washington. Despite his father's attempts to intervene on his behalf, Frank Tape was eventually transferred from his home post in St. Louis, Missouri, to a post in Seattle.[117]

The middle-class racisms that portrayed Chinese Americans as a chief source of corruption and bribery dogged the bureau's ability to fulfill its mission until well into the twentieth century. Employment as an interpreter continued to serve as a path for social mobility for Chinese American men, but their presence at the margins kept the bureau inadequately staffed and under bureaucratic suspicion. The targeting of the Chinese Bureau's Chinese American interpreters constituted an ongoing racial project that brightened what had previously been blurred racial boundaries in San Francisco's middle class.

Conclusion

While stories about the dangers of Chinese labor had been commonplace among White tradesmen and laborers in the West since the 1850s, the final decades of the nineteenth century saw the emergence of new stories about the racial threat posed by Chinese immigrants. For White San Franciscans, the danger now stemmed not only from the population of seemingly unassimilable racial outsiders but also from seemingly assimilated Americanized Chinese—the small but visible population of foreign- and US-born Chinese who demonstrated both a familiarity with middle-class culture and a desire for full American citizenship. As historian Mae Ngai has aptly noted, Chinese American immigrant brokers within San Francisco's racialized economic order were situated between inclusion and exclusion. Their position of relative privilege, evinced by hard-won entry into White spaces, was built chiefly on the large-scale exclusion of Chinese immigrants from full citizenship and equality before the law. As with any group, some sought profit from exploiting their countrymen and countrywomen, taking advantage of their desire to avoid overzealous and racist immigration laws. The reactions of the public and the press to the presence of Chinese Americans in the Immigration Bureau's Chinese Bureau reflected new understandings of the race-class nexus and reinforced the need to clearly define racial boundaries in a changing landscape.

Journalists covering the corruption trials of Chinese interpreters and the employment of Chinese American men in the Chinese Bureau helped to popularize new racial storylines about middle-class identity and mobility that fit the regional needs of the West Coast. Beginning in the 1890s, newspaper accounts of crimes involving Chinese American federal interpreters helped link Chinese Americans' middle-class mobility in the popular mind to "Chinese" crimes like immigrant smuggling, drug peddling, and forced prostitution—reflecting and reinforcing existing White beliefs about Chinese racial inferiority. The Richard Williams corruption trial and the issues it raised about race, class, and manliness provided an important cultural resource for Whites looking to ward off what they saw as the occupational encroachment of Chinese American men into middle-class jobs. Williams's conviction on extortion charges and the revelations about his racial background and his disorderly family life made a clear statement about the corrupting influence of people of Chinese blood on middle-class institutions. This theme of corruption returned in the story of ex-interpreter Hippolytus Eça da Silva's alleged seduction of a bureau stenographer for the purpose of securing information about a federal investigation. Press descriptions of Da Silva's Chineseness, though vehemently denied by him, gave further grounding to claims by Immigration Bureau administrators that Chinese American interpreters were the source of "corruption" and "malfeasance" in the Chinese Bureau. Stories about Chinese corruption also included seemingly respectable merchants like Lee Toy and immigrant brokers like Joseph Tape, whose ties to "honest" clerks like Herman Lowe suggested that influence could extend from Chinatown's underworld into even a middle-class government workplace like the Immigration Bureau.

Press coverage of the controversies at the Chinese Bureau also signaled important changes in the ways people understood and maintained racial boundaries between Whites and Chinese. The presence of Americanized Chinese men like Lowe and Park in middle-class workplaces required new justifications for racial segregation and new strategies for enforcing it. By the early twentieth century, stories about Chinese criminality, moral corruption, and sexual predation had become such a foundational part of Whites' narratives about Chinese American social mobility that even Lowe, whose humble origins and "honest" path to social mobility were remarkably similar to those of many White men in his era, was not immune to charges of corruption. In fact, Lowe's appointment and those of his brothers-in-law were interpreted by the press, government officials, and the public as evidence of corruption that resulted in the continued illegal entry of Chinese immigrants. Taken together, press and official accounts of corruption investigations suggested that, despite their having secured federal employment, Chinese American men lacked the honesty and integrity—the manliness— required for such jobs. At the same time, false press claims that there were "many white men" who were qualified and ready to work as interpreters fueled the idea that Chinese Americans' ability to access these jobs endangered the economic as well as the social prospects of middle-class White men.

In response to the visibility of such mixed-race Chinese men as Williams, Gardner, and Da Silva, middle-class Whites attempted to brighten the racial boundaries between Whites and Chinese that had been crossed and blurred in the cosmopolitan environment of late nineteenth-century San Francisco. Williams's efforts to portray himself as a middle-class White man of means had been nearly successful, so the move by federal agents and bureau officials to ban Chinese employees after public revelations of Williams's Chinese ancestry seemed to reaffirm the brightness of racial boundaries in the face of a successful attempt at boundary crossing. Yet, almost immediately, press descriptions of the mixed-race Gardner as a "White" man—seemingly prompted by a shortage of qualified White men to serve as Chinese interpreters—directly contradicted this logic, suggesting an ongoing blurriness with respect to mixed-race Chinese men in the Chinese Bureau.

Beyond the dangers Americanized Chinese were thought to pose to middle-class men's labor, accounts produced by middle-class Whites portrayed them as a potential threat to sexual boundaries between the races. The White women who figured in the Williams and Da Silva trials—Isabelle Williams, Mary Monferran, and Agnes Burbank—embodied the apparent fate awaiting White women who crossed racial boundaries with Chinese men. Isabelle Williams not only had given birth to a mixed-race child but was also suspected of helping to conceal her husband's crimes. Williams's mother, Monferran, had, of course, also been revealed to have birthed a mixed-race child—one whose social ambitions to pass himself off as a middle-class White man of means ended with his conviction and transportation to prison. Burbank had been ruined by her association with Da Silva, losing her federal job and her racial honor by taking up with a mixed-race man who, in addition to his smuggling and "slave trading," had shown a disregard for manly self-control by abandoning his family and making marriage proposals to multiple women.

Though separated by time and distance, the brightening of racial boundaries and class boundaries in response to Chinese American mobility mirrored their brightening in response to African American mobility. In both cities, Whites developed and mobilized new narratives about the perceived damage done to middle-class workplaces by introducing non-White workers. As they did in response to the increasingly common presence of Black mail carriers, Whites associated the visibility of mixed-race and full-blooded Chinese men among the ranks of federal interpreters with political corruption, their own economic displacement, the degradation of middle-class identity, and the threat of miscegenation. The political and economic exigencies of the early exclusion era, however, both required and allowed for minor adjustments in the logic of racial classification and the placement of racial boundaries. Compared with the gradually blurred and brightened racial distinctions between Anglos and Tejanos in San Antonio, boundaries between Whites and Chinese in San Francisco were almost consistently bright, with both native-born Whites and European immigrants regularly invoking a shared whiteness against the invasion of "Asiatic" races like the Chinese. While concerns about mobility among Tejano policemen never explicitly invoked the threat of miscegenation, theirs was nevertheless understood as a dangerous and subordinate type of manliness that required careful control.

Conclusion

Between 1870 and 1910, White middle-class workers embraced narratives about the dangers of social mobility among those they deemed racial outsiders. In different parts of the country, White populations (consisting primarily of native-born Anglo Protestants and immigrants of European origin) used "deep stories" linking economic, moral, political, and sexual dangers to clarify and defend racialized class distinctions in a changing social landscape. Narratives about upwardly mobile populations of Blacks in the South, Mexicans in the US-Mexico borderlands, and Chinese in the West helped middle-class Whites in these regions make sense of unsettling changes to both the nation's class hierarchy and its racial structure. Popular representations of Black, Mexican, and Chinese men occupying middle-class jobs reveal the growing anxieties the White middle class had about preserving its position in a changing social order. These stories specifically drew on ideas about middle-class manliness, presumed to be White, to portray some groups' efforts to enter the middle class as particularly dangerous and concerning.

While these regionally specific efforts to shore up racial boundaries against social change generally cohered with a national racial ideology of White supremacy, they were often focused on articulating the symbolic and social distinctions around a particular non-White population. The Black-White boundary in the postslavery South, the Mexican-White boundary in the US-Mexico borderlands, and the Chinese-White boundary on the West Coast were regional manifestations of this ideology—each demonstrating specific properties of brightness or blurriness and sustained through different processes that fixed or altered its position. In analyzing these cases, I have considered the important similarities and differences that are the product of distinct but not unrelated histories of racial slavery, territorial expansion, colonialism, and Indigenous removal.

The popularity of these narratives in different regional urban contexts underscores the importance of race-class narratives for sustaining or promoting change in the racial order. In cities like Atlanta, San Antonio, and San Francisco, narratives featuring socially ambitious, criminally inclined, and sexually predatory non-White (or racially ambiguous) men were surprisingly common. Containing similar plots with different racial "villains," these stories underscore the malleability of a racial structure that is simultaneously durable—one that individuals and groups continually refit and adapt by connecting "deep" racial schemata to various collections of resources. These stories also reveal the importance of organizational settings like schools, neighborhoods, and workplaces as pivotal sites through which new mechanisms of racial inequality and new racial meanings are generated, enacted, and revised.[1]

For Whites in the South and in the West, the bright racial boundaries separating them from African Americans and Chinese immigrants were reflected and reinforced in popular claims about the dangers that upwardly mobile men from these groups posed to White men's livelihood and White women's sexual purity. In expressing their opposition to the employment of Charles Penney, an African American, and Herman Lowe, a Chinese American, in white-collar jobs in federal agencies, White journalists, politicians, and investigators developed similar narratives that portrayed the men as morally deficient inferiors whose employment stole jobs from "deserving" White men and jeopardized their economic standing. These voices similarly claimed that Black mail carriers and mixed-race Chinese interpreters put White women in sexual danger, whether they were in the workforce or in the home. For Anglos in the Southwest, blurred racial boundaries between them and the region's Mexican-origin population found expression in gradually changing representations of Tejano men and their relationship to social order in the Anglo-dominated US-Mexico borderlands. In the 1870s and 1880s, White journalists applauded the bravery of men like Juan Cardenas, Jacobo Coy, and Rafael Martinez in defending White San Antonians from a largely non-White urban criminal class. Within a decade, however, stories about Mexican men's penchant for violent crime and vice overshadowed these heroic representations and even portrayed Tejano lawmen as prone to some of these same behaviors. In each of these cases, Whites used arguments about the connections among race, class, and manliness in middle-class labor to mark, defend, or partially shift prevailing understandings of racial difference.

The Race-Class Nexus, Class Mobility, and Boundaries

Stuart Hall's famous insight about race as the "modality" through which class is lived in racialized societies has a particular salience when thinking about middle-class identity and mobility.[2] Scholarly research analyzing non-White racial groups' contemporary experiences with securing a middle-class position, defending it against economic uncertainty, and enacting it through everyday interactions in public spaces sheds light on the complex interactions between class dynamics and racial dynamics in people's lived experiences. A rich literature in social history places many of these contemporary works in historical context, documenting the existence of consciously middle-class populations of skilled, nonmanual, and professional workers among African Americans, Mexican Americans, and Asian Americans before World War II. These histories describe the aforementioned groups' varied encounters—often in different regional contexts—with navigating an evolving racial structure while at the same time pursuing aspirations for middle-class stability. Comparative and relational studies of race and racism in the United States have carefully documented important similarities and differences in African Americans', Asian Americans', and Latines' larger experiences with racial segregation in labor markets, housing, schools, and public spaces, yet few have considered parallels in these groups' experiences with middle-class mobility.[3]

Historical analyses have also highlighted the important variations in group experiences with race, racialization, and racism that produced different patterns of inclusion and exclusion. Works acknowledging the unsettled nature of racial categories and meanings across time and place have considered this variability's impact on patterns of social mobility, citing the case of those European groups who "became White" by the mid-twentieth century. These scholars have drawn on the social science literature on ethnoracial boundaries to describe the workings of a dynamic racial structure.[4] Boundary properties like brightness or blurriness and processes like boundary shifting or boundary crossing have been useful for understanding the movements and shifts within whiteness. Scholars have, however, devoted less attention to identifying the parallels and divergencies in how Whites brightened, blurred, or shifted racial boundaries between themselves and the different groups of people they regarded as reliably—if not consistently—non-White when confronted with their movement into middle-class jobs, spaces, and identities.

In this book, I have explored how narratives about non-White men and middle-class mobility shored up White supremacy during a period of marked economic and demographic change. I take it as a given that an analysis of different racial formations requires attention to the particular group-making strategies actors utilize, the boundary properties they invoke, and the processes they activate. These repertoires enact general trends of how bright or blurred the boundaries of racial categories are and in the positioning of people relative to those boundaries—shifting or crossing. The historical evidence presented here also supports the idea that fully understanding the long history of racial inequality in the United States requires us to adequately consider the importance of region in the production of distinct racial formations.

The case of Atlanta's African American postal workers demonstrates how that city's Whites mobilized strategies that enforced the bright and relatively impermeable Black-White racial boundary in urban spaces. Atlanta's rapid economic expansion and physical growth made it important as a regional center and capital of the New South. During the 1880s, this growth generated new, albeit restricted, labor opportunities for Black men—including a federal employment sector subject to new civil service laws but still subject to political patronage. Together, their workings challenged the labor market's rigid racial structure that restricted Blacks—reliable Republican voters—to only the most menial and least desirable jobs. White journalists, politicians, and ordinary citizens responded by depicting Black men's access to even low-level white-collar employment as dangerous, a narrative that deployed newly popular stories about Black men as thieves and rapists for a new socioeconomic landscape. Whites described Charles Penney's appointment to a postal clerkship as an economic catastrophe for White men and a mortal threat to White women. Linking the occupational mobility of Black men like Penney to the downward occupational trajectories of White men identified it as a threat to White men's economic livelihood, a cornerstone of White supremacy. Rumors of Penney's physical proximity to Mary Lyon, a White woman, suggested that Black men's movement into white-collar work presented sexual hazards to White working women.

Local and state officials found in these stories a powerful tool for mobilizing Whites around efforts to disenfranchise Black voters, and to extend policies of racial separation in the state's cities and towns. Within months of the reports, journalists and politicians had revised these stories to feature Black men employed as letter carriers as usurpers of White, middle-class manliness. In these newer versions of the narrative, literate, educated, and ambitious Black men like Eugene Martin and Julius King were cast as dangerous "after-the-war negroes" who, in addition to being criminally inclined, also failed to show Whites proper deference as they moved freely through what White residents desired to be a thoroughly segregated Atlanta. By the century's end, White newspapers throughout the state routinely invoked the threat of Black letter carriers as sexual predators—an absolute danger to both urban and rural Whites—whose presence supposedly justified both legal and extralegal forms of violence in public spaces.

These stories about Black postal clerks and mail carriers fortified bright racial boundaries while giving form to White men's anxieties about a new racial landscape. In the New South, formerly enslaved Black men, and their sons alongside them, actively pursued middle-class lives and middle-class masculinities. For Atlanta's growing population of Black men educated in missionary schools and colleges, federal employment meant the means to claim, enact, and, when necessary, defend new identities as urban middle-class workers. With higher levels of education and the security of federal employment, Black men like Mark Anthony Thomas, Eugene Martin, and George White could not only enact claims to middle-class manliness but also secure their class position as middle-class homeowners. White men and women saw in these actions a threat to their already precarious position in the industrialized New South. Ultimately, the Black-White racial boundary was deeply strengthened and brightened through stories that, though originating in response to Black occupational mobility within a particular workplace, would be taken up and used by a wide range of social actors to justify the violent defense of White supremacy.

In the case of San Antonio's Tejano lawmen, Whites responded to assertions of middle-class identities among Mexicans with boundary repertoires that moved between brightness and blurriness. The largest and most ethnically diverse city in Texas before the 1890s, San Antonio had long been the site of cultural, political, and economic encounters between US-origin and Mexican-origin communities. By the late nineteenth century, the city's Mexican-origin Tejano population had experienced profound changes. Their numbers and their social status declined in the face of continuing waves of Anglo American settlers who tended to treat all Mexicans—even those who had been considered part of the region's landed White elite—as non-White racial inferiors. Yet some of this class managed to sustain its social position in San Antonio's new urban economy through employment in the now-Anglo-dominated city and county government. As the city contended with a new urban criminal class that White residents portrayed as largely—though not exclusively—non-White, White journalists, local officials, and everyday citizens regarded Tejano policemen as safe and reliable defenders of law and order. At the same time that the local press regularly began linking San Antonio's crime and vice to the city's "Mexican Quarter," it also commended Tejano policemen—omitting any reference to their Mexican origins—for protecting the city's law-abiding White population from

"Mexican" thieves, alleged Black rapists, or White "desperadoes." Yet for the Southern-born Anglo Americans who made up the majority of San Antonio's population in the final decades of the nineteenth century, the idea of "Mexicans" occupying positions of authority in a purportedly American city occasionally became difficult to reconcile.

In the 1890s and 1900s, the blurred racial boundary between Mexican and White appeared to become *brighter*—becoming more significant and institutionalized. Tejano men like Rafael Martinez, Juan Garza, and brothers Andrés and Jacobo Coy continued to find jobs in law enforcement a reliable path to the middle class, sometimes moving between law enforcement and other forms of white-collar employment. The press also continued to blur racial boundaries by omitting references to Tejano policemen's Mexican origins. At the same time, stories in the Anglo press about Tejano policemen's involvement in cases of corruption or public misconduct expressed doubts about their previously assumed whiteness. Initially regarded as heroes, Martinez and Jacobo Coy would later be charged with actions that were inconsistent with middle-class manliness and that undermined, rather than upheld, the rule of law. While the Spanish-language press expressed concerns over the mistreatment of Mexicans by Anglo officers, coverage in the Anglo press seemed to suggest that even Tejanos who worked to suppress non-White criminality lacked the command of middle-class manliness shown by White men. For San Antonio's Anglo residents, stories about the city's Tejano lawmen emerged as a crucial site in struggles over the Mexican-White racial boundary.

Finally, the case of San Francisco's Chinese American immigration interpreters shows how White journalists, politicians, and workers could—and occasionally did—sanction individual boundary crossing when the need arose, even as they simultaneously mobilized strategies that brightened racial distinctions. Chinese immigrants had been central to San Francisco's growth since the 1860s. During the exclusion era beginning in the 1880s, those remaining in what was the largest Chinese settlement in the nation continued to provide the city's Whites with a source of cheap labor. The emergence and growth of a federal enforcement apparatus overseeing Chinese immigration created new occupational opportunities for the small but visible population of US-born Chinese Americans and foreign-born Americanized Chinese who learned to navigate racial boundaries in pursuit of class mobility. While federal interpreter jobs in the Chinese Bureau were initially restricted to White men, Richard Williams's 1896 corruption trial indicates that the agency had become a site of racial boundary crossing. Like the anti-Chinese labor organizations that blamed any number of social ills on Chinese immigrants White journalists, politicians, and prosecutors used Williams's case to warn about the corrupting influence of Chinese men's social ambitions. The controversies over Williams and later John Endicott Gardner Jr. reflected Whites' anxieties about the apparent ease with which mixed-race Chinese men crossed racial boundaries in the workplace and in private, claiming a middle-class manliness that threatened White men and White women and violated the law. According to press accounts, trial witnesses, and the suggestions of federal investigators, Williams's criminal ties were deeply linked to the "Chinese blood" he had tried to conceal with the help of his mother and his wife—both of whom were White women. These stories helped brighten the Chinese-White racial boundary and undergirded the US Treasury's ban on employing anyone of Chinese ancestry in the agencies overseeing Chinese immigration. Within months, however, the scarcity of qualified Chinese-speaking White men prompted some journalists and politicians to express support for classifying the mixed-race Gardner as White.

During the 1900s, Whites continued to make use of stories about the dangers of Chinese social mobility in San Francisco's Immigration Bureau. The corruption trials of Hippolytus Eça da Silva and Lee Toy reinforced links between race and class by recounting for the public the perils that even—perhaps especially—the most assimilated Chinese-origin men presented to Whites. Newspaper reports, witness testimonies, and prosecutors' statements all suggested that, in addition to having acquired their middle-class status by cooperating with Chinese immigration smugglers, these men violated prohibitions against social and, in Da Silva's case, sexual contact between the races. Even as salaried interpreter positions became available for Chinese American men like Herman Lowe, Frank Tape, and Edward Park, White journalists, politicians, and federal officials continued to invoke stories about alleged Chinese criminality and illegitimate social mobility as a powerful resource for resisting Chinese American advancement in the immigration service. White officials in the Immigration Bureau would resurrect these narratives—along with older ones about Chinese "racial temperament"—to justify mandatory transfers of Chinese American interpreters and disrupt what was becoming a reliable mobility pathway for Chinese American men. These efforts both mirrored and strengthened dominant narratives about the existential threat Chinese immigration allegedly posed to the nation's Whites.

Comparing Whites' public responses to social mobility among African American men in Atlanta, Tejano men in San Antonio, and Chinese American men in San Francisco sheds light on these different boundary repertoires and encourages us to rethink long-held assumptions about historical parallels among groups durably or consistently marked as non-White. In Atlanta and San Francisco, White journalists, politicians, pundits, and everyday actors told similar stories about Black postal workers and Chinese immigration interpreters. In both cases, non-White men with middle-class aspirations were said to be especially dangerous because they undermined White men's economic position and sexually endangered White women. These stories contributed to Whites' vigorous defense of racial boundaries through everyday interactions, public campaigns, and formal policies. In San Francisco, however, the willingness of White elites to blur the color line or sanction individual crossings shows a marked difference between the two cases. The blurring of racial boundaries was more expected in the US-Mexico borderlands. Yet Anglos shifted their understanding of Tejano policemen from "off-White" to non-White as the population of Mexican immigrants in the region increased. Though the defense of these racial boundaries was not identical to that of boundaries pertaining to Chinese men or African American men, popular claims about Mexican men's criminality were not unlike those that emerged about Black men and Chinese men in this era.

Historical research on race in the United States and its territories has shown how White populations across the country—in their interactions with African Americans, Spanish-speaking peoples, Asian immigrants, and Indigenous populations of the Pacific—engaged in distinct but not unrelated processes of race-making. Considering these histories through the lens of boundary properties and processes offers a useful way of understanding the diverse trajectories of inclusion and exclusion among differently racialized groups. It also helps to describe changes in the content of the multiple racial projects that sustain or challenge the racial order. This analytical approach offers important insights into differently racialized groups' diverse experiences with the intersection of race and middle-class mobility. In this book, I have focused my attention on how people developed and refit race-class narratives about class mobility as both the US class structure and the racial order underwent far-reaching change at the beginning of the twentieth century. These narratives applied *within* as well as *through* new settings like the middle-class workplace, where they also articulated with gendered ideas about class identity—that is, "manliness."

Middle-Class Racisms: Looking Back to Look Forward

As we near completion of the first quarter of the twenty-first century, there are echoes of the late nineteenth-century conjuncture of economic crisis, sociodemographic change, and appeals to nationalist populism. Social scientists and policy researchers have described profound structural shifts taking place in the American middle class—those whose incomes fall between the 20th and 60th percentiles of the US income distribution. Researchers at the Brookings Institution report that the middle class is undergoing both demographic and economic changes. As of 2019, although non-Hispanic Whites remained overrepresented in the upper-middle class or top income quintile, as they have since the 1980s, the middle of the income distribution is more race plural than at any time in the recent past. The racial composition of those in the first, second, and middle-income quintiles reflects that of the nation as a whole, with non-Hispanic Whites representing 59 percent, African Americans 12 percent, Hispanics 18 percent, and Asian Americans 7 percent of the total.[5] By 2042, non-Hispanic Whites are expected to be in the minority of the nation's middle classes.

At the same time that increasing income inequality, rising costs, and the loss of stable, middle-class jobs in some economic sectors have undermined people's expectations about middle-class stability and increased fears of downward social mobility, these demographic changes continue to alter the racial makeup of the middle class.[6] Yet while some argue the nation has supposedly entered a "post-racial era," these fears are understood and expressed in people's understandings of race. Sociologists like Arlie Hochschild have pointed to the "deep stories" that have become popular among many working-class and middle-class Whites, stories that claim (among other things) harm from employment policies and college admission criteria that "unfairly" favor racial minorities.[7] Scholarship in the humanities and the social sciences, meanwhile, also continues to document how people's experiences with middle-class mobility and belonging still vary along racial lines. Widely circulated news stories and social media posts have shown African Americans, Latines, Asian Americans, Muslims, and others being subjected to a range of acts of racial intimidation or even violence in middle-class spaces (public parks, gated communities, college dormitories, shopping centers, places of worship) often—but by no means exclusively—at the hands of people who self-identify as White. These incidents were particularly significant in the context of a 2016 presidential election that highlighted the anxieties of White workers, especially those who had fallen out of the middle class in recent years. Researchers analyzing the social origins of people charged with storming the nation's capital on January 6, 2021, describe a population that was not only overwhelmingly White in racial origin but also middle class—professionals, business owners, white-collar workers, and public-sector workers.[8]

Sociologist Les Back has observed that, while the social bases of middle-class racisms are often new, with new populations targeted or new settings invoked, their forms tend to reproduce familiar themes of displacement and the "perfidy of outsiders" in the stories people tell about race and class.[9] By focusing on Whites' responses to changes in the face of middle-class mobility and identity during the late nineteenth and early twentieth centuries—a period of economic uncertainty and new encounters with populations of African Americans, Asians, Mexicans, and other non-Whites who, like themselves, asserted identities that signified middle-class belonging—this book has attempted to contribute to an archive of middle-class racisms. It specifically considers how understandings of the race-class nexus were developed and expressed through stories about middle-class workplaces, neighborhoods, and public spaces.

Emerging as the dominant form of racism in the aftermath of the Civil War, constitutionalized segregation supposedly offered Whites a rational, modern, and even "genteel" way to mark and preserve racial boundaries in a changing racial landscape. Save for the use of physical force required to ensure adherence to the law, most believed that legally sanctioned racial separation in the public sphere sustained the "natural" racial order without the overt physical violence that necessarily accompanied slavery and wars of expansion and settlement. Yet historians tell us that in the decade following the period examined here, the Ku Klux Klan, the best-known of the many violent White supremacist organizations born out of a desire to terrorize Southern Blacks during Reconstruction, experienced a marked resurgence, growing its membership to between 4 million and 6 million members nationally. The organization's leaders effectively recruited among the middle classes of Anglo Protestant Whites—families headed by small-business owners, professionals, merchants, and artisans—who had notably begun to experience a marked decline in economic position, for which they readily blamed not only African Americans but an expansive body of cultural and racial villains against whom they directed varying tactics of intimidation and violence: Jews, Catholics, communists, and immigrants.[10] A wide range of academic and mainstream scholars who write about racism in the post–civil rights era have tended to describe middle-class racisms as primarily "covert," "subtle," "masked," and generally nonviolent, in supposed contrast to more direct, "unvarnished," and physically violent working-class racisms that garner public attention.[11] But as this book has shown, this view bypasses a long and complex history in which middle-class Whites in different regions of the United States actively and explicitly constructed, sustained, altered, and defended racial distinctions in middle-class neighborhoods, public spaces, and workplaces using methods that ranged from violent to nonviolent. Newspaper stories; popular fictional accounts in print, on stage, and, later, in film; public monuments; and even many lynching photographs and postcards with a "posed" nature are all powerful records of the range of "acceptable" middle-class racisms that emerged during the end of the nineteenth century and extended well into the start of the twentieth.[12] By now, there should be no doubt that even with the range of understandings about the nature of racial boundaries, certain segments of the American middle class have, at various points in history, not only explicitly embraced ideologies of White supremacy but also been moved to many different public forms of violence in its defense.

APPENDIX

Collective Biographical Data Used in This Study

African American mail carriers and postal clerks in Atlanta, 1875–1910

Name	Birth year	First recorded service year	Last recorded service year	Position held
Ammonetti, George J., Sr.	1870	1899	1905	Mail carrier
Amos, Moses	1866	1901	1905	Postal clerk
Andrews, Grant	—	1892	1892	Mail carrier
Anthony, Alvin F.	1880	1909	1911	Postal clerk
Bass, Elijah	1857	1885	1897	Postal clerk
Beall [Bell], John	1868	1891	1903	Mail carrier
Boswell, William Reese	1879	1907	1911	Mail carrier; postal clerk
Briscoe, Henry	1874	1901	1911	Mail carrier
Brooks, Robert D	1877	1906	1906	Mail carrier
Carey, Ulysses S.	1880	1903	1905	Railroad postal clerk
Carey, Walter E.	1878	1903	1905	Railroad postal clerk
Carthorn, Linwood A.	1882	1905	1911	Mail carrier
Cater, Charles C.	1856	1885	1887	Clerk; Railroad postal clerk
Cooke, Virgil L.	1864	1891	1892	Mail carrier
Covington, Walter R.	1876	1901	1909	Mail carrier
Craddock, Robert L.	1865	1903	1911	Mail carrier
Crawford, Joseph	1877	1903	1905	Mail carrier
Donald, James T.	1879	1905	1911	Mail carrier
Dozier, Wilson H.	1868	1895	1905	Mail carrier
Drakeford, Edmond	1869	1895	1905	Mail carrier
Fagan, John T.	1873	1905	1910	Mail carrier
Gibson, John C.	1861	1891	1899	Mail carrier
Gilbert, William J.	1887	1909	1911	Mail carrier
Goosby, Robert	—	1891	1891	Mail carrier
Goosby, William H.	1867	1891	1893	Mail carrier
Grant, Thomas	1866	1905	1911	Mail carrier

(continued)

(*continued*)

Name	Birth year	First recorded service year	Last recorded service year	Position held
Greene, John H.	1862	1891	1905	Mail carrier
Greenwood, John B.	1866	1891	1905	Mail carrier
Greenwood, Thornton T.	1856	1881	1905	Mail carrier
Griggs, Richard B.	1881	1905	1905	Mail carrier
Grimes, Cornelius L.	1871	1903	1909	Mail carrier
Heard, Rell G.	1875	1906	1909	Mail carrier
Holmes, Thomas W.	1881	1901	1905	Mail carrier
Jackson, John W.	—	1891	1891	Mail carrier
Jones, John N.	1868	1905	1909	Mail carrier
Joplin, Clarence E.	1859	1883	1885	Mail carrier
Joyce, Lewis S.	1870	1891	1903	Postal clerk
King, Julius C.	1882	1905	1911	Mail carrier
King, William H.	1869	1899	1905	Mail carrier
Landrum, Lafayette	1863	1891	1905	Mail carrier
Lofton, Augustus G.	1864	1891	1909	Mail carrier
Logan, Walter S.	1873	1891	1909	Mail carrier
Luckie, Henry J.	1882	1906	1908	Mail carrier
Luckie, Solomon S.	1866	1901	1911	Mail carrier
Martin, Eugene M.	1858	1891	1911	Mail carrier
Martin, George W., Jr.	—	1891	1893	Mail carrier
McCray, Stephen P.	1859	1891	1891	Postal clerk
McCray, Thaddeus B.	1867	1885	1887	Postal clerk
McDonald, William	1877	1905	1907	Mail carrier
McHenry, Jackson, Jr.	1884	1905	1911	Mail carrier
Meade, Edward L.	1862	1891	1891	Mail carrier
Mitchell, Calvin	1878	1901	1905	Mail carrier
Moody, Robert	—	1889	1889	Mail carrier
Parker, James B.	1858	1883	1886	Mail carrier
Payne, Thomas W.	1872	1891	1905	Mail carrier
Penney, Charles C.	1865	1889	1893	Postal clerk
Phillips, James Knox, Jr.	1864	1891	1909	Mail carrier
Reynolds, St. Elmo	1883	1905	1911	Mail carrier
Rhodes, Edward S.	1884	1903	1905	Mail carrier
Rosette, William C.	1868	1905	1911	Mail carrier
Rucker, Amos	1840	1885	1887	Postal clerk
Rucker, Augustus	1875	1905	1911	Postal clerk

Name	Birth year	First recorded service year	Last recorded service year	Position held
Shelton, John C.	—	1879	1885	Mail carrier
Simmons, William H.	1888	1905	1909	Postal clerk
Smith, Sylvanus	1862	1897	1905	Mail carrier
Strong, John W.	—	1891	1893	Postal clerk
Tabb, Artaway J.	1859	1888	1891	Mail carrier
Tate, George W.	1862	1885	1911	Mail carrier; postal clerk
Thomas, Joseph	1856	1891	1899	Mail carrier
Thomas, Marcus A.	1867	1885	1911	Postal clerk
Thomas, R. Lee	1865	1891	1905	Mail carrier
Toliver, Dudley L.	1877	1901	1905	Postal clerk
Tompkins, Henry T.	1874	1901	1905	Mail carrier
Walton, Claybourne Warren, Jr.	1870	1891	1892	Mail carrier
Ware, Samuel A.	1880	1909	1911	Mail carrier
Watts, Walter S.	1883	1905	1909	Mail carrier
Westmoreland, William G.	1867	1903	1905	Mail carrier
White, George W.	1857	1885	1911	Mail carrier
White, Reuben W.	1865	1891	1905	Mail carrier
Williams, Henry H.	1854	1910	1911	Postal clerk
Wimbish, Christopher Columbus	1851	1876	1911	Postal clerk
Wynn, William A.	1867	1894	1905	Mail carrier

Sources: Official Register (1885, vol. 2; 1887, vol. 2; 1889, vol. 2; 1891, vol. 2; 1893, vol. 2; 1895, vol. 2; 1897, vol. 2; 1899, vol. 2; 1901, vol. 2; 1903, vol. 2; 1905, vol. 2; 1907, vol. 2; 1909, vol. 2; 1911, vol. 2); 1870 Census of the United States, Atlanta, Fulton County; 1880 Census of the United States, Atlanta, Fulton County; 1900 Census of the United States, Atlanta, Fulton County; 1910 Census of the United States, Atlanta, Fulton County; James W. Beasley Publisher, *Atlanta City Directory for 1875*; R. L. Polk and Company, *Atlanta City Directory for 1888*; R. L. Polk and Company, *Atlanta City Directory for 1889*; Saunders, *Atlanta City Directory for 1890*; Saunders, *Atlanta City Directory for 1893*; Saunders, *Atlanta City Directory for 1895*; Maloney Directory, *Atlanta City Directory 1900*; Foote and Davies, *Atlanta City Directory 1906*; Sholes, *Sholes' Directory*; Weatherbee, *Atlanta City Directory for 1883*; Weatherbee, *Atlanta City Directory for 1888*.

Mexican American police officers in San Antonio, 1872–1910

Name	Birth year	First recorded service year	Last recorded service year	Position held
Barrera, Francisco (Frank)	1852	1900	1910	Policeman
Barrera, Juan E.	1832	1872	1872	Policeman
Cadena, Celedonio V.	1849	1890	1899	Policeman
Cadena, José Maria	1823	1872	1872	Policeman
Cardenas, Juan T.	1844	1870	1909	Policeman; assistant city marshal; police captain
Cassiano, José, Jr.	1866	1900	1910	Police detective
Cevallos, Pedro	1832	1860	1877	Policeman
Chavez, Ignacio	1851	1895	1899	Policeman
Chavez, Jose G.	1853	1895	1899	Policeman
Coy, Andrés (Andreas) S.	1842	1880	After 1910	Policeman; assistant city marshal; police captain
Coy, Jacobo (Jacob) S.	1841	1880	1897	Policeman; deputy sheriff
Cruz, David T.	1887	1910	After 1910	Policeman
Diaz, Bonifacio	1856	1901	1905	Policeman
Diaz, Domingo	1856	1891	1910	Sheriff; policeman
Esparza, Francisco	1864	1887	1887	Policeman
Espinoza, Luciano	1860	1901	1905	Policeman
Galan, Francisco	1836	1870	1895	Policeman
Galan, Norberto	1865	1908	1910	Policeman
Garcia, Mariano M.	1833	1885	1885	Policeman
Garza, Fernando G.	1846	1887	1887	Policeman
Garza, Antonio	—	1889	1889	Policeman
Garza, Juan (John) M.	1841	1910	1910	Policeman
Gonzales, Jacinto	1851	1895	1895	Policeman
Guerrero, Angel	1857	1909	1910	Policeman
Herrera, Antonio	1858	1890	1905	Sheriff; policeman
Leal, Luciano	1854	1910	1910	Policeman
Luceo, Manuel B.	1862	1910	1910	Policeman

(continued)

Name	Birth year	First recorded service year	Last recorded service year	Position held
Martinez, Rafael R.	1842	1881	1895	Policeman; constable; jailer
Montes, Alejo	1852	1900	1910	Policeman
Morin, Eduardo (Edward A.)	1867	1899	1905	Policeman; sheriff
Ortiz, Nicolas	1873	1910	1910	Policeman
Perez, Alejo	1834	1875	1889	Policeman; assistant city marshal
Perez, Desiderio	1879	1901	1901	Policeman
Perez, Romualdo	1862	1892	1895	Policeman
Quintana, Gerónimo (Jerome)	1870	1890	1899	Policeman; sheriff
Quintero, Calixto	1867	1910	1910	Policeman
Robalin, Luz (Lucero)	1866	1900	1909	Policeman
Sanchez, Manuel	—	1880	1889	Policeman
Serna, Albert I.	1874	1910	1910	Policeman
Torres, Modesto	1863	1887	1892	Policeman; jailer; sheriff
Vidal, Alejandro	1872	1910	1910	Policeman
Zapata, Fernando	1875	1910	After 1910	Policeman

Sources: Mooney and Morrison, *Directory*; Morrison and Fourmy, *General Directory* (1879, 1881, 1883, 1885, 1887); Johnson and Chapman, *General Directory*; Appler, *General Directory* (1893, 1895, 1897, 1899, 1901); Appler, *General Directory and Blue Book* (1903, 1905, 1907, 1908, 1909); Texas Publishing, *Directory of the City*; 1870 Census of the United States, San Antonio, Bexar County; 1880 Census of the United States, San Antonio, Bexar County; 1900 Census of the United States, San Antonio, Bexar County; 1910 Census of the United States, San Antonio, Bexar County; San Antonio Police History Archive.

Chinese-origin and Chinese American interpreters for the San Francisco
Immigration Bureau, 1894–1920

Name	Birth year	First recorded service year	Last recorded service year	Position held
Da Silva, Hippolytus L. Eça	1871	1900	1903	Interpreter, US Immigration Bureau
Gardner, John Endicott, Jr.	1863	1897	1912	Interpreter, US Customs Service; interpreter and inspector, US Customs
Lowe, Herman	1875	1905	After 1920	Interpreter, US Immigration Bureau
Park, Edward L.	1881	1906	1917	Interpreter, US Immigration Bureau
Williams, Richard S.	1861	1894	1896	Interpreter, US Customs Service; Chinese inspector, US Customs Service

Sources: Official Register (1893, vol. 1; 1895, vol. 1; 1897, vol. 1; 1899, vol. 1; 1901, vol. 1; 1903, vol. 1; 1905, vol. 1; 1907, vol. 1; 1909, vol. 1; 1911, vol. 1); 1870 Census of the United States, San Francisco, San Francisco County; 1880 Census of the United States, San Francisco, San Francisco County; 1900 Census of the United States, San Francisco, San Francisco County; 1910 Census of the United States, San Francisco, San Francisco County; 1920 Census of the United States, Berkeley, Alameda County; H. S. Crocker Company, Crocker-Langley San Francisco Directory, 1891; H. S. Crocker Company, Crocker-Langley San Francisco Directory, 1896.

Notes

Introduction

1. 1900 United States Census, Atlanta, Fulton, Georgia, digital image s.v. "Mark A. Thomas," Ancestry.com; US Department of Commerce and Labor, Bureau of the Census, *Official Register* (hereafter cited as *Official Register*) (1899), 2:445; Bullock, *Atlanta City Directory for 1899*, 1504, digital image s.v. "Mark A. Thomas"; Sanborn-Perris Map Company, *Sanborn Fire Insurance Map from Atlanta*, 47–48. Although available census records indicate that Thomas was identified as "Mulatto," the enumerator for the 1900 census identified him and his family as being among the racially mixed block's White residents. See 1880 United States Census, Atlanta, Fulton, Georgia, digital image s.v. "Mark Thomas," Ancestry.com; and 1910 United States Census, Atlanta, Fulton, Georgia, digital image s.v. "Marcus Thomas," Ancestry.com.

2. Throughout this text, I capitalize the racial categories used at the turn of the century, such as "Black," "White," or "Mexican," and treat them as proper nouns when they refer to a particular group or individual. This practice acknowledges that racial categories signify complex histories, collective identities, and social positions within racially structured social systems like that of the United States. I also recognize that racial categories are regionally specific. In the case of Texas and the Southwest, I use the term "Anglos" to refer to non-Hispanic Whites of both US and European immigrant origin residing in the region and use the term "White" to refer to the nationally institutionalized racial category. The term "Tejanos" refers to Texans of Mexican descent, whether US-born or made citizens by the Treaty of Guadalupe Hidalgo. "Mexican," used as a regional racial category, referred to all people of Mexican origin regardless of nativity. Occasionally in the text, I will refer to specific groups within these populations.

3. Sanborn-Perris Map Company, *Sanborn Fire Insurance Map from San Antonio*, 4, 6; 1900 United States Census, San Antonio, Bexar, Texas, 8–9, digital image s.v. "Juan T. Cardenas," Ancestry.com.

4. "West of the San Pedro," *San Antonio Express*, November 5, 1880, 4; "Shot Him for a Robber," *San Antonio Daily Express*, October 28, 1893, 3; McEachin, "Our Mexican Citizens," 15; De León, *Tejano Community*, 103.

5. Jewell, "'Injurious Effect.'"

6. 1900 United States Census, San Francisco, San Francisco County, California, digital image s.v. "Herman Lowe," Ancestry.com; Condit, "Americanized Chinese."

7. Ngai, *Lucky Ones*, 148; *Official Register* (1905), 1:522, 1094.

8. Painter, *Standing at Armageddon*, xxiii–xxviii; Archer and Blau, "Class Formation," 30–32; Blumin, *Emergence of the Middle Class*, 258–97; Wiebe, *Search for Order*, 11–43.

9. See US Census Office, *Eleventh Census: 1890*; Hunt, *Special Census Report*; and Hunt, *Occupations at the Twelfth Census*. The data in these reports provide useful but

incomplete information about race and occupation. The 1890 report distinguishes between "Native White" and "Foreign White" people and those with parents from either or both groups. African Americans ("Negroes") are identified as part of a "Colored" category that also included Japanese, Chinese, and "Civilized Indians." People of Mexican origin would have likely been classified under the foreign-born White category. The 1900 report followed a similar logic, but with some added detail. For "Persons of Foreign Parentage," only the following countries of origin were identified: Austria-Hungary, Canada (English), Canada (French), Germany, Great Britain, Ireland, Italy, Poland, Russia, Scandinavia, and "other countries." Mexico was not identified as a country of origin, even in those cities with large concentrations of Mexican-origin workers. See "Use of Terms in General and Analytical Tables," in Hunt, *Occupations at the Twelfth Census*, xxviii.

10. Richardson, *Christian Reconstruction*; Mora, *Border Dilemmas*; Hoffnung-Garskof, *Racial Migrations*; Maddox, *Citizen Indians*; Go, *American Empire*.

11. Jacobson, *Barbarian Virtues*; F. James Davis, *Who Is Black?*; Du Bois, *Souls of Black Folk*, 372.

12. Winant, *Racial Conditions*, 40; Robinson, *Black Marxism*, 26–27; Roediger, *Wages of Whiteness*.

13. These works include Roediger, *Towards the Abolition of Whiteness*; Saxton, *Rise and Fall of the White Republic*; Arnesen, "Up from Exclusion White"; Lott, *Love and Theft*.

14. Trotter, *Workers on Arrival*; John Weber, *From South Texas*; Menchaca, *Naturalizing Mexican Immigrants*, 118–22; Benton-Cohen, *Borderline Americans*; Gardner, "Working on White Womanhood"; Nicholas W. Mason, "Anti-Chinese Mob Violence"; Lew-Williams, *Chinese Must Go*, 129–31; McMath, *American Populism*, 171–75.

15. Blair Murphy Kelley, *Right to Ride*; Kibler, *Censoring Racial Ridicule*; Sueyoshi, *Discriminating Sex*; Gross, *What Blood Won't Tell*; Lui, *Chinatown Trunk Mystery*, 176–82.

16. Omi and Winant, *Racial Formation*, 124–25; Jung, *Beneath the Surface*; Lewis, "'What Group?'"; Beisel and Kay, "Abortion, Race, and Gender"; Ray, "Theory of Racialized Organizations."

17. Weatherwax, "Mocking the 'Other'"; "Our New Citizens—Ben Monowski," no. 1–3, 1882, Arnold and Deanne Kaplan Collection of Early American Judaica, Call No. Arc.MS.56, Colenda Digital Repository, University of Pennsylvania Libraries, https://colenda.library.upenn.edu; "Our New Citizens—German," nos. 1–4, 1882, #20.1–20.4, http://www.tradecards.com/articles/series/index.html.

18. Lamont and Molnár, "Study of Boundaries"; Alba, *Blurring the Color Line*; Wimmer, *Ethnic Boundary Making*, 58–63.

19. Ray, "Theory of Racialized Organizations," 51–53; Diamond and Lewis, "Race and Discipline."

20. Rabinowitz, *Race Relations*, 66; Barr, "Occupational and Geographic Mobility"; De León, *Tejano Community*, 87–112; Mei, "Socioeconomic Developments."

21. Goldberg, *The Threat of Race*, 69–70.

22. Anderson, "Idea of Chinatown"; Ling, *Chinese Chicago*; Bronstein, "Segregation, Exclusion"; Brooks, *Alien Neighbors, Foreign Friends*; Bow, *Partly Colored*.

23. Almaguer, *Racial Fault Lines*; Gross, "The Caucasian Cloak"; Lim, *Porous Borders*; Molina, *How Race Is Made*; Menchaca, *Recovering History, Constructing Race*.

24. Dorsey, *To Build Our Lives*; Jewell, *Race, Social Reform*; Godshalk, *Veiled Visions*.

25. De León, *The Tejano Community*, 25–28; Ramos, *Beyond the Alamo*; David J. Weber, *Foreigners*, 146–47.

26. McClain, *In Search of Equality*; Wong and Chan, *Claiming America*; Lee, *At America's Gates*; Sandmeyer, *Anti-Chinese Movement*.

27. Pachucki, Pendergrass, and Lamont, "Boundary Processes"; Lamont and Molnár, "Study of Boundaries."

28. Zolberg and Woon, "Why Islam Is like Spanish"; Wimmer, *Ethnic Boundary Making*, 58–61; Fox and Guglielmo, "Defining America's Racial Boundaries."

29. Gerteis, "Populism, Race," 199–200; Somers, "Narrativity, Narrative Identity," 608; Franzosi, "Narrative Analysis."

30. Sewell, "Historical Events."

31. Brodkin, *How Jews Became White*; Roediger, *Working toward Whiteness*.

32. Arnesen, "Whiteness"; Guterl, "Note on the Word White"; Guglielmo, *White on Arrival*; Gross, *What Blood Won't Tell*, 230–31.

33. Here I would include Glenn, *Unequal Freedom*; Molina, *How Race Is Made*; Kurashige, *Shifting Grounds of Race*; Lim, *Porous Borders*; Fox, *Three Worlds of Relief*; and Pulido, *Black, Brown, Yellow*.

34. My research methods have been informed by the work of a number of historians and historical sociologists who analyze articulations of race, class, and gender, including Donovan, *White Slave Crusades*; Muhammad, *Condemnation of Blackness*; Lui, *Chinatown Trunk Mystery*; and Heap, *Slumming*.

35. Verboven, Carlier, and Dumolyn, "Short Manual."

36. Bonnell, "Uses of Theory."

37. Back, "All the World's," 54–58; Clayton, "Thinking Spatially," 495n5.

Chapter One

1. Gould, "Tariffs and Markets"; Maggor, "American Capitalism."

2. Maggor, "American Capitalism," 208.

3. Archer and Blau, "Class Formation," 29. See Doyle, *New Men, New Cities*, 88–92; Lands, *Culture of Property*, 23–24; Haydu, *Citizen Employers*; Zunz, *Making America Corporate*; and Decker, *Fortunes and Failures*.

4. Shefter, "Trade Unions," 202.

5. Sobek, "Occupations," 2-38–2-39.

6. Bederman, *Manliness and Civilization*, 12; Hofstadter, *Age of Reform*, 216.

7. Painter, *Standing at Armageddon*, xv.

8. Foner, *Reconstruction*, 564–601; Rabinowitz, *Race Relations*; Du Bois, *Black Reconstruction in America*, 670–709.

9. Higham, *Strangers in the Land*, 87–89; Jacobson, *Whiteness of a Different Color*; Beisel and Kay, "Abortion, Race, and Gender."

10. Lee, *At America's Gates*; Saxton, *Indispensable Enemy*.

11. Haas, *Conquests and Historical Identities*; Gross, "Caucasian Cloak," 337; Mora, *Border Dilemmas*, 135–41.

12. Hofstadter, *Age of Reform*, 216–18; Bederman, *Manliness and Civilization*, 12.

13. Smith-Rosenberg, *Disorderly Conduct*, 177–78; McGovern, "American Woman's"; Freedman, "New Woman."

14. Bederman, *Manliness and Civilization*, 13–14.

15. US Bureau of the Census, *Historical Statistics*, 11–12.

16. Aron, *Ladies and Gentlemen*.

17. Warner, *Streetcar Suburbs*; Sennett, *Families against the City*; Domosh, *Invented Cities*; Doyle, *New Men, New Cities*; Garb, *City of American Dreams*; Decker, *Fortunes and Failures*, 214–15, 224–26.

18. Rutenbeck, "Newspapers Trends"; Evensen, "Journalism."

19. Goldberg, *Threat of Race*, 89–90.

20. Muhammad, *Condemnation of Blackness*; Nicholas Sean Hall, "'Wasp's' Troublesome Children'"; Hernández, *City of Inmates*; Carrigan and Webb, *Forgotten Dead*.

21. Stuart Hall, "Race, Articulation and Societies"; Winant, *Racial Conditions*, 33–36, 39–43; powell, "Race and Class Nexus."

22. Bonilla-Silva, "Rethinking Racism"; Omi and Winant, *Racial Formation*; Feagin, *Systemic Racism*.

23. Sewell, "Theory of Structure."

24. Beisel and Kay, "Abortion, Race, and Gender," 503–504; Lewis, "'What Group?,'" 629–32; Jung, *Beneath the Surface*, 35–36; Ray, "Theory of Racialized Organizations," 27, 32–33.

25. Sewell, "Theory of Structure," 17–19; Beisel and Kay, "Abortion, Race, and Gender," 504.

26. Powell, "Race and Class Nexus," 355. With apologies to powell, I have adopted Eduardo Bonilla-Silva's usage of "race-class nexus." See Bonilla-Silva, "Toward a New Political Praxis" and "Hegemonic Racism and Democracy," 19.

27. Jung, *Beneath the Surface*, 35–36; Ray, "Theory of Racialized Organizations," 34.

28. Omi and Winant, *Racial Formation*, 125; Omi and Winant, "Once More, with Feeling."

29. Somers, "Narrative Constitution of Identity"; Steinmetz, "Reflections on the Role"; Franzosi, "Narrative Analysis," 519–20.

30. Bonilla-Silva, "Structure of Racism," 1366; Gerteis, "Possession of Civic Virtue."

31. Robin D. G. Kelley, "'We Are Not'"; Gerteis, *Class and the Color Line*, 200–201; Roediger, *Working toward Whiteness*.

32. Lamont, *Dignity of Working Men*; Pachucki, Pendergrass, and Lamont, "Boundary Processes"; Wimmer, *Ethnic Boundary Making*; Loveman, *National Colors*; Alba and Nee, *Remaking the American Mainstream*.

33. Beisel, "Shifting Moral Boundary," 107–8; Lamont, *Dignity of Working Men*.

34. Fox and Guglielmo, "Defining America's Racial Boundaries," 331.

35. Wimmer, *Ethnic Boundary Making*, 58–60.

36. Zolberg and Woon, "Why Islam Is like Spanish," 8–9; Wimmer, *Ethnic Boundary Making*, 61; Alba, *Blurring the Color Line*, 19–20.

37. Roediger, *Working toward Whiteness*; Brodkin, *How Jews Became White*; Orsi, "Religious Boundaries."

38. Alba, *Blurring the Color Line*. See also Alba, "'Bright vs. Blurred Boundaries"; and Wimmer, *Ethnic Boundary Making*, 61.

39. Arnesen, "Whiteness"; Gross, *What Blood Won't Tell*; Guglielmo, *White on Arrival*; Painter, *History of White People*.

40. Fox and Guglielmo, "Defining America's Racial Boundaries," 366.

41. Lacy, *Blue-Chip Black*; Vallejo, *Barrios to 'Burbs*; Clerge, *New Noir*; Yu, "Revisiting the Bamboo Ceiling"; Margaret M. Chin, *Stuck*; Wingfield, *No More Invisible Man*; Neckerman, Carter, and Lee, "Segmented Assimilation."

42. Back, "All the World's," 57.

43. Glenn, *Unequal Freedom*; Go, *American Empire*; Fox, *Three Worlds of Relief*; Kurashige, *Shifting Grounds of Race*; Lim, *Porous Borders*; Arvin, *Possessing Polynesians*.

44. Molina, *How Race Is Made*; Gilmore, "Fatal Couplings"; Benton-Cohen, *Borderline Americans*; Goldberg, *Threat of Race*, 66–67. See also Cheng, *Changes Next Door*; Garcia, *World of Its Own*; and Pulido, *Black, Brown, Yellow*.

45. Du Bois, *Black Reconstruction in America*; Rabinowitz, *Race Relations*, 61–96; Ruef, *Between Slavery and Capitalism*; Doyle, *New Men, New Cities*.

46. Gatewood, *Aristocrats of Color*; Butler, *Entrepreneurship and Self-Help*; Yellin, *Racism*.

47. Hale, *Making Whiteness*; Blair Murphy Kelley, *Right to Ride*; Driskell, *Schooling Jim Crow*.

48. Stampp, *Era of Reconstruction*, 196; The brightness and inflexibility of the Black-White boundaries were such that covert strategies of boundary crossing or "passing" became a central theme in African Americans' experience with social mobility. See Saperstein and Gullickson, "'Mulatto Escape Hatch'?"

49. Gibson, "Population of the 100 Largest"; Rabinowitz, *Race Relations*, 19–20; Carter, *Black Side*; Dittmer, *Black Georgia*, 12–13.

50. Rabinowitz, *Race Relations*, 62–70.

51. Mixon, *Atlanta Riot*.

52. Bonacich, "Background to Asian Immigration."

53. Lee, *At America's Gates*; Lew-Williams, *Chinese Must Go*; Pfaelzer, *Driven Out*.

54. Ngai, *Lucky Ones*; Wong and Chan, *Claiming America*; Marcus and Chen, "Inside and outside Chinatown."

55. Mei, "Socioeconomic Developments"; Pascoe, "Gender Systems in Conflict"; Woo, "Chinese Protestants"; Lui, *Chinatown Trunk Mystery*.

56. Ngai, "'Slight Knowledge'"; Ngai, "History as Law."

57. Gibson, "Population of the 100 Largest," 35.

58. Mei, "Socioeconomic Developments," 370; Chen, *Chinese San Francisco*, 50, 59–60.

59. Saxton, *Indispensable Enemy*; Trauner, "Chinese as Medical Scapegoats"; Gardner, "Working on White Womanhood"; Shah, *Contagious Divides*; Lew-Williams, *Chinese Must Go*.

60. Brooks, *Alien Neighbors, Foreign Friends*, 19.

61. Ngai, *Lucky Ones*; Brooks, *Alien Neighbors, Foreign Friends*, 23–25; Jewell, "'Injurious Effect.'"

62. Barrera, *Race and Class*; Griswold-Del Castillo, *La Familia*; Thomas D. Hall, *Social Change*.

63. Gonzales, *Hispanic Elite*.

64. Sheridan, *Los Tucsonenses*, 41–54, 93; Benton-Cohen, *Borderline Americans*, 27–29; Casas, *Married to a Daughter*; Montejano, *Anglos and Mexicans*.

65. See Barr, "Occupational and Geographic Mobility"; and Johnson, *In the Loop*, 120.

66. Arreola, *Tejano South Texas*, 145; Garcia, *Rise of the Mexican American*, 29.

67. De León, *Tejano Community*, 97–99; Garcia, *Rise of the Mexican American*, 22–23; Martinez, "Voice of the People"; Dewey, *Pesos and Dollars*.

68. Buitron, *Quest for Tejano Identity*; Kenneth Mason, *African Americans*; Menchaca, *Naturalizing Mexican Immigrants*; Orozco, *Agent of Change*.

69. Ray, "Theory of Racialized Organizations," 46–48.

Chapter Two

1. "Did Not Indict Dr. E. C. Ripley," *Atlanta Constitution*, June 5, 1906, 11.

2. Crowe, "Racial Massacre in Atlanta"; Mixon, *Atlanta Riot*.

3. White, *Man Called White*, 10–12; Janken, *Walter White*, 13–17.

4. Ruef, *Between Slavery and Capitalism*, 75–77.

5. Muhammad, *Condemnation of Blackness*, 15–34; Flowe, *Uncontrollable Blackness*.

6. Yellin, *Racism in the Nation's Service*, 22; John A. Davis and Golightly, "Negro Employment."

7. Colored American, *Colored American Republican Text Book*, 37.

8. Bacote, "Negro Officeholders in Georgia," 222–25; Jones, "Black Political Empowerment"; Watts, "Black Political Progress"; Bacote, *Story of Atlanta University*; Richardson, *Christian Reconstruction*; Gatewood, *Aristocrats of Color*, 90–92.

9. Dittmer, *Black Georgia*, 90–92.

10. Rubio, *There's Always Work*, 44–47, 324nn11–12.

11. According to city directories, African American men had been employed in Atlanta as regular letter carriers as early as 1875, though more may have been employed as substitute carriers, assigned to carry out the urban routes of regular carriers during periods when additional labor was needed. See James W. Beasley Publisher, *Beasley's Atlanta City Directory*, 318.

12. *Official Register* (1881), 2:679; Sholes, *Sholes' Directory*, 40–41.

13. *Official Register* (1885), 2:701, 787.

14. *Official Register* (1911), 2:80.

15. *Official Register* (1891), 2:996. Black men also continued to be employed as substitute carriers at the rate of one dollar per day.

16. *Official Register* (1891), 2:865.

17. *Official Register* (1901), 2:452.

18. The only category of postal employees that Black men dominated numerically was those listed as "laborers" employed by the post office—six out of the eight were Black. See *Official Register* (1901), 2:734.

19. Mikusko and Miller, *Carriers*, 60; Dodson, "Affairs at Coon City," *Postal Record* 3, no. 1 (November 1889): 14; Dodson, "Affairs at Coon City," *Postal Record* 3, no. 2 (December 1889): 21. See also Rubio, *There's Always Work*, 49.

20. *Postal Record* 4, no. 2, (February 1891): 37

21. "Banquet to Captain Maddox," *Atlanta Constitution*, July 17, 1898, 12; "Letter Carriers' Banquet," *Atlanta Constitution*, January 19, 1899, 9.

22. *Postal Record* 11 no. 2 (February 1898): 53; *Postal Record* 11, no. 7 (July 1898): 188; "Carriers Elect Officers: Annual Election of Gate City Branch, No. 172, Held Yesterday Morning," *Atlanta Constitution*, December 14, 1903, 10; "Letter Carriers Meet," *Atlanta Constitution*, June 14, 1905, 11E.

23. *Official Register* (1881), 2:679; *Official Register* (1883), 2:741; *Official Register* (1885), 2:787; *Official Register* (1887), 2:838; *Official Register* (1889), 2:922; Painter, *Standing at Armageddon*, 30–31.

24. 1880 United States Census, District 567, Henry County, Georgia, digital image s.v. "Charles C. Cater," Ancestry.com; Weatherbee, *Weatherbee's Atlanta City Directory for 1883*, 263, digital image s.v. "Charles C. Cater," Ancestry.com; *Official Register* (1883), 2:741; *Official Register* (1885), 2:787; *Official Register* (1887), 2:838; Weatherbee, *Weatherbee's Atlanta City Directory for 1888*, 986, digital image s.v. "Charles C. Cater," Ancestry.com.

25. Adams, *General Catalogue*, 139; Connelly and Fais, *City Directory of Chattanooga*, 521, digital image s.v. "Artaway Tabb," Ancestry.com.

26. *Official Register* (1901), 2:734; *Official Register* (1911), 2:80.

27. *Official Register* (1885), 2:701; *Official Register* (1887), 2:745; *Official Register* (1889), 2:819.

28. Moore, "Jim Crow in Georgia"; Dittmer, *Black Georgia*, 16–21.

29. *Official Register* (1909), 2:78–79.

30. Hodes, "Sexualization of Reconstruction Politics"; Dowd-Hall, "'Mind That Burns'"; Bederman, *Manliness and Civilization*, 57–60.

31. 1870 United States Federal Census, Chattanooga, Ward 4, Hamilton, Tennessee, digital image s.v. "Ernest Penney," Ancestry.com; 1880 Federal Census, Atlanta, Fulton, Georgia, digital image s.v. "Ernest Penney," Ancestry.com.

32. *Catalogue of the Officers and Students* (1882–83), 2, 5; *Catalogue of the Officers and Students* (1881–82), 9; *Catalogue of the Officers and Students* (1880–81), 20.

33. *Official Register* (1889), 2:819, 922; "A Negro Appointee," *Atlanta Constitution*, August 6, 1889, 8.

34. Van Riper, *History*, 103–4.

35. "A Negro Appointee," *Atlanta Constitution*, August 6, 1889, 8; *Official Register* (1889), 2:819; R. L. Polk and Company, *Atlanta City Directory for 1889*, 824, digital image s.v. "Wilson N. Sturges"; R. L. Polk and Company, *Atlanta City Directory for 1889*, 896, digital image s.v. "S.P. Richards and Son," Ancestry.com.

36. "A Negro Appointee," *Atlanta Constitution*, August 6, 1889, 8; Harold E. Davis, *Henry Grady's New South*, 153–55.

37. "That Negro Appointee," *Atlanta Constitution*, August 7, 1889, 5.

38. Maclachlan, "Women's Work," 8, 30–40, 271–276, 286–289; "Our Girls—Found in Factory and Shop," *Atlanta Daily Constitution*, June 16, 1881, 1.

39. Hickey, *Hope and Danger*, 15–19, 25–29.

40. "General Lewis's Bond," *Atlanta Constitution*, August 9, 1889, 4.

41. "General Lewis and the Postoffice [sic]," *Atlanta Constitution*, August 7, 1889, 4.

42. "An Ebony-Hued Clerk," *Savannah Morning News*, August 6, 1889, 2; "That Negro Appointee," *Henry County Weekly* (Hampton, GA), August 9, 1889, 2; "A Colored Appointee," *Fayetteville (GA) News*, August 9, 1889, 3.

43. "Postmaster Lewis's Insult," *Atlanta Constitution*, August 7, 1889, 4.

44. "A Negro Appointee," *Atlanta Constitution*, August 6, 1889, 4.

45. "Two More Appointments Were Made by Postmaster Lewis Yesterday," *Atlanta Constitution*, August 8, 1889, 4.

46. "A Negro Appointee," *Atlanta Constitution*, August 6, 1889, 4; "That Negro Appointee," *Atlanta Constitution*, August 7, 1889, 5.

47. "Postmaster Lewis's Insult," 5.

48. "General Lewis's Bond," 4.

49. "Mr. Lyon Denies," *Athens Weekly Banner*, August 20, 1889, 5.

50. "Talks and Talkers," *Atlanta Constitution*, August 10, 1885, 9; "Two More Appointments," 4.

51. "Burned in Effigy," *Atlanta Constitution*, August 9, 1889, 5.

52. "Postmaster Lewis and Buck Hung in Effigy," *Athens Weekly Banner*, August 14, 1889, 1; "Burned in Effigy," 5; "Some Street Scenes—Which Created a Good Deal of Excitement," *Atlanta Constitution*, August 13, 1889, 5. Northern papers, taking notice of the controversy, roundly criticized White Atlantans as "ridiculous" and foolish and were joined by *Constitution* editor Henry W. Grady, who called the protests "especially unwise, impolitic and unnecessary," even as he shared their sentiments about the alleged insult done to Mary Lyon. See "The Thursday Night Demonstration," *Atlanta Constitution*, August 11, 1889, 14.

53. "Thursday Night Demonstration," 14; "Who Loves the Nigger?," *Atlanta Constitution*, August 11, 1889, 8; "Latest Telegraphic News—Buck and Lewis Hung in Effigy by the Outraged Citizens of Atlanta" and "A Whole City Insulted," *Daily Times Enterprise* (Thomasville, GA), August 10, 1889, 2.

54. "That Negro Appointee," *Atlanta Constitution*, August 7, 1889, 5.

55. "He Was Insulted," *Athens Weekly Banner*, August 13, 1889, 2.

56. "Two More Appointments," 4.

57. "The Atlanta Postoffice [sic] Still at White Heat," *Athens Weekly Banner*, August 14, 1889, 1.

58. "General Lewis and the Club," *Atlanta Constitution*, September 15, 1889, 20.

59. "What Was the Motive," *Savannah Tribune*, August 31, 1889, 1.

60. "Southern Chivalry," *Washington (DC) Bee*, August 24, 1889, 2.

61. "General Lewis and the Club," 20.

62. *Atlanta City Directory for 1895* (Washington, DC: Franklin Printing), 1022, digital image s.v. "Charles C. Penny," Ancestry.com.

63. "Negro Clerks and Carriers Being Appointed to Positions in the Atlanta Postoffice [sic]," *Atlanta Constitution*, November 19, 1889, 7; "Negro Clerks and Carriers," *Henry County Weekly* (Hampton, GA), November 22, 1889, 2.

64. "One of Lewis's Angels," *Atlanta Constitution*, March 19, 1890, 3; "A Negro Carrier Arrested," *Savannah Morning News*, March 19, 1890, 2; "Martin Rearrested," *Atlanta Constitution*, April 4, 1890, 2.

65. "One of Lewis's Angels," 3.

66. "One of Lewis's Angels," 3.

67. "One of Buck's Pets," *Columbus (GA) Enquirer-Sun*, March 19, 1890, 1; *Gwinnett Herald* (Lawrenceville, GA), April 8, 1890, 2.

68. "The Revenue Service in Georgia," *Athens Weekly Banner*, March 18, 1890, 2.

69. R. L. Polk and Company, *Atlanta City Directory for 1889*, 723, digital image s.v. "Daniel Martin," Ancestry.com; H. G. Saunders, *Atlanta City Directory for 1890*, 1178, digital image s.v. "Christopher C. Wimbish," Ancestry.com.

70. "Martin Rearrested," 2; "Jailed in Default of a Bond," *Savannah Morning News*, April 5, 1890, 2; "The Negro Postal Clerk," *Atlanta Constitution*, April 5, 1890, 7.

71. "An Educated Young Negro," *Atlanta Constitution*, May 21, 1891, 7.

72. "Educated Young Negro," 7; "Not a Graduate," *Atlanta Constitution*, May 22, 1891, 7.

73. Saunders, *Atlanta City Directory for 1893*, 926, digital image s.v. "Nelson Martin," Ancestry.com.

74. "He Robbed the Mails—Cunning Theft of a Young Negro Mail Carrier," *Atlanta Constitution*, April 20, 1892, 2.

75. "Robbed the Mails," *Atlanta Constitution*, July 3, 1892, 17.

76. 1880 United States Census, Stone Mountain, DeKalb, Georgia, digital image s.v. "Eugene Martin," Ancestry.com; R. L. Polk and Company, *Atlanta City Directory for 1889*, 1013, 723, digital image s.v. "Eugene Martin," Ancestry.com; Saunders, *Atlanta City Directory for 1890*, 872, digital image s.v. "Eugene Martin," Ancestry.com; H. G. Saunders, *Atlanta City Directory for 1891*, 808, digital image s.v. "Eugene Martin," Ancestry.com.

77. "Martin Arrested," *Atlanta Constitution*, December 14, 1893, 10; "Georgia and Florida," *Savannah Morning News*, December 15, 1893, 6.

78. "Martin Arrested."

79. "Martin Released," *Atlanta Constitution*, December 15, 1893, 9.

80. "Martin Endorsed," Atlanta Constitution, December 16, 1893, 5.

81. "Martin Released."

82. "Martin Released."

83. "Martin Released."

84. "Martin Endorsed"; *Postal Record* 19, no. 1 (January 1906): 42.

85. "Newsy Notes," *Atlanta Constitution*, March 3, 1895, 14; "Negro Mail Carrier Arrested," *Atlanta Constitution*, December 5, 1896, 2; "Tired of Living," *Atlanta Constitution*, December 9, 1894, 14; "Newsy Notes," *Atlanta Constitution*, March 2, 1895, 3; "Another Indictment," *Atlanta Constitution*, March 14, 1895, 3; "Not Caught Twice," *Atlanta Constitution*, April 18, 1895, 1; "Colonel John L. Cooper Wins a Legal Victory," December 16, 1897, 3; untitled article, *Savannah Morning News*, December 9, 1894, 5; "In the United States Court," *Savannah Morning News*, May 10, 1893, 8; "Another One Gone," *Atlanta Constitution*, February 3, 1893, 8; "Is He Guilty?," *Athens Weekly Banner*, January 31, 1893, 4; "He Is in Trouble," *Athens Weekly Banner*, March 21, 1893, 1.

86. "Arrest of a Negro Mail Carrier," *Columbus (GA) Enquirer-Sun*, March 13, 1890, 1.

87. "Rural Delivery Carriers for Bibb," *Atlanta Constitution*, April 24, 1899, 3.

88. "Postmaster Notified," *Atlanta Constitution*, April 24, 1899, 3.

89. "Rural Delivery for Bibb County," *Atlanta Constitution*, March 29, 1899, 3; "Hertz Will Hold His Office," *Savannah Morning News*, April 23, 1899, 6; "Crushed by

Machinery—the Famous Lindsay Case—Will Have No Negro Carriers," *Savannah Morning News*, April 30, 1899, 7.

90. Litwack, *Trouble in Mind*, 280; Wells-Barnett, *Lynch Law in Georgia*, 9–10.

91. "No Rural Delivery for Bibb County," *Atlanta Constitution*, June 14, 1899, 3.

92. Cater, "To Pick Up Again."

93. "Bostonians Given Facts," *Savannah Morning News*, May 23, 1899, 7.

94. "Ex-Governor Northen Meets Colored Bishop in Debate," *Atlanta Constitution*, May 23, 1899, 3–4; "Bostonians Given Facts," 1, 7.

95. Dowd-Hall, *Revolt against Chivalry*, xx, 150; "Ex-Governor Northen," 3; "Deep Interest in Northen's Address," *Atlanta Constitution*, May 24, 1899, 1; "Northen and Arnett," *Baltimore Sun*, May 24, 1899, 2; "The Negro in the South," *New York Times*, May 23, 1899, 8; "The Government Arraigned," *Walker County Messenger* (LaFayette, GA), June 1, 1899, 7; "The Great Georgian's Great Speech," *Austin American Statesman*, May 28, 1899, 10; "Boston Is Impressed," *Baltimore Sun*, May 24, 1899, 2; "Boston Audience Is Highly Pleased," *Atlanta Constitution*, June 19, 1899, 5; "Ex-Governor Northen on Lynching," *Chicago Tribune*, May 23, 1899, 5; "Ex-Governor Northen on Lynching," *New York Times*, May 24, 1899, 6; "Ex-Governor Northen's Speech," *Atlanta Constitution*, May 27, 1899, 4; "White Man's View," *Baltimore Sun*, May 23, 1899, 1.

96. "Macon Won't Have a Rural Free Delivery," *Atlanta Constitution*, July 13, 1899, 2; "No Rural Delivery for Bibb County," *Atlanta Constitution*, July 14, 1899, 3; "Bartlett's Rural Delivery Scheme," *Savannah Morning News*, July 14, 1899, 4; "War Trophies for Atlanta—No Rural Delivery," *Savannah Morning News*, July 13, 1899, 1.

97. "No Rural Delivery for Bibb County," 3.

98. "War Trophies for Atlanta," 1.

99. "Where the Responsibility Lies," *Atlanta Constitution*, May 18, 1903, 6; "National Affairs," *Union Recorder* (Milledgeville, GA), May 19, 1903, 6; "That Tenn Incident," *Waynesboro (GA) True Citizen*, May 16, 1903, 1.

100. "Fears Negro Postman," *Baltimore Sun*, Mary 12, 1903, 2; "Rumors vs. Facts," *Baltimore Sun*, Mary 27, 1903, 4; "No Negroes Are Wanted as Carriers," *Atlanta Constitution*, May 8, 1903, 1; "Masked Men Threaten Negro Mail Carrier," *New York Times*, May 8, 1903, 1; "Race Troubles End Mail Route," *Chicago Tribune*, May 8, 1903, 1.

101. "News from the Capitol," *Tammany Times* (New York, NY), May 16, 1903, 2.

102. "Democrats Must Give Ticket Big Majority," *Atlanta Constitution*, November 6, 1904, B2.

103. "Apoligies [sic] Won't Pay Fines," *Atlanta Constitution*, August 10, 1904, 7.

104. "Trial Waived by Dr. Ripley—Well Known Physician Accused of Assaulting Mail Carrier in Uniform," *Atlanta Constitution*, May 19, 1906, 10.

105. "Did Not Indict Dr. E. C. Ripley," *Atlanta Constitution*, June 5, 1906, 11; "No Bill Was Found against Dr. Ripley," *Atlanta Georgian*, June 5, 1906, 3; "Uniform Cut No Figure," *Dade County Sentinel* (Trenton, GA), June 8, 1906, 1; "Uniform Was Non-protective," *Clayton (GA) Tribune*, June 14, 1906, 1. A grand jury convening the following month apparently concurred, refusing to bring charges against Ripley, who was also cleared by a federal jury in October 1908. See "Federal Jury Clears Ripley," *Atlanta Constitution*, October 28, 1908, 10.

106. "Trolley Car Scene of Lively Scrimmage," *Atlanta Georgian*, July 21, 1906, 2.

107. "Negro Fined Heavily," *Atlanta Constitution*, March 9, 1909, 3; "Tampering with Mail: Negro Is Charged," *Atlanta Georgian*, August 1, 1906, 9; "The Real Truth Obscured," *Macon (GA) Telegraph*, May 17, 1907, 4; "Negro Mail Carrier Held," *Atlanta Georgian and News*, December 21, 1908, 5; "Carrier Force Is Now Completely Composed of Blacks," *Americus (GA) Times-Recorder*, February 8, 1908, 1; "Letter from 'a Friend,'" *Watson's Weekly Jeffersonian* (Atlanta), August 7, 1907, 7.

108. "Edwards' Refusal to See Delegation of Negro Carriers Excites Indignation in Savannah," *Augusta Herald*, May 20, 1907, 1; "Edwards Replies to Criticisms," *Waynesboro (GA) True Citizen*, June 1, 1907, 2; "Negro Letter Carrier Assaulted at Savannah," *Atlanta Georgian*, July 27, 1907, 3.

109. "Letter from 'A Friend,'" 7.

110. "In Uncle Sam's Service," *Augusta Herald*, November 18, 1909, 6; R. L. Ballantine, "More Light on the Inside Workings of the Augusta Post Office," *Augusta Herald*, November 30, 1909, 6.

111. "Letter Carrying in Uncle Sam's Service," *Augusta Herald*, November 30, 1909, 6.

112. Bruce, *Plantation Negro as Freeman*; Macon, *Uncle Gabe Tucker*, 41–42; Joel Chandler Harris, *Uncle Remus*, 262–65.

Chapter Three

1. The term "Bexareño" has been used by historians of the Texas-Mexico borderlands to identify Spanish Mexican settlers residing in the presidio San Antonio de Béxar, which would later become the city of San Antonio in Bexar County, Texas. See Ramos, *Beyond the Alamo*, 6–8; de la Teja, *Faces of Béxar*; and de la Teja and Wheat, "Béxar."

2. "Bloody Tragedy," *San Antonio Light*, March 12, 1884, 1; "The Thompson-Fisher Tragedy," *San Antonio Daily Express*, March 14, 1884, 3.

3. "Assassins," *San Antonio Light*, March 14, 1884, 1; "Sensational Rumors," *San Antonio Daily Express*, March 14, 1884, 4.

4. "Transferred to the County Jail," *San Antonio Light*, March 15, 1884, 1; "From San Antonio—Mexicans Released on Bond," *Galveston Daily News*, March 18, 1884, 4.

5. Gómez, *Manifest Destinies*, 12–13.

6. See Ramos, *Beyond the Alamo*; and Valerio-Jiménez, *River of Hope*.

7. De León, *Tejano Community*, 29–49; Stewart and De León, *Not Room Enough*, 41–44.

8. Carrigan and Webb, *Forgotten Dead*, 51–56. See also De León, *They Called Them Greasers*.

9. Ramsdell, *Reconstruction in Texas*, 371–72; *San Antonio Police Department Illustrated*, 27; Perrin, "Crime and Order."

10. Stewart and De León, *Not Room Enough*, 9.

11. See Alonzo, *Tejano Legacy*; De León, *Tejano Community*; Morales, "Tejano-Anglo Alliance"; Mendoza, "'For Our Own'"; and Tijerina, "Foreigners."

12. Stewart and De León, *Not Room Enough*, 37; Ramos, *Beyond the Alamo*, 244–47; Thompson, *Tejanos in Gray*, xvi–xx.

13. Baum and Miller, "Ethnic Conflict," 63–64; Johnson, "Frugal and Sparing," 35–36; Gibson, "Population of the 100 Largest."

14. US Census Office, *Report on the Population*, 592–95; Johnson, *In the Loop*, 121.

15. Baum and Miller, "Ethnic Conflict," 72; Barr, "Occupational and Geographic Mobility."

16. See Land and Thomas, *Historical and Descriptive Review*; De León, *Tejano Community*, 96–98; Martinez-Catsam, "'Los Precios Mas Baratos,'" 94; and Dewey, *Pesos and Dollars*.

17. Pilcher, "Who Chased Out?," 181–84.

18. Barr, "Occupational and Geographic Mobility," 396–403; Stewart and De León, *Not Room Enough*, 37; Kenneth Mason, *African Americans*, 51–52, 56–59.

19. David J. Weber, *Foreigners*, 145–46, 272n21; McDonald, *José Antonio Navarro*, 221–22; Matovina, "Between Two Worlds."

20. De León, *Tejano Community*, 89–90; Knight, "Cart War"; Ramos, *Beyond the Alamo*, 238–44.

21. "The People of Goliad and the Cart War Again," *Southern Intelligencer*, January 6, 1858, 3; Stewart and De León, *Not Room Enough*, 25; Ramos, *Beyond the Alamo*, 238–39.

22. Winkler, *Journal of the Secession Convention*, 122, 401–2.

23. Kenneth Mason, *African Americans*, 35–38.

24. Cantrell, "'Our Very Pronounced Theory.'"

25. Ramos, *Beyond the Alamo*, 216–22; De León, *Tejano Community*, 101–4; Stewart and De León, *Not Room Enough*, 44.

26. Perrin, "Crime and Order," 84–85.

27. Department of the Interior, Census Office, *Report on the Social Statistics*, 132.

28. Morrison and Fourmy, *General Directory* (1885), 47; US Bureau of the Census, *Statistics of Cities* (1905), 68; US Bureau of the Census, *Statistics of Cities* (1907), 320; US Bureau of the Census, *Statistics of Cities* (1909), 390.

29. Waller, "Callaghan Machine," 110; City of San Antonio, Texas, *Annual Message of Marshall Hicks*, 39–40.

30. US Bureau of the Census, *Statistics of Cities* (1906), 75; US Bureau of the Census, *Statistics of Cities* (1908), 138.

31. Texas Publishing, *Directory of the City*, 94, Ancestry.com; City Council of San Antonio, *Annual Message of Bryan Callaghan*, 44.

32. Go, "Imperial Origins," 1222–23.

33. De León, *Tejano Community*, 103–4. I arrived at this figure using searches for the keywords "police," "policeman," and "detective" in the following city directories digitized on Ancestry.com: Mooney and Morrison, *Directory*; Morrison and Fourmy, *General Directory* (1879, 1881, 1883, 1885, 1887); Johnson and Chapman, *General Directory*; Appler, *General Directory* (1893, 1895, 1897, 1899, 1901); Appler, *General Directory and Blue Book* (1903, 1905, 1907, 1908, 1909); Texas Publishing, *Directory of the City*.

34. See Baum and Miller, "Ethnic Conflict," 72–73, 79–80; Waller, "Callaghan Machine"; and Edelen, "Bryan Callaghan II."

35. Waller, "Callaghan Machine," 66; Baum and Miller, "Ethnic Conflict," 64–66.

36. Kenneth Mason, *African Americans*, 105–6; Waller, "Callaghan Machine," 112–14.

37. "Shot by a Policeman," *San Antonio Light*, May 29, 1884, 1; "The Verdict," *San Antonio Light*, May 30, 1884, 1; 1870 United States Census, San Antonio, Bexar, Texas,

digital image s.vv. "Henry Smith" and "David Reed," Ancestry.com; Texas Publishing, *Directory of the City*, 94, Ancestry.com.

38. Appler, *General Directory and Blue Book* (1905); Texas Publishing, *Directory of the City*, 94.

39. 1870 United States Census, Karnes, Texas, digital image s.v. "Trinidad Coy," Ancestry.com; 1860 United States Census, Karnes, Texas, digital image s.v. "Trinidad Coy," Ancestry.com.

40. 1860 United States Census, San Antonio, Bexar, Texas, digital image s.v. "Maximo Cadena," Ancestry.com; 1860 United States Census, Bexar, Texas, digital image s.v. "Jose Maria Chavez," Ancestry.com. By 1870, Chavez's father, Jose Maria, is listed in the 1870 census as having assets valued at $6,500. See 1870 United States Census, Bexar, Texas, digital image s.v. "J M Chavez," Ancestry.com.

41. 1860 United States Census, San Antonio, Bexar, Texas, digital image s.v. "Anavato Martinez," Ancestry.com; 1870 United States Census, San Antonio, Bexar, Texas, digital image s.v. "Anavato Martinez," Ancestry.com.

42. A keyword search of city directories and US Census records using "police" or "policeman" indicates that approximately six African American men served as police officers between 1880 and 1900. These appointments resulted from Reconstruction-era Black voters' support of Mayor James French, who broke with state Republicans in his willingness to protect Black interests. See Kenneth Mason, *African Americans*, 95–106.

43. Perrin, "Crime and Order," 95–97; City Council of San Antonio, *Annual Message of Bryan Callaghan*, 44; City of San Antonio, Texas, *Annual Message of Marshall Hicks*, 103–4, 199; Theodore Harris, *Charter and Ordinances*, 302.

44. Morrison and Fourmy, *General Directory* (1883), 133; Appler, *General Directory* (1897), 216; Appler, *General Directory* (1893), 241.

45. Morrison and Fourmy, *General Directory* (1887), 368, digital image s.v. "Modesto Torres," Ancestry.com; Appler, *General Directory* (1893), 615, digital image s.v. "Modesto Torres," Ancestry.com; Appler, *General Directory* (1897), 559, digital image s.v. "Modesto Torres," Ancestry.com; Appler, *General Directory* (1901), 524, digital image s.v. "Modesto Torres," Ancestry.com; 1900 United States Census, San Antonio, Bexar, Texas, digital image s.v. "Modesto Torres," Ancestry.com.

46. This included José Cassiano, who held the position of "Market Master" at a salary of seventy-five dollars per month; Louis A. Morín, who received fifty dollars per month as a clerk for the city engineer; and T. Rodriguez, who received sixty dollars per month as the city assessor's clerk. See City of San Antonio, Texas, *Annual Message of Marshall Hicks*, 197–98.

47. Perrin, "Crime and Order," 93–95.

48. De León, *Tejano Community*, 103; Morrison and Fourmy, *General Directory* (1881), 97, digital image s.v. "Juan E. Barrera," Ancestry.com; Appler, *General Directory* (1893), 241, digital image s.v. "Juan E. Barrera," Ancestry.com.

49. 1910 United States Census, San Antonio, Bexar, Texas, digital image s.v. "Celedonio Cadena," Ancestry.com; 1900 United States Census, San Antonio, Bexar, Texas, digital image s.v. "Antonio Herrera," Ancestry.com; 1910 United States Census, San Antonio, Bexar, Texas, digital image s.v. "Antonio Herrera," Ancestry.com; *San Antonio*

Police Department Illustrated, 43; "Elect Chairman Pro Tem for the Commissioners," *San Antonio Daily Express*, December 13, 1908, 14.

50. Johnson and Chapman, *General Directory*, 138, digital image s.v. "Jacob S. Coy," Ancestry.com.

51. 1900 United States Census, San Antonio, Bexar, Texas, digital image s.v. "Luz Robalín," Ancestry.com; Texas Publishing, *Directory of the City*, 903, digital image s.v. "Luz Robalín," Ancestry.com.

52. Appler, *Directory of the City of San Antonio, 1908*, 370, digital image s.v. "Norberto Galan," Ancestry.com.

53. Appler, *Directory for the City of San Antonio, 1908*, 346, digital image s.v. "Luciano Espinoza," Ancestry.com.

54. "Recorder's Court Notes," *San Antonio Light*, July 31, 1883, 2; "Rays of Light," *San Antonio Daily Light*, December 2, 1884, 4; "Will Throw Hot Water," *San Antonio Light*, January 19, 1885, 1; "That Nigger Shooter," *San Antonio Light*, March 6, 1885, 1.

55. "Our City Guardians—the Police Department of San Antonio and Its Record for 1887," *San Antonio Express*, February 20, 1888, 3; "Local Affairs," *San Antonio Daily Express*, September 18, 1873, 3.

56. Perrin, "Crime and Order," 78–79, 302–5; Kenneth Mason, *African Americans*, 169–72.

57. Perrin, "Crime and Order," 76–80.

58. Kenneth Mason, *African Americans*, 170–71; Perrin, "Crime and Order," 72–75; untitled article, *San Antonio Daily Herald*, April 20, 1875, 2.

59. Carrigan and Webb, *Forgotten Dead*; De León, *They Called Them Greasers*, 37, 45–46, 69; Kitch, *Specter of Sex*, 99–100; Pierce, *Making the White Man's West*, 216–20; Varon, *Before Chicano*, 61–65. For examples of the popularity of discussions of Mexican criminality in Anglo American newspapers, see Arnoldo De León's essential resource *Apuntes Tejanos*.

60. Perrin, "Crime and Order," 352–55; "The Poor in Our Midst," *San Antonio Express*, December 1, 1876, 4; Ana Luisa R. Martinez, "Voice of the People," 42–43; Everett, *San Antonio*, 32–43; Pilcher, "Who Chased Out?," 177.

61. Mickle, "Wanderings in West Texas" (July 27, 1879), 4; Mickle, "Wanderings in West Texas" (August 5, 1879), 4.

62. Mickle, "Wanderings in West Texas" (July 27, 1879), 4.

63. "No Mexicans Need Apply," *San Antonio Express*, August 7, 1883, 1.

64. "Indignant Mexicans," *San Antonio Express*, August 8, 1883, 1; "Kerbel vs. Mexicans," *San Antonio Express*, August 8, 1883, 1.

65. "The Mexican Indignation Meeting," *San Antonio Express*, August 9, 1883, 4; "Outraged," *San Antonio Light*, August 9, 1883, 1.

66. "Mexican Indignation Meeting," 4; "San Pedro Park: A Question of Social Rights for Mexicans," *Fort Worth Daily Gazette*, August 19, 1883, 8.

67. "Die Aufregung bei den Mexikanern" (The excitement among the Mexicans), *Freie Press für Texas* (San Antonio), August 9, 1883, 4 (Google Translate trans., unless otherwise noted); "Krieg zwischen Deutschland und Mexiko" (War between Germany and Mexico), *Der Deustche Correspondent* (Baltimore), August 17, 1883, 1; "Greasers Excited," *Maysville (KY) Evening Bulletin*, August 13, 1883, 1; "An Insult to Mexican

Citizens," *New Orleans Daily Picayune*, August 9, 1883, 1; "The Lessee of a San Antonio Park Having Ejected from His Premises Several Disorderly Mexicans, the Entire Mexican Populace Has Become Enraged," *New Orleans Daily Picayune*, August 11, 1883, 1. Foreign language translations by author.

68. Walton, *Life and Adventures*, 208.

69. "Bloody Tragedy," *San Antonio Light*, March 12, 1884, 1.

70. "Bloody Tragedy," 1; "The Thompson-Fisher Tragedy," *San Antonio Daily Express*, March 14, 1884, 3.

71. Mickle, "Wanderings in West Texas" (July 27, 1879), 4.

72. *San Antonio Police Department Illustrated*, 27.

73. *San Antonio Police Department Illustrated*, 17.

74. "Directory of Societies," *San Antonio Light*, August 27, 1885, 3; Santleben and Affleck, *Texas Pioneer*, 319–20.

75. Barnes, *Combats and Conquests*, 143. Barnes wrote that Cardenas was a senior captain in Sibley's Brigade, a Confederate army cavalry unit organized in San Antonio that included several prominent Anglo Americans. See also Nelson, *Three-Cornered War*.

76. Editorial, *San Antonio Herald*, February 28, 1868, 2; "Announcements," *San Antonio Herald*, August 11, 1868, 3.

77. "A Devil Who Wants Burning at the Stake," *Galveston Daily News*, August 23, 1881, 1; "A Fiend's Deed," *San Antonio Express*, August 23, 1881, 3; "Angriff auf ein Junges Mädchen" (Attack on a young girl), *Der Freie Press für Texas*, August 27, 1881, 4.

78. "Fiend's Deed," 3.

79. "Fiendish Crime," *San Antonio Daily Express*, October 22, 1884, 3; "A Brutal Black," *Austin Daily Statesman*, October 23, 1884, 4; "A Negro Fiend," *Galveston Daily News*, October 22, 1884, 1; "Loud for Lynching," *Dallas Weekly Herald*, October 23, 1884, 1; "A Brutal Outrage," *San Antonio Light*, October 22, 1884, 1.

80. "Fiendish Crime," 3; "Negro Fiend," 1.

81. "A Big Haul by the Police," *San Antonio Express*, October 10, 1883, 4; "A Big Haul by the Police," *San Antonio Light*, October 10, 1883, 1; "A Big Haul by the Police," *Galveston Daily News*, October 11, 1883, 1.

82. "A Big Haul by the Police," *San Antonio Express*, October 10, 1883, 4.

83. "Killed by an Officer," *San Antonio Express*, April 17, 1888, 5; "Shot by an Officer," *Galveston Daily News*, April 15, 1888, 1; "Killed," *San Antonio Daily Light*, April 15, 1888, 4.

84. Ana Luisa R. Martinez, "Voice of the People," 175–77.

85. Martinez, 88–89, 161–63; Walraven, "Ambivalent Americans," 192–93.

86. "Letter to the Editor," *El Regidor* (Austin, TX), January 18, 1890, 4.

87. "La policía" (Police), *El Regidor*, April 12, 1890, 4 (Author's translation).

88. "Shot Him for a Robber," *San Antonio Daily Express*, October 28, 1893, 3; "Killed in the Road," *San Antonio Daily Light*, October 28, 1893, 8; "Dr. Fanning erschießt einen Mexikaner" (Dr. Fanning Shoots a Mexican), *Freie Presse für Texas*, October 28, 1893, 4.

89. "Shot Him for a Robber," 3.

90. "Dr. Fanning Out on Bail," *San Antonio Daily Express*, October 29, 1893, 6; "Condemned Dr. Fanning," *San Antonio Daily Light*, October 30, 1893, 4; "Allerlei" (Various), *Freie Presse für Texas*, October 30, 1893, 4.

91. "A Mexican Mass Meeting," *Galveston Daily News*, October 29, 1893, 3.

92. "Dr. Fanning Out on Bail," 6; "Asesinato de Juan Salas" (Murder of Juan Salas), *El Regidor*, November 4, 1893, 1.

93. "The Salas Inquest," *San Antonio Daily Light*, November 1, 1893, 8.

94. "Asesinato de Juan Salas," 1.

95. "Dr. Fanning on Trial Today," *San Antonio Daily Light*, April 3, 1894, 5; "Fanning Found Not Guilty," *San Antonio Daily Express*, April 4, 1894, 5; "Dr. Frank Fanning Acquitted for Killing Juan Salas," *San Antonio Daily Light*, April 4, 1894, 7; "Frank Fanning Acquitted," *Galveston Daily News*, April 4, 1894, 4; "Allerlei" (Various), *Freie Press für Texas*, April 4, 1894, 4.

96. "Asesinato de Juan Salas," 1.

97. McEachin, "Our Mexican Citizens," 15.

98. Flores, "Our Mexican Citizens," 15.

99. De León, *In Re Ricardo Rodriguez*, 1–16; Gross, "Texas Mexicans"; Boyle, *Federal Reporter*, 347.

100. "Grand Jury Report," *San Antonio Daily Express*, September 27, 1887, 5; untitled article, *Galveston Daily News*, October 1, 1887, 4; "Duties of Officers," *Brenham (TX) Daily Banner*, September 28, 1887, 2.

101. "Duties of Officers," 2.

102. "An Outrage on a Citizen," *San Antonio Express*, July 23, 1886, 8.

103. "City News," *San Antonio Daily Express*, May 18, 1887, 3.

104. "Women Warriors," *San Antonio Express*, June 6, 1887, 3; "Almost a Tragedy," *Fort Worth Daily Gazette*, June 15, 1887, 3; "Almost a Tragedy," *Austin Weekly Statesman*, June 16, 1887, 1.

105. "The Constable Indicted," *San Antonio Express*, November 13, 1891, 5; "Demanda" (Demand), *El Regidor*, February 28, 1891, 4 (Author's translation); untitled article, *San Antonio Daily Express*, February 25, 1891, 8; untitled article, *San Antonio Daily Light*, February 25, 1891, 8.

106. "Constable Indicted," 5.

107. "Martinez Has to Go," *San Antonio Express*, November 25, 1891, 6.

108. "Police Heads Will Fall," *San Antonio Express*, February 24, 1901, 8.

109. City of San Antonio, *Annual Message of Marshall Hicks*, 40; "City Police Appointments," *San Antonio Daily Express*, March 12, 1901, 8.

110. "Mr. William Aubrey Gratuitously Insults the Mexicans" (Mr. William Aubrey, insulta a los mexicanos gratuitamente), *El Regidor*, April 27, 1905, 1 (Author's translation). Although Aubrey's remarks do not appear to have been reported in any of the city's Anglo papers, coverage and editorials of the contest between the Democrats and the People's Party made reference to occasional calls to bigotry during the campaign. See "Out in the Opening," *San Antonio Daily Light*, April 23, 1905, 5; "800 Enthusiasts Cheer Democrats and Platform," *San Antonio Gazette*, April 21, 1905, 1.

111. "Is This Economy?," *San Antonio Gazette*, November 4, 1905, 4; "Caught on the Curb" and "The Deadly Paralell [sic]," *San Antonio Gazette*, November 11, 1905, 10; "How Do You Stand?," *San Antonio Gazette*, November 11, 1905, 8; "Wants San Antonio's Czar to Take Notice," *San Antonio Gazette*, November 11, 1905, 8; "Mr. Voter, Please Read," *San Antonio Gazette*, November 11, 1905, 6.

112. "Three Matters before Commission Are Decided," *San Antonio Express*, December 28, 1906, 12; "Charge of Affray," *San Antonio Express*, February 3, 1907, 17; "City Detective Resigns," *San Antonio Express*, February 20, 1907, 14; "Detective Is Fined," *San Antonio Express*, February 7, 1907, 10.

113. "Por cuestión política" (For a Political Question), *El Regidor*, February 7, 1907, 3 (Author's translation); "Policeman Fires Shots in Attempt to Make Arrest," *San Antonio Daily Express*, February 2, 1907, 14; "Two Policemen Are Indicted by Grand Jury," *San Antonio Daily Express*, February 14, 1907, 5.

114. "Flores Case Dismissed," *San Antonio Daily Express*, February 10, 1907, 5; "Jose [sic] Quintana Is Fined in County Court," *San Antonio Daily Express*, March 7, 1907, 10; "Policía multado" (Policeman fined), *El Regidor*, March 14, 1907, 2 (Author's translation).

115. "De interes para los votantes" (Of interest to voters), *El Regidor*, May 9, 1907, 1.

116. "De interes para los votantes," 1.

117. Fox and Guglielmo, "Defining America's Racial Boundaries," 352.

118. Montejano, *Anglos and Mexicans*, 82–84; San Miguel, "From a Dual"; Martinez-Catsam, "Los Precios Mas Baratos."

119. Monica Muñoz Martinez, *Injustice Never Leaves You*, 4; Orozco, *Agent of Change*, 9.

Chapter Four

1. "No Chinese in the Customs Service," *San Francisco Chronicle*, November 7, 1896, 13.

2. "Collector Wise Not Consulted," *San Francisco Chronicle*, December 19, 1896, 9.

3. "North Gives Chinese a Job," *San Francisco Chronicle*, April 4, 1905, 16.

4. Shah, *Contagious Divides*, 101; Lui, *Chinatown Trunk Mystery*, 17–51; Ling, *Chinese Chicago*, 30–33, 46–50.

5. Wong, "Cultural Defenders and Brokers"; Chan, "Race, Ethnic Culture"; Ngai, *Lucky Ones*.

6. Lui, *Chinatown Trunk Mystery*, 137.

7. Ngai, "'Slight Knowledge,'" 11.

8. Lee, *At America's Gates*, 141.

9. Walker, "Economic Opportunity," 260.

10. Haydu, *Citizen Employers*, 67.

11. Yong Chen, *Chinese San Francisco*, 55–56.

12. Sandmeyer, *Anti-Chinese Movement*, 47–56; Saxton, *Indispensable Enemy*, 104–12.

13. California State Senate, Special Committee on Chinese Immigration, *Chinese Immigration*; US Congress, *Appendix to the Congressional Record*, 40–45; Salyer, *Laws as Harsh as Tigers*, 9–10; Catherine Lee, "Where the Danger Lies."

14. Peffer, *If They Don't Bring*.

15. McClain, *In Search of Equality*, 43–44; Saxton, *Indispensable Enemy*, 261; Lee, *At America's Gates*, 55–57, 188–89.

16. Yong Chen, *Chinese San Francisco*, 46–47; Shah, *Contagious Divides*, 21; Daniels, *Pioneer Urbanites*, 13.

17. See Anderson, "Idea of Chinatown"; Shah, *Contagious Divides*.

18. Yong Chen, *Chinese San Francisco*, 50, 58–59; Farwell, *Chinese at Home*, 136.

19. Farwell, *Chinese at Home*, 203–4; "A New Danger," *San Francisco Chronicle*, July 22, 1878, 2.

20. Farwell, *Chinese at Home*, 12–13.

21. Shah, *Contagious Divides*, 101–2; Riis, *How the Other Half*, 92–103; Lui, *Chinatown Trunk Mystery*, 17–20.

22. Farwell, *Chinese at Home*, 15–16; Shah, *Contagious Divides*, 95–96.

23. Decker, *Fortunes and Failures*, 96–97; Walker, "Economic Opportunity," 260.

24. Walker, "Economic Opportunity," 262; Haydu, *Citizen Employers*, 63; Burchell, *San Francisco Irish*.

25. Mei, "Socioeconomic Developments," 381–82; Marcus and Chen, "Inside and outside Chinatown," 369–71; Ngai, "History as Law."

26. Mei, "Socioeconomic Developments," 382; Ngai, "'Slight Knowledge,'" 15–17.

27. Wen-Hsien Chen, "Chinese under Both Exclusion," 88–89; Perkins, "Reminiscences," 183–84.

28. Lee, *At America's Gates*, 59; Lehlbach, *Chinese Immigration*, 252–53, 269–71; *Official Register* (1885), 1:148; *Official Register* (1889), 1:39; *Official Register* (1893), 1:63; *Official Register* (1899), 1:62–63; *Official Register* (1901), 1:1153.

29. *Official Register* (1891), 1:47–48; *Official Register* (1895), 1:59.

30. *Official Register* (1897), 1:59–60; *Official Register* (1899), 1:62–63; *Official Register* (1903), 1:1183; Coolidge, *Chinese Immigration*, 313–14.

31. Lee, *At America's Gates*, 76; Coolidge, *Chinese Immigration*, 313–14.

32. *Official Register* (1901), 1:186; *Official Register* (1903), 1:1183; *Official Register* (1905), 1:1094; *Official Register* (1907), 1:63; *Official Register* (1909), 1:76; *Official Register* (1911), 1:74.

33. Ngai, "'Slight Knowledge,'" 20–21; "Notable Californians," *San Francisco Chronicle*, January 16, 1915, 69.

34. Edward L. Park remained at the San Francisco offices and kept a home in the suburb of Berkeley. A successful grocer before joining the Immigration Bureau, he did not return to small business after leaving the Customs Service in 1917, instead becoming a traveling agent for a company selling marble. 1920 United States Census, Berkeley, Alameda, California, digital image s.v. "Edward L. Park," Ancestry.com; Ngai, *Lucky Ones*, 217–18.

35. 1880 United States Census, San Francisco, San Francisco, California, digital image s.v. "Richard Williams," Ancestry.com.

36. "California, U.S., Voter Registers, 1866–1898," digital image s.v. "Richard S. Williams" (1882), 194, Ancestry.com; H. S. Crocker Company, *Crocker-Langley San Francisco Directory* (1891), 1436, digital image s.v. "Richard S. Williams," Ancestry.com.

37. "Wise on the Rack," *San Francisco Chronicle*, April 16, 1894, 12.

38. "Wise on the Rack," 12. *Official Register* (1895), 1:59.

39. H. S. Crocker Company, *Crocker-Langley San Francisco Directory* (1896), 1633, digital image s.v. "Richard S. Williams," Ancestry.com.

40. "Garter Was Angry," *San Francisco Chronicle*, March 11, 1894, 17.

41. "Wise on the Rack," 12; *Official Register* (1895), 1:77.

42. Mei, "Socioeconomic Developments," 381; "How Little Pete Outwitted Wise," *San Francisco Chronicle*, January 4, 1896, 8; "Wong Sam against Williams," *San Francisco Chronicle*, March 17, 1896, 11.

43. "Wise and Foote Confer," *San Francisco Call*, March 28, 1896, 5.

44. "Wong Sam against Williams," 11; "Wise and Foote Confer," 5; Ngai, "'Slight Knowledge,'" 10.

45. "Strange Story of Witness Schwartz," *San Francisco Chronicle*, April 2, 1896, 10.

46. "Strange Story of Witness Schwartz," 10. Wise also denied that Williams had attempted to conceal his purchase of property in San Francisco and nearby Alameda County by listing his stepfather, a French-born window cleaner named Henry Monferran, as the buyer. Monferran's suicide at Golden Gate Park made headlines when, in addition to his connection to Williams, he was found to hold titles to several properties including Williams's Pacific Heights home. See "In Monferran's [sic] Name," *San Francisco Examiner*, April 2, 1896, 8.

47. "Wise Anxious for Moore's Scalp," *San Francisco Chronicle*, March 6, 1896, 10; "Moore Accepts the Challenges," *San Francisco Chronicle*, March 7, 1896, 11; "Investigating Williams," *San Francisco Examiner*, March 21, 1896, 14; "Dick Williams Indicted," *San Francisco Call*, April 3, 1896, 5; "Williams Is Dismissed," *San Francisco Call*, June 24, 1896, 9.

48. "Dick Williams Indicted," 5; "Bay Gleanings," *Sacramento Evening Bee*, April 4, 1896, 2.

49. "Moore Is After Big Game," *San Francisco Chronicle*, August 19, 1896, 9; "No Tale Is Told of Williams' Wealth," *San Francisco Examiner*, August 25, 1896, 16; "Telltale Bank Book Kept Out," *San Francisco Chronicle*, August 25, 1896, 16.

50. "Williams Had Money in Bank," *San Francisco Call*, August 23, 1896, 32.

51. "Wise Comes to Williams' Rescue," *San Francisco Call*, September 1, 1896, 11.

52. "Wise Comes to Williams' Rescue."

53. "Two Charges to Be Dropped," *San Francisco Chronicle*, August 27, 1896, 16.

54. "Moore Is After Big Game," 9.

55. "Williams Guilty of Extortion," *San Francisco Call*, September 4, 1896, 8; "Williams Must Go to San Quentin," *San Francisco Chronicle*, September 23, 1896, 9; "Convicted of Extortion," *Sacramento Evening Bee*, September 3, 1896, 8.

56. "Williams Will Not Confess to Foote," *San Francisco Chronicle*, September 25, 1896, 12.

57. "Williams in San Quentin," *San Francisco Call*, September 26, 1896, 7.

58. "Dick Williams Gets One Year," *San Francisco Call*, May 1, 1898, 32; *Williams v. United States* 168 U.S. 382, Nos. 266, 267 (1897).

59. "Williams Is Dismissed," 9; "Loui [sic] Quong Implicated," *San Francisco Chronicle*, August 22, 1896, 9; "Louie Quong Dismissed," *San Francisco Call*, October 17, 1896, 11.

60. Ngai, *Lucky Ones*, 60–61; Condit, *Chinaman*, 170–80.

61. "And Still They Come," *San Francisco Call*, December 31, 1896, 7; "Dong Sum Pardoned," *San Francisco Chronicle*, December 9, 1896, 7; "One Year for Contempt," *San Francisco Chronicle*, December 10, 1896, 8; "The Missing Witness Returns," *San Francisco Chronicle*, December 4, 1896, 8; "Louie Quong Dismissed," 11; "A Bevy of

Slave Girls—the City of Puebla Brings a Number of Chinese Women," *San Francisco Chronicle*, December 30, 1896, 9; "Wailing Women in Chinatown," *San Francisco Chronicle*, March 23, 1897, 14.

62. "No Chinese in the Customs Service," *San Francisco Chronicle*, November 7, 1896, 13; "Was Told to Obey His Orders," *San Francisco Examiner*, November 29, 1896, 11; "Disobedience of Orders Charged," *San Francisco Chronicle*, November 13, 1896, 9.

63. "No Chinese in the Customs Service," 13.

64. "Interpreter Huff Exonerated," *San Francisco Chronicle*, January 29, 1897, 5; "A Complete Exoneration," *San Francisco Call*, February 21, 1897, 30.

65. "Light on Dark Ways," *San Francisco Chronicle*, November 3, 1898, 9; "Major Moore Ordered to Investigate," *San Francisco Call*, November 4, 1898, 14; "Miss Cameron Had Married Meredith," *San Francisco Call*, November 5, 1898, 12; "Strange Story Told by a Chinese Slave," *San Francisco Call*, November 15, 1898, 4; "Story of a Slave Girl," *San Francisco Chronicle*, November 14, 1898, 10; "Huff Says It Is False," *San Francisco Chronicle*, November 15, 1898, 10; "Dismissal of Meredith Has Been Ordered," *San Francisco Call*, February 25, 1899, 4.

66. "Disobedience of Orders Charged," *San Francisco Chronicle*, November 13, 1896, 9.

67. Ngai, *Lucky Ones*, 76–78, 250n76; Con and Wickberg, *From China to Canada*, 58.

68. Con and Wickberg, *From China to Canada*, 58; Ngai, *Lucky Ones*, 76–78, 250n76.

69. "Collector Wise Not Consulted," *San Francisco Chronicle*, December 19, 1896, 9.

70. "Chinese Females—an Alarmingly Large Number of This Class Have Arrived Recently," *San Francisco Call*, December 30, 1896, 7; "Collector Wise Not Consulted," 9.

71. *Official Register* (1897), 1:59; "Dr. Gardner's Hands Untied at Last," *San Francisco Call*, November 16, 1898, 7; *Official Register* (1899), 1:62.

72. Lee, *At America's Gates*, 54–55; Converse J. Smith and John W. Linck to John P. Jackson, February 24, 1899, 3–4, File 53108/9A, Record Group 85, Records of the Immigration and Naturalization Service, Collector of Chinese Customs Cases, National Archives.

73. John P. Jackson to Secretary of the Treasury, March 30, 1899, 23–24, File 53108/9B, Record Group 85, Records of the Immigration and Naturalization Service, Irregular Application of Chinese Exclusion Act, National Archives; Linck and Smith to Jackson, February 24, 1899, 16, 53108/9A.

74. Jackson to Secretary of the Treasury, March 30, 1899, 23, 53108/9B. Meredith, who was also one of Harry S. Huff's close associates, was later terminated after being found guilty of having aided and abetted traffickers. See Lee, *At America's Gates*, 214–15; and "Dismissal of Meredith Has Been Ordered," 4.

75. "Angel Island Men Score Dr. John Gardner," *San Francisco Chronicle*, September 23, 1916, 4; "Angel Island Smuggling Ring Long Suspected," January 28, 1917, 27–28; "Gardner Given Bad Name in Testimony," *San Francisco Chronicle*, January 29, 1917, 1–2.

76. 1900 United States Census, San Francisco, San Francisco, California, digital image s.v. "Hippolito Eca da Silva," Ancestry.com.

77. Teng, *Eurasian*, 265n13; Dikötter, *Discourse of Race*, 11, 17; de Piña-Cabral, *Between China and Europe*, 39; Montalto de Jesus, *Historic Macao*, 41–42.

78. Li, "'New Woman'"; Ives, "Overlooked No More."

79. *Official Register* (1901), 1:186; Prince and Keller, *US Customs Service*, 173–74; Lee, *At America's Gates*, 85.

80. "Interpreter Da Silva Out," *San Francisco Call*, March 5, 1904, 16.

81. Ngai, *Lucky Ones*, 95–96.

82. "Indict Alleged Slave Trader," *San Francisco Call*, September 18, 1904, 36.

83. Frank Dunn to Bureau of Immigration, September 16, 1904, quoted in "Memorandum: Canton Section 6 Certificate, Chinese to St. Louis Fair, etc." F. P. Sargent, May 8, 1906, 4, Casefile 57204/2, Record Group 85, Records of the Immigration and Naturalization Service, Series A: Subject Correspondence Files, Part 1: Asian Immigration and Exclusion, 1906–1913, [Miscellaneous Memos Regarding Employees], National Archives.

84. "To Investigate North's Office," *San Francisco Chronicle*, September 4, 1904, 41; "Ring Brings in Slave Women," *San Francisco Call*, September 18, 1904, 36; "Alleged Buyer of Chinese Women in Jail," *San Francisco Examiner*, September 19, 1894, 7.

85. "Ring Brings in Slave Women," *San Francisco Chronicle*, September 7, 1904, 16.

86. "Ring Brings in Slave Women," *San Francisco Chronicle*, September 7, 1904, 16.

87. "Arrested in St. Louis," *Los Angeles Times*, September 21, 1904, 3; "Da Silva Arrives in Charge of Murphy," *San Francisco Call*, September 27, 1904, 6; "Da Silva Turned Over," *Los Angeles Times*, September 28, 1904, 3; "Love Letters Hold Secrets," *San Francisco Call*, October 1, 1904, 16; "Da Silva Is Now in County Jail," *San Francisco Chronicle*, September 27, 1904, 14.

88. "Ring Brings in Slave Women," *San Francisco Chronicle*, September 7, 1904, 16.

89. "Da Silva in County Jail," *San Francisco Examiner*, September 27, 1904, 4.

90. "Da Silva Is Now in County Jail," 14.

91. "Da Silva Arrives in Charge of Murphy," 7.

92. "Tells Story of a Dual Courtship," *San Francisco Chronicle*, September 30, 1904, 9.

93. "Da Silva's Master Role Hypnotizing of Women," *San Francisco Examiner*, September 30, 1904, 5.

94. Lui, *Chinatown Trunk Mystery*, 49–50, 82; Shah, *Contagious Divides*, 74; Gabriel J. Chin and Ormonde, "War against Chinese Restaurants," 681.

95. "Da Silva's Master Role," 5.

96. "Hired as Waiters, but Destined for Slavery," *San Francisco Examiner*, January 25, 1905, 13; "Slave Relates Her Sad Story," *San Francisco Call*, January 25, 1905, 16; "Comes Over as a Slave," *San Francisco Chronicle*, January 26, 1905, 9; "Shortridge Says Man May Hit a Woman," *San Francisco Chronicle*, February 2, 1905, 16.

97. "Lee Toy and Da Silva Acquitted by Jury," *San Francisco Chronicle*, February 3, 1905, 16; "Says North Was Remiss," *San Francisco Examiner*, February 7, 1905, 5; "More Scandal in North's Bureau," *San Francisco Chronicle*, February 7, 1905, 16; "Chinese Exclusion—Official Aid Extended to the Importing Ring," *San Francisco Chronicle*, February 9, 1905, 6, 9.

98. "Stenographer Accused of Betraying Secrets," *San Francisco Examiner*, February 10, 1905, 5; "North Suspends Miss Burbank," *San Francisco Call*, February 10, 1905, 11; "Miss Burbank Is Now under Fire," *San Francisco Chronicle*, February 10, 1905, 16.

99. "Love in Chinese Bureau Ends in Wedding," *San Francisco Examiner*, August 17, 1905, 2.

100. Ngai, *Lucky Ones*, 102.

101. "North Gives Chinese a Job," *San Francisco Chronicle*, April 4, 1905, 16; "Chinese Blood Goes into the Bureau," *San Francisco Morning Call*, April 4, 1905, 7.

102. Ngai, *Lucky Ones*, 144–45.

103. "North Gives Chinese a Job," 16.

104. Ngai, "History as Law and Life"; Martinez-Cola, *Bricks before Brown*, 79–105.

105. "Chinese Blood Goes into the Bureau," 7.

106. "North Gives Chinese a Job," 16.

107. "Native-Born Chinese Couple Plan an Elaborate Wedding," *San Francisco Call*, November 1, 1901, 11. Park's paper is mistakenly referred to as the *Chinese Herald*. See Stellmann, "Yellow Journals," 199.

108. *Official Register* (1907), 1:434, 522.

109. Lee, *At America's Gates*, 85; Asiatic Exclusion League of San Francisco, *Proceedings*, 24.

110. "Chinese Interpreters Prefer to Remain Here," *San Francisco Call*, June 4, 1907, 9.

111. "Three Interpreters Are Ordered Transferred," *San Francisco Call*, June 3, 1907, 13.

112. Ngai, "'Slight Knowledge,'" 17; "Chinese Interpreters Warned against Graft," *San Francisco Call*, June 18, 1907, 13.

113. *Official Register* (1905), 1:1096.

114. F. P. Sargent to John Endicott Gardner, June 3, 1907, 2, Casefile 15053/C1, Record Group 85, Records of the Immigration and Naturalization Service, Collector of Chinese Customs Cases, National Archives.

115. John Endicott Gardner to F. P. Sargent, October 5, 1907, 2, Casefile 15053/C1, Record Group 85, Records of the Immigration and Naturalization Service, Collector of Chinese Customs Cases, National Archives.

116. F. P. Sargent to Commissioner General of Immigration, October 24, 1907, 2, Casefile 15053/1-C, Record Group 85, Records of the Immigration and Naturalization Service, Collector of Chinese Customs Cases, National Archives.

117. Ngai, *Lucky Ones*, 122, 128; *Official Register* (1911), 1:515, 624, 765.

Conclusion

1. Jung, *Beneath the Surface*, 25–35; Ray, "Theory of Racialized Organizations," 35–37.

2. Hall, "The Politics of Mugging," 394.

3. See Neckerman, Carter, and Lee, "Segmented Assimilation"; and Román, *Race and Upward Mobility*.

4. Alba and Maggio, "Demographic change and assimilation"; Roediger, *Working toward Whiteness*.

5. Pulliam, Reeves, and Shiro, "Middle Class"; Reeves and Busette, "Middle Class."

6. Teresa A. Sullivan, Warren, and Westbrook, *Fragile Middle Class*; Boushey and Hersh, *American Middle Class*; Kochhar, "American Middle Class."

7. Hochschild, *Strangers*, 92–93, 137–38; Polletta and Callahan, "Deep Stories."

8. Chicago Project on Security and Threats, *American Face of Insurrection*; Pape, "Jan. 6 Insurrectionists."

9. Back, "All the World's," 57.

10. Blee, *Women of the Klan*; MacLean, *Behind the Mask*; McVeigh, "Structural Incentives"; Rhomberg, "Class, Race"; Rable, *There Was No Peace*; Richard, *Not a Catholic Nation*; Pegram, *One Hundred Percent American*.

11. Haney-López, *Dog Whistle Politics*; DiAngelo, *Nice Racism*; Shannon Sullivan, *Good White People*; Bonilla-Silva, "New Racism"; Roediger, *Sinking Middle Class*.

12. Hale, *Making Whiteness*; Wood, "Lynching Photography"; Deverell, *Whitewashed Adobe*; Gonzales-Day, *Lynching in the West*; Pfaelzer, *Driven Out*; Chang, "Dreaming," 45–49; Flores, *Remembering the Alamo*, 95–107; Domby, *False Cause*.

Bibliography

Archival Collections

Georgia Historic Newspapers, https://gahistoricnewspapers.galileo.usg.edu/
Library of Congress, Chronicling America: Historic American Newspapers,
     https://chroniclingamerica.loc.gov/
San Antonio Police History Archive, https://sanantoniopolicehistoryarchive.org/
Texas Digital Newspaper Program, Portal to Texas History, University of
     North Texas Libraries, https://texashistory.unt.edu/explore/collections
     /TDNP/
US National Archives, Washington, DC (accessed through ProQuest History Vault)
     Records of the Immigration and Naturalization Service, Series A: Subject
         Correspondence Files, Part 1: Asian Immigration and Exclusion, 1906–1913,
         [Chinese Exclusion Laws—California] Casefile 53108/9A, 1898–1899; Record
         Group 85
     Records of the Immigration and Naturalization Service, Series A:
         Subject Correspondence Files, Part 1: Asian Immigration and Exclusion,
         1906–1913, [Chinese "Matter," California] Casefile 53108/9B, 1899; Record
         Group 85
     Records of the Immigration and Naturalization Service, Series A: Subject
         Correspondence Files, Part 1: Asian Immigration and Exclusion, 1906–1913,
         [Miscellaneous Memos Regarding Employees] Casefile 52704/2 cont.—
         Selections Relating to Oriental Immigration Only, 1906 and undated; Record
         Group 85
     Records of the Immigration and Naturalization Service, Series A: Subject
         Correspondence Files, Part 1: Supplement: Asian Immigration and Exclusion,
         1898–1941, [Various Chinese Interpreters, 1907–1924] Casefile 53360/34,
         [June 1907–May 1924]; Record Group 85
     Records of the Immigration and Naturalization Service, Series A: Subject
         Correspondence Files, Part 1: Asian Immigration and Exclusion, 1906–1913,
         [Statistics regarding Chinese immigration to San Francisco, California,
         Hawaii, and United States] Casefile 52704/2 [Jan 01, 1906–Dec 31, 1906];
         Record Group 85
     Records of the Immigration and Naturalization Service, Series A: Subject
         Correspondence Files, Part 1: Asian Immigration and Exclusion, 1906–1913,
         [Miscellaneous Memos Regarding Employees] Casefile 52704/2 cont.—
         Selections Relating to Oriental Immigration Only. 1906 and undated;
         Record Group 85

Federal Census Schedules (Accessed through Ancestry.com)

Atlanta

1870
1880
1900
1910

San Antonio

1860
1870
1880
1900
1910

San Francisco

1880
1900
1910
1920

City Directories (Accessed through Ancestry.com)

Atlanta

Bullock, V. V. *Atlanta City Directory for 1899*. Atlanta: Franklin Printing.
Foote and Davies. *Atlanta City Directory 1906*. Atlanta: Foote and Davies, 1906.
James W. Beasley Publisher. *Beasley's Atlanta City Directory for 1875*. Atlanta: James W. Beasley, 1875.
Maloney Directory. *Atlanta City Directory 1900*. Atlanta: Maloney Directory, 1900.
R. L. Polk and Company. *Atlanta City Directory for 1888*. Atlanta: Constitution Publishing, 1888.
———. *Atlanta City Directory for 1889*. Atlanta: Constitution Publishing, 1889.
———. *Atlanta City Directory for 1891*. Atlanta: Constitution Publishing, 1891.
Saunders, H. G. *Atlanta City Directory for 1890*. Atlanta: Constitution Publishing, 1890.
———. *Atlanta City Directory for 1893*. Atlanta: Constitution Publishing, 1893.
———. *Atlanta City Directory for 1895*. Atlanta: The Franklin Printing and Publishing Company, 1895.
Sholes. *Sholes' Directory of the City of Atlanta for 1881*. Vol. 5. Atlanta: H. H. Dickson Printer, 1881.
Weatherbee. *Weatherbee's Atlanta City Directory for 1883*. Atlanta: C. F. Weatherbee, 1883.
———. *Weatherbee's Atlanta City Directory for 1888*. Atlanta: C. F. Weatherbee, 1888.

San Antonio

Appler, Jules A. *Jules A. Appler's General Directory and Blue Book of the City of San Antonio for 1903-1904*. San Antonio, TX: Jules A. Appler, 1903.

————. *Jules A. Appler's General Directory and Blue Book of the City of San Antonio, 1905-1906*. San Antonio, TX: Jules A. Appler, 1905.

————. *Jules A. Appler's General Directory and Blue Book of the City of San Antonio, 1907-1908*. San Antonio, TX: Jules A. Appler, 1907.

————. *Jules A. Appler's General Directory and Blue Book of the City of San Antonio, 1908*. San Antonio, TX: Jules A. Appler, 1908.

————. *Jules A. Appler's General Directory and Blue Book of the City of San Antonio, 1909*. San Antonio, TX: Jules A. Appler, 1909.

————. *Jules A. Appler's General Directory of the City of San Antonio for 1892-93*. San Antonio, TX: Jules A. Appler, 1893.

————. *Jules A. Appler's General Directory of the City of San Antonio for 1895-'96*. San Antonio, TX: Jules A. Appler, 1895.

————. *Jules A. Appler's General Directory of the City of San Antonio for 1897-'98*. San Antonio, TX: Jules A. Appler, 1897.

————. *Jules A. Appler's General Directory of the City of San Antonio for 1899-1900*. San Antonio, TX: Jules A. Appler, 1899.

————. *Jules A. Appler's General Directory of the City of San Antonio for 1901-02*. San Antonio, TX: Jules A. Appler, 1901.

Johnson and Chapman. *Johnson and Chapman's General Directory of the City of San Antonio for the Year 1891*. San Antonio, TX: Johnson and Chapman, 1891.

Mooney and Morrison. *Mooney and Morrison's Directory of the City of San Antonio, for 1877-78*. Galveston, TX: Galveston News, 1877.

Morrison and Fourmy. *Morrison and Fourmy's General Directory of the City of San Antonio, 1879-1880*. Galveston, TX: Morrison and Fourmy, 1879.

————. *Morrison and Fourmy's General Directory of the City of San Antonio, 1881-82*. Austin, TX: Morrison and Fourmy, 1881.

————. *Morrison and Fourmy's General Directory of the City of San Antonio, 1883-84*. Galveston, TX: Morrison and Fourmy, 1883.

————. *Morrison and Fourmy's General Directory of the City of San Antonio, 1885-86*. Galveston, TX: Morrison and Fourmy, 1885.

————. *Morrison and Fourmy's General Directory of the City of San Antonio, 1887-88*. Galveston, TX: Morrison and Fourmy, 1887.

Texas Publishing. *Directory of the City of San Antonio, 1910-11*. San Antonio, TX: Texas Publishing, 1910.

San Francisco

H. S. Crocker Company. *Crocker-Langley San Francisco Directory, 1891*. San Francisco: H. S. Crocker, 1891.

————. *Crocker-Langley San Francisco Directory, 1896*. San Francisco: H. S. Crocker, 1896.

Chattanooga

Connelly and Fais. *City Directory of Chattanooga, Tennessee 1894.* Chattanooga, TN: Connelly and Fais, 1894.

Newspapers

Atlanta

Atlanta Daily Constitution
Atlanta Georgian
Watson's Weekly Jeffersonian

Other Cities in Georgia

Americus Times-Recorder
Athens Weekly Banner
Augusta Herald
Clayton Tribune
Columbus Enquirer-Sun
Dade County Sentinel (Trenton, GA)
Daily Times Enterprise
  (Thomasville, GA)
Fayetteville News
Gwinnett Herald (Lawrenceville, GA)

Henry County Weekly (Hampton, GA)
Macon Telegraph
Savannah Morning News
Savannah Tribune
Union Recorder (Milledgeville, GA)
Walker County Messenger
  (LaFayette, GA)
Waynesboro True Citizen

San Antonio

El Regidor
Freie Press für Texas
San Antonio Daily Express
San Antonio Daily Herald
San Antonio Daily Light

San Antonio Express
San Antonio Gazette
San Antonio Herald
San Antonio Light

Other Cities in Texas

Austin Daily Statesman
Brenham Daily Banner
Dallas Weekly Herald

Fort Worth Daily Gazette
Galveston Daily News
Southern Intelligencer (Austin, TX)

San Francisco

San Francisco Call
San Francisco Chronicle
San Francisco Daily Call

San Francisco Examiner
San Francisco Gazette

Other Cities in California

Los Angeles Times
Sacramento Evening Bee

Other US Newspapers

Baltimore Sun
Chicago Tribune
Der Deutsche Correspondent (Baltimore)
Maysville (KY) Evening Bulletin

New Orleans Daily Picayune
New York Times
Washington (DC) Bee

Published Government Reports

California State Senate, Special Committee on Chinese Immigration. *Chinese Immigration: The Social, Moral, and Political Effect of Chinese Immigration: Testimony Taken before a Committee of the Senate of the State of California, Appointed April 3d, 1876.* Sacramento, CA: State Printing Office, 1876.

Department of the Interior, Census Office. *Report on the Social Statistics of Cities.* Pt. 2, *The Southern and the Western States.* Washington, DC: Government Printing Office, 1887.

Farwell, W. B. *The Chinese at Home and Abroad: The Report of the Special Committee of the Board of Supervisors of San Francisco on the Condition of the Chinese Quarter of That City.* San Francisco: A. L. Bancroft, 1885.

Hunt, William Chamberlin. *Occupations at the Twelfth Census.* Washington, DC: Government Printing Office, 1904.

———. *Special Census Report on the Occupations of the Populations of the United States at the Eleventh Census: 1890.* Washington, DC: Government Printing Office, 1896.

Lehlbach, Herman. *Chinese Immigration.* March 2, 1891. Joint Select Committee on Immigration and Naturalization. Washington, DC: Government Printing Office, 1891.

US Bureau of the Census. *Statistics of Cities Having a Population of over 25,000, 1902 and 1903.* Washington, DC: Government Printing Office, 1905.

———. *Statistics of Cities Having a Population of over 30,000: 1904.* Washington, DC: Government Printing Office, 1906.

———. *Statistics of Cities Having a Population of over 30,000: 1905.* Washington, DC: Government Printing Office, 1907.

———. *Statistics of Cities Having a Population of over 30,000: 1906.* Washington, DC: Government Printing Office, 1908.

———. *Statistics of Cities Having a Population of over 30,000: 1907.* Washington, DC: Government Printing Office, 1909.

US Census Office. *Report on the Population of the United States at the Eleventh Census: 1890.* Washington, DC: Government Printing Office, 1895–97.

US Congress. *Appendix to the Congressional Record: The Proceedings and Debates of the 43rd Congress, 2d Session*. 1875. Washington, DC: Government Printing Office, 1876.

US Congress, House of Representatives, Select Committee on Immigration and Naturalization. *Investigation of Chinese Immigration*. 51st Cong., 2d. Sess. Report No. 4048. Washington, DC: Government Printing Office, 1891.

Government Directories (Accessed through Ancestry.com unless otherwise noted)

US Department of Commerce and Labor, Bureau of the Census. *Official Register of the United States, Containing a List of the Officers and Employés in the Civil, Military, and Naval Service of the United States and List of Vessels, July 1, 1881*. Vol. 2. Washington, DC: Government Printing Office, 1881.

———. *Official Register of the United States, Containing a List of the Officers and Employés in the Civil, Military, and Naval Service of the United States and List of Vessels, July 1, 1883*. Vol. 2. Washington, DC: Government Printing Office, 1883.

———. *Official Register of the United States, Containing a List of the Officers and Employés in the Civil, Military, and Naval Service of the United States and List of Vessels, July 1, 1885*. Vols. 1–2. Washington, DC: Government Printing Office, 1885.

———. *Official Register of the United States, Containing a List of the Officers and Employés in the Civil, Military, and Naval Service of the United States and List of Vessels, July 1, 1887*. Vols. 1–2. Washington, DC: Government Printing Office, 1887.

———. *Official Register of the United States, Containing a List of the Officers and Employés in the Civil, Military, and Naval Service of the United States and List of Vessels, July 1, 1889*. Vols. 1–2. Washington, DC: Government Printing Office, 1889.

———. *Official Register of the United States, Containing a List of the Officers and Employés in the Civil, Military, and Naval Service of the United States and List of Vessels, July 1, 1891*. Vols. 1–2. Washington, DC: Government Printing Office, 1891.

———. *Official Register of the United States, Containing a List of the Officers and Employés [sic] in the Civil, Military, and Naval Service of the United States and List of Vessels, July 1, 1893*. Vols. 1–2. Washington, DC: Government Printing Office, 1893. https://catalog.hathitrust.org/Record/011712478

———. *Official Register of the United States, Containing a List of the Officers and Employees in the Civil, Military, and Naval Service of the United States and List of Vessels, July 1, 1895*. Vols. 1–2. Washington, DC: Government Printing Office, 1895.

———. *Official Register of the United States, Containing a List of the Officers and Employees in the Civil, Military, and Naval Service of the United States and List of Vessels, July 1, 1897*. Vols. 1–2. Washington, DC: Government Printing Office, 1897.

———. *Official Register of the United States, Containing a List of the Officers and Employees in the Civil, Military, and Naval Service of the United States and List of Vessels, July 1, 1899*. Vols. 1–2. Washington, DC: Government Printing Office, 1899.

———. *Official Register of the United States, Containing a List of the Officers and Employees in the Civil, Military, and Naval Service of the United States and List of Vessels, July 1, 1901*. Vols. 1–2. Washington, DC: Government Printing Office, 1901.

———. *Official Register of the United States, Containing a List of the Officers and Employees in the Civil, Military, and Naval Service of the United States and List of Vessels, July 1, 1903*. Vols. 1–2. Washington, DC: Government Printing Office, 1903.

———. *Official Register of the United States, Containing a List of the Officers and Employees in the Civil, Military, and Naval Service of the United States and List of Vessels, July 1, 1905*. Vols. 1–2. Washington, DC: Government Printing Office, 1905.

———. *Official Register of the United States, Containing a List of the Officers and Employees in the Civil, Military, and Naval Service of the United States and List of Vessels, July 1, 1907*. Vols. 1–2. Washington, DC: Government Printing Office, 1907.

———. *Official Register of the United States, Containing a List of the Officers and Employees in the Civil, Military, and Naval Service of the United States and List of Vessels, July 1, 1909*. Vols. 1–2. Washington, DC: Government Printing Office, 1909.

———. *Official Register of the United States, Containing a List of the Officers and Employees in the Civil, Military, and Naval Service of the United States and List of Vessels, July 1, 1911*. Vols. 1–2. Washington, DC: Government Printing Office, 1911.

Published Primary Sources

Asiatic Exclusion League of San Francisco. *Proceedings of the Asiatic Exclusion League of San Francisco*. San Francisco: Organized Labor Press, 1910.

Atlanta University. *Catalogue of the Offers and Students of Atlanta University, Atlanta, Georgia, with a Statement of the Courses of Study, Expenses, Etc. 1880–81*. Atlanta, GA: Constitution Book and Job Printing Establishment, 1881.

———. *Catalogue of the Offers and Students of Atlanta University, Atlanta, Georgia, with a Statement of the Courses of Study, Expenses, Etc. 1881–82*. Atlanta, GA: Constitution Book and Job Printing Establishment, 1882.

———. *Catalogue of the Offers and Students of Atlanta University, Atlanta, Georgia, with a Statement of the Courses of Study, Expenses, Etc. 1882–83*. Atlanta, GA: Constitution Book and Job Printing Establishment, 1883.

Barnes, Charles Merritt. *Combats and Conquests of Immortal Heroes: Sung in Song and Told in Story*. San Antonio, TX: Guessaz and Ferlet, 1910.

Boyle, Peyton, ed. *The Federal Reporter: Cases Argued and Determined in the Circuit and District Courts of the United States*. Permanent Edition, July–October 1897. St. Paul, MN: West Publishing, 1897.

Bruce, Philip A. *The Plantation Negro as Freeman: Observations on His Character, Condition, and Prospects in Virginia*. New York: G. P. Putnam's Sons, 1889.

City Council of San Antonio. *Annual Message of Bryan Callaghan, Mayor of the City of San Antonio and Review of Reports of City Officers for Fiscal Year Ending May 31, 1910*. San Antonio, TX: J. A. Appler.

City of San Antonio, Texas. *Annual Message of Marshall Hicks, Mayor of the City of San Antonio, and Review of Reports of City Officers for Fiscal Year Ending June, 1901*. San Antonio, TX: Guessaz and Ferlet, 1901.

Colored American. *The Colored American Republican Text Book: A Book of Facts and Figures, Showing What the Republican Party Has Done for the Afro-American*. Washington, DC: Colored American, 1900.

Condit, Ira M. "Americanized Chinese." *Woman's Work for Woman and Our Mission Field*, April 1902, 219–21.

———. *The Chinaman as We See Him, and Fifty Years of Work for Him*. Chicago: F. H. Revell Company, 1900.

Coolidge, Mary Roberts. *Chinese Immigration*. New York: H. Holt and Company, 1909.

Dodson, Peter. "Affairs at Coon City." *Postal Record: A Journal for Postal Employes* [sic] 3, no. 1 (November 1889): 14.

———. "Affairs at Coon City." *Postal Record: A Journal for Postal Employes* [sic] 3, no. 2 (December 1889): 21.

Flores, Antonio D. "Our Mexican Citizens." *Collier's Once a Week*, October 6, 1894, 15.

Harris, Joel Chandler. *Uncle Remus: His Songs and His Sayings*. New York: D. Appleton, 1898.

Harris, Theodore. *Charter and Ordinances of the City of San Antonio: Comprising All Ordinances of a General Character in Force August 7th, 1899*. San Antonio, TX: San Antonio Printing, 1899.

Land and Thomas. *Historical and Descriptive Review of the Industries of San Antonio, 1885: Commerce, Trade and Manufactures, Manufacturing Advantages, Business and Transportation Facilities, Together with Sketches of the Representative Business Houses and Manufacturing Establishments in the "Alamo City."* 1885; repr., San Antonio, TX: N. Brock, 1977.

Macon, John A. *Uncle Gabe Tucker: Or Reflections, Song and Sentiment in the Quarters*. Philadelphia: J. B. Lippincott, 1883.

McEachin, Hector. "Our Mexican Citizens." *Collier's Once a Week*, September 8, 1894, 15.

Mickle, Hans. "Wanderings in West Texas." *San Antonio Express*, July 27, 1879, 4.

———. "Wanderings in West Texas." *San Antonio Express*, August 5, 1879, 4.

Ramsdell, Charles William. *Reconstruction in Texas*. New York: Columbia University Press, 1910.

San Antonio Police Department Illustrated. N.p., 1901.

Sanborn-Perris Map Company. *Sanborn Fire Insurance Map from Atlanta, Fulton County, Georgia*. New York: Sanborn-Perris Map Company, 1899.

———. *Sanborn Fire Insurance Map from San Antonio, Bexar County, Texas*. New York: Sanborn Map Company, 1896. https://www.loc.gov/item/sanborn08740_004/.

Santleben, A., and Isaac Dunbar Affleck. *A Texas Pioneer: Early Staging and Overland Freighting Days on the Frontiers of Texas and Mexico*. New York: Neale, 1910.

Stellmann, Louis J. "Yellow Journals: San Francisco's Oriental Newspapers." *Sunset* 24, no. 1 (1910): 197–201.

Wells-Barnett, Ida. *Lynch Law in Georgia: A Six Weeks' Record in the Center of Southern Civilization, as Faithfully Chronicled by the "Atlanta Journal" and the "Atlanta Constitution."* Chicago: Chicago Colored Citizens, 1899.

Winkler, Ernest William, ed. *Journal of the Secession Convention of Texas*. 1861; Austin, TX: Texas Library and Historical Commission and Texas State Library, printed by Austin Printing, 1912.

Secondary Sources

Acuña, Rodolfo. *Occupied America: A History of Chicanos*. 3rd ed. New York: Harper and Row, 1988.

Adams, Myron W. *General Catalogue of the Officers and Students of Atlanta University, 1867–1929*. Atlanta: Atlanta University Press, 1929.

Alba, Richard. *Blurring the Color Line: The New Chance for a More Integrated America*. Cambridge, MA: Harvard University Press, 2009.

———. "'Bright vs. Blurred Boundaries': Second-Generation Assimilation and Exclusion in France, Germany, and the United States." *Ethnic and Racial Studies* 28, no. 1 (2005): 20–49.

Alba, Richard, and Christopher Maggio. "Demographic Change and Assimilation in the Early 21st-Century United States." *Proceedings of the National Academy of Sciences* 119, no. 13 (2022): 1–11.

Alba, Richard, and Victor Nee. *Remaking the American Mainstream: Assimilation and Contemporary Immigration*. Cambridge, MA: Harvard University Press, 2009.

Almaguer, Tomás. *Racial Fault Lines: The Historical Origins of White Supremacy in California*. Berkeley: University of California Press, 1992.

Alonzo, Armando C. *Tejano Legacy: Rancheros and Settlers in South Texas, 1734–1900*. Albuquerque: University of New Mexico Press, 1998.

Anderson, Kay J. "The Idea of Chinatown: The Power of Place and Institutional Practice in the Making of a Racial Category." *Annals of the Association of American Geographers* 77, no. 4 (1987): 580–98.

Archer, Melanie, and Judith R. Blau. "Class Formation in Nineteenth-Century America: The Case of the Middle Class." *Annual Review of Sociology* 19, no. 1 (August 1993): 17–41.

Arnesen, Eric. "Whiteness and the Historians' Imagination." *International Labor and Working-Class History* 60 (Fall 2001): 3–32.

———. "Up from Exclusion: Black and White Workers, Race, and the State of Labor History." *Reviews in American History* 26, no. 1 (March 1998): 146–74.

Aron, Cindy S. *Ladies and Gentlemen of the Civil Service: Middle-Class Workers in Victorian America*. New York: Oxford University Press, 1987.

Arreola, Daniel D. *Tejano South Texas: A Mexican American Cultural Province*. Austin: University of Texas Press, 2010.

Arvin, Maile Renee. *Possessing Polynesians: the Science of Settler Colonial Whiteness in Hawaii and Oceania*. Durham, NC: Duke University Press, 2020.

Back, Les. "All the World's a Corporate Stage." *Soundings* 2000, no. 15 (2000): 54–58.

Bacote, Clarence A. "Negro Officeholders in Georgia under President McKinley." *Journal of Negro History* 44, no. 3 (1959): 217–39.

———. *The Story of Atlanta University: A Century of Service, 1865–1965*. Atlanta: Atlanta University Press, 1969.

Barr, Alwyn. "Occupational and Geographic Mobility in San Antonio, 1870–1900." *Social Science Quarterly* 51, no. 2 (1970): 396–403.

Barrera, Mario. *Race and Class in the Southwest: A Theory of Racial Inequality*. Notre Dame, IN: University of Notre Dame Press, 1979.

Barrett, James R., and David Roediger. "Inbetween Peoples: Race, Nationality and the New Immigrant Working Class." In *American Exceptionalism? US Working-Class Formation in an International Context*, edited by Rick Halpern and Johnathan Morris, 181–220. London: Palgrave Macmillan, 1997.

Baum, Dale F., and Worth Robert Miller. "Ethnic Conflict and Machine Politics in San Antonio, 1892–1899." *Journal of Urban History* 19, no. 4 (1993): 63–84.

Bederman, Gail. *Manliness and Civilization: A Cultural History of Gender and Race in the United States, 1880–1917*. Chicago: University of Chicago Press, 1995.

Beisel, Nicola. "Constructing a Shifting Moral Boundary: Literature and Obscenity in Nineteenth-Century America." In *Cultivating Differences: Symbolic Boundaries and the Making of Inequality*, edited by Michele Lamont and Marcel Fournier, 104–28. Chicago: University of Chicago Press.

Beisel, Nicola, and Tamara Kay. "Abortion, Race, and Gender in Nineteenth-Century America." *American Sociological Review* 69, no. 4 (2004): 498–518.

Benton-Cohen, Katherine. *Borderline Americans: Racial Division and Labor War in the Arizona Borderlands*. Cambridge, MA: Harvard University Press, 2009.

Blee, Kathleen M. *Women of the Klan: Racism and Gender in the 1920s*. Berkeley: University of California Press, 1991.

Blumin, Stuart M. *The Emergence of the Middle Class: Social Experience in the American City, 1760–1900*. New York: Cambridge University Press, 1989.

Bonacich, Edna. "U.S. Capitalist Development: A Background to Asian Immigration." In *Labor Immigration under Capitalism: Asian Workers in the United States before World War II*, edited by Lucie Cheng and Edna Bonacich, 79–129. Berkeley: University of California Press, 1984.

Bonilla-Silva, Eduardo. "The New Racism: Racial Structure in the United States, 1960s–1990s." In *Race, Ethnicity, and Nationality in the United States: Toward the Twenty-First Century*, edited by Paul Wong, 55–101. London: Routledge, 2021.

———. "Rethinking Racism: Toward a Structural Interpretation." *American Sociological Review* 62, no. 3 (1997): 465–80.

———. "The Structure of Racism in Color-Blind, 'Post-racial' America." *American Behavioral Scientist* 59, no. 11 (2015): 1358–76.

———. "Toward a New Political Praxis for Trumpamerica: New Directions in Critical Race Theory." *American Behavioral Scientist* 63, no. 13 (2019): 1776–88.

———. "'Racists,' 'Class Anxieties,' Hegemonic Racism, and Democracy in Trump's America." *Social Currents* 6, no. 1 (2019): 14–31.

Bonnell, Victoria E. "The Uses of Theory, Concepts and Comparison in Historical Sociology." *Comparative Studies in Society and History* 22, no. 2 (1980): 156–73.

Boushey, Heather, and A. S. Hersh. *The American Middle Class, Income Inequality, and the Strength of Our Economy: New Evidence in Economics*. Washington, DC: Center for American Progress, 2012.

Bow, Leslie. *Partly Colored: Asian Americans and Racial Anomaly in the Segregated South*. New York: New York University Press, 2010.

Brodkin, Karen. *How Jews Became White Folks and What That Says about Race in America*. New Brunswick, NJ: Rutgers University Press, 1998.

Bronstein, Daniel. "Segregation, Exclusion, and the Chinese Communities in Georgia, 1880s–1940." In *Asian Americans in Dixie*, edited by Khyati Y. Joshi and Jigna Desai, 107–30. Urbana: University of Illinois Press, 2013.

Brooks, Charlotte. *Alien Neighbors, Foreign Friends: Asian Americans, Housing, and the Transformation of Urban California*. Chicago: University of Chicago Press, 2009.

Buitron, Richard. *The Quest for Tejano Identity in San Antonio, Texas, 1913–2000*. London: Routledge, 2012.

Burchell, Robert Arthur. *The San Francisco Irish, 1848–1880*. Berkeley: University of California Press, 1980.

Butler, John Sibley. *Entrepreneurship and Self-Help among Black Americans: A Reconsideration of Race and Economics*. Albany: State University of New York Press, 1991.

Cantrell, Gregg. "'Our Very Pronounced Theory of Equal Rights to All': Race, Citizenship, and Populism in the South Texas Borderlands." *Journal of American History* 100, no. 3 (2013): 663–90.

Carrigan, William D., and Clive Webb. *Forgotten Dead: Mob Violence against Mexicans in the United States, 1848–1928*. Oxford: Oxford University Press, 2013.

Carter, Edward R. *The Black Side: A Partial History of the Business, Religious and Educational Side of the Negro in Atlanta, Georgia*. Atlanta: n.p., 1894.

Casas, María Raquél. *Married to a Daughter of the Land: Spanish-Mexican Women and Interethnic Marriage in California, 1820–80*. Reno: University of Nevada Press, 2009.

Cater, Casey. "To Pick Up Again the Cross of Missionary Work: W. J. Northen's Politics of Race, Religion, and Reform, 1890–1911." *Georgia Baptist History* 21 (2008): 23–41.

Chan, Sucheng. "Race, Ethnic Culture, and Gender in the Construction of Identities among Second-Generation Chinese Americans, 1880s–1930s." In *Claiming America: Constructing Chinese American Identities during the Exclusion Era*, edited by K. Scott Wong and Sucheng Chan, 127–64. Philadelphia: Temple University Press, 1998.

Chang, Robert S. "Dreaming in Black and White: Racial-Sexual Policing in the Birth of a Nation, the Cheat, and Who Killed Vincent Chin." *Asian Law Journal* 5 (1998): 41–62.

Chen, Yong. *Chinese San Francisco: A Trans-Pacific Community, 1850–1943*. Stanford, CA: Stanford University Press.

Cheng, Wendy. *The Changes Next Door to the Díazes: Remapping Race in Suburban California*. Minneapolis: University of Minnesota Press, 2013.

Chicago Project on Security and Threats. *American Face of Insurrection: Analysis of Individuals Charged for Storming the US Capitol on January 6, 2021*. Chicago: Chicago Project on Security and Threats, 2022. https://cpost.uchicago.edu/publications/american_face_of_insurrection/.

Chin, Gabriel J., and John Ormonde. "The War against Chinese Restaurants." *Duke Law Journal* 67, no. 4 (2017): 681–741.

Chin, Margaret M. *Stuck: Why Asian Americans Don't Reach the Top of the Corporate Ladder*. New York: New York University Press, 2020.

Clayton, John. "Thinking Spatially: Towards an Everyday Understanding of Inter-ethnic Relations." *Social and Cultural Geography* 10, no. 4 (June 2009): 481–98.

Clerge, Orly. *The New Noir: Race, Identity, and Diaspora in Black Suburbia*. Berkeley: University of California Press, 2019.

Con, Harry, and Edgar Wickberg. *From China to Canada: A History of the Chinese Communities in Canada*. Toronto: McClelland and Stewart in association with the Multiculturalism Directorate, Department of the Secretary of State and the Canadian Government Publishing Centre, Supply and Services Canada, 1982.

Crowe, Charles. "Racial Massacre in Atlanta: September 22, 1906." *Journal of Negro History* 54, no. 2 (1969): 150–73.

Daniels, Douglas H. *Pioneer Urbanites: A Social and Cultural History of Black San Francisco*. Berkeley: University of California Press, 1990.

Davis, F. James. *Who Is Black? One Nation's Definition*. University Park: Pennsylvania State University Press, 1991.

Davis, Harold E. *Henry Grady's New South: Atlanta, a Brave and Beautiful City*. Tuscaloosa: University of Alabama Press. 1990.

Davis, John A., and Cornelius L. Golightly. "Negro Employment in the Federal Government." *Phylon* 6, no. 4 (1945): 337–46.

Decker, Peter R. *Fortunes and Failures: White-Collar Mobility in Nineteenth-Century San Francisco*. Cambridge, MA: Harvard University Press, 1978.

de la Teja, Jesús F. *Faces of Béxar: Early San Antonio and Texas*. College Station: Texas A&M University Press, 2016.

de la Teja, Jesus F., and John Wheat. "Béxar: Profile of a Tejano Community, 1820–1832." In *Tejano Origins in Eighteenth-Century San Antonio*, edited by Gerald E. Pyo and Gilberto Hinojosa, 1–24. Austin: University of Texas Press.

De León, Arnoldo. *In Re Ricardo Rodriguez: An Attempt at Chicano Disfranchisement in San Antonio, 1896–1897*. San Antonio, TX: Caravel, 1979.

———. *Apuntes Tejanos Volume 1: An Index of Items Related to Mexican Americans in Nineteenth Century Texas Extracted from the San Antonio Express (1869) and the San Antonio Herald (1855–1878)*. Ann Arbor: University Microfilms International, 1978.

———. *The Tejano Community, 1836–1900*. Albuquerque: University of New Mexico Press, 1982.

———. *They Called Them Greasers: Anglo Attitudes toward Mexicans in Texas, 1821–1900*. Austin: University of Texas Press, 1983.

de Piña-Cabral, João. *Between China and Europe: Person, Culture and Emotion in Macao*. UK: Routledge, 2020.

Deverell, William. *Whitewashed Adobe: The Rise of Los Angeles and the Remaking of Its Mexican Past*. Berkeley: University of California Press, 2004.

Dewey, Alicia Marion. *Pesos and Dollars: Entrepreneurs in the Texas-Mexico Borderlands, 1880–1940*. College Station: Texas A&M University Press, 2014.

Diamond, John B., and Amanda E. Lewis. "Race and Discipline at a Racially Mixed High School: Status, Capital, and the Practice of Organizational Routines." *Urban Education* 54, no. 6 (2019): 831–59.

DiAngelo, Robin. *Nice Racism: How Progressive White People Perpetuate Racial Harm*. Boston: Beacon, 2021.

Dikötter, Frank. *The Discourse of Race in Modern China*. New York: Oxford University Press, 2015.

Dittmer, John. *Black Georgia in the Progressive Era, 1900–1920*. Urbana: University of Illinois Press, 1980.

Domby, Adam H. *The False Cause: Fraud, Fabrication, and White Supremacy in Confederate Memory*. Charlottesville: University of Virginia Press, 2020.

Domosh, Mona. *Invented Cities: The Creation of Landscape in Nineteenth-Century New York and Boston*. New Haven, CT: Yale University Press, 1996.

Donovan, Brian. *White Slave Crusades: Race, Gender, and Anti-vice Activism, 1887–1917*. Urbana: University of Illinois Press, 2006.

Dorsey, Allison. *To Build Our Lives Together: Community Formation in Black Atlanta, 1875–1906*. Athens: University of Georgia Press, 2004.

Dowd-Hall, Jacqueline. *Revolt against Chivalry: Jessie Daniel Ames and the Women's Campaign against Lynching*. New York: Columbia University Press, 1993.

———. "'The Mind That Burns in Each Body': Women, Rape, and Racial Violence." In *Powers of Desire: The Politics of Sexuality*, edited by Ann Snitow, Christine Stansell, and Sharon Thompson, 328–49. New York: Monthly Review Press, 1983.

Doyle, Don Harrison. *New Men, New Cities, New South: Atlanta, Nashville, Charleston, Mobile, 1860–1910*. Chapel Hill: University of North Carolina Press, 1990.

Driskell, Jay W., Jr. *Schooling Jim Crow: The Fight for Atlanta's Booker T. Washington High School and the Roots of Black Protest Politics*. Charlottesville: University of Virginia Press, 2014.

Du Bois, W. E. B. *Black Reconstruction in America, 1860–1880*. 1935; Cleveland: Meridian Books, 1968.

———. *The Souls of Black Folk: Essays and Sketches*. Chicago: A. C. McClurg, 1903.

Evensen, Bruce J. "Journalism." In *A Companion to the Gilded Age and Progressive Era*, edited by Christopher McKnight Nichols and Nancy C. Unger, 178–89. New York: John Wiley and Sons, 2017.

Everett, Donald E. *San Antonio: The Flavor of Its Past, 1845–1898*. San Antonio, TX: Trinity University Press, 1975.

Feagin, Joe. *Systemic Racism: A Theory of Oppression*. New York: Routledge, 2013.

Flores, Richard R. *Remembering the Alamo: Memory, Modernity, and the Master Symbol*. Austin: University of Texas Press, 2002.

Flowe, Douglas J. *Uncontrollable Blackness: African American Men and Criminality in Jim Crow*. Chapel Hill: University of North Carolina Press, 2020.

Foner, Eric. *Reconstruction: America's Unfinished Revolution, 1863–1877*. New York: Harper Perennial, 2014.

Fox, Cybelle. *Three Worlds of Relief: Race, Immigration, and the American Welfare State from the Progressive Era to the New Deal*. Princeton, NJ: Princeton University Press, 2012.

Fox, Cybelle, and Thomas A. Guglielmo. "Defining America's Racial Boundaries: Blacks, Mexicans, and European Immigrants, 1890–1945." *American Journal of Sociology* 118, no. 2 (2012): 327–79.

Franzosi, Roberto. "Narrative Analysis—or Why (and How) Sociologists Should Be Interested in Narrative." *Annual Review of Sociology* 24, no. 1 (1998): 517–54.

Freedman, Estelle B. "The New Woman: Changing Views of Women in the 1920s." *Journal of American History* 61, no. 2 (1974): 372–93.

Garb, Margaret. *City of American Dreams: A History of Home Ownership and Housing Reform in Chicago, 1871-1919*. Chicago: University of Chicago Press, 2005.

Garcia, Matt. *A World of Its Own: Race, Labor, and Citrus in the Making of Greater Los Angeles, 1900-1970*. Chapel Hill: University of North Carolina Press, 2001.

Garcia, Richard A. *Rise of the Mexican American Middle Class: San Antonio, 1929-1941*. College Station: Texas A&M University Press, 1991.

Gardner, Martha Mabie. "Working on White Womanhood: White Working Women in the San Francisco Anti-Chinese Movement, 1877-1890." *Journal of Social History* 33, no. 1 (1999): 73–95.

Gatewood, Willard B. *Aristocrats of Color: The Black Elite, 1880-1920*. Fayetteville: University of Arkansas Press, 1990.

Gerteis, Joseph. *Class and the Color Line: Interracial Class Coalition in the Knights of Labor and the Populist Movement*. Durham, NC: Duke University Press, 2007.

———. "Populism, Race, and Political Interest in Virginia." *Social Science History* 27, no. 2 (2003): 197–227.

———. "The Possession of Civic Virtue: Movement Narratives of Race and Class in the Knights of Labor." *American Journal of Sociology* 108, no. 3 (2002): 580–615.

Gibson, Campbell. "Population of the 100 Largest Cities and Other Urban Places in the United States: 1790 to 1990." Population Division Working Paper No. 27, US Census Bureau, June 1998. https://purl.fdlp.gov/GPO/LPS2100.

Gilmore, Ruth Wilson. "Fatal Couplings of Power and Difference: Notes on Racism and Geography." *Professional Geographer* 54, no. 1 (2002): 15–24.

Glenn, Evelyn Nakano. *Unequal Freedom: How Race and Gender Shaped American Citizenship and Labor*. Cambridge, MA: Harvard University Press, 2002.

Go, Julian. *American Empire and the Politics of Meaning: Elite Political Cultures in the Philippines and Puerto Rico during U.S. Colonialism*. Durham, NC: Duke University Press, 2008.

———. "The Imperial Origins of American Policing: Militarization and Imperial Feedback in the Early 20th Century." *American Journal of Sociology* 125, no. 5 (March 2020): 1193-1254.

Godshalk, David Fort. *Veiled Visions: The 1906 Atlanta Race Riot and the Reshaping of American Race Relations*. Chapel Hill: University of North Carolina Press, 2006.

Goldberg, David Theo. *The Threat of Race: Reflections on Racial Neoliberalism*. New York: John Wiley and Sons, 2009.

Gómez, Laura E. *Manifest Destinies: The Making of the Mexican American Race*. New York: New York University Press, 2007.

Gonzales, Manuel G. *The Hispanic Elite of the Southwest*. El Paso: Texas Western Press, 1989.

Gonzales-Day, Ken. *Lynching in the West, 1850-1935*. Durham, NC: Duke University Press, 2006.

Gould, Lewis L. "Tariffs and Markets in the Gilded Age." *Reviews in American History* 2, no. 2 (June 1974): 266–71.

Griswold-Del Castillo, Richard. *La Familia: Chicano Families in the Urban Southwest, 1848 to the Present*. Notre Dame, IN: University of Notre Dame Press, 1991.

Gross, Ariela J. "The Caucasian Cloak: Mexican Americans and the Politics of Whiteness in the Twentieth-Century Southwest." *Georgetown Law Journal* 95, no. 2 (2006): 337–92.

———. "Texas Mexicans and the Politics of Whiteness." *Law and History Review* 21, no. 1 (Spring 2003): 195–205.

———. *What Blood Won't Tell: A History of Race on Trial in America*. Cambridge, MA: Harvard University Press, 2009.

Guglielmo, Thomas A. *White on Arrival: Italians, Race, Color, and Power in Chicago, 1890-1945*. New York: Oxford University Press, 2003.

Guterl, Matthew Pratt. "A Note on the Word White." *American Quarterly* 56, no. 2 (2004): 439–47.

Haas, Lisbeth. *Conquests and Historical Identities in California, 1769-1936*. Berkeley: University of California Press, 1995.

Hale, Grace Elizabeth. *Making Whiteness: The Culture of Segregation in the South, 1890-1940*. New York: Vintage, 2010.

Hall, Nicholas Sean. "'The Wasp's 'Troublesome Children': Culture, Satire, and the Anti-Chinese Movement in the American West." *California History* 90, no. 2 (2013): 42–67.

Hall, Stuart. "The Politics of Mugging." In *Policing the Crisis: Mugging, the State and Law and Order*, edited by Stuart Hall, Chas Critcher, Tony Jefferson, John Clarke, and Brian Roberts. London: Macmillan, 1982.

———. "Race, Articulation and Societies Structured in Dominance." In *Sociological Theories: Race and Colonialism*, by UNESCO, 305–44. Paris: UNESCO, 1980.

Hall, Thomas D. *Social Change in the Southwest, 1350-1880*. Lawrence: University Press of Kansas, 1989.

Haney-López, Ian. *Dog Whistle Politics: How Coded Racial Appeals Have Reinvented Racism and Wrecked the Middle Class*. Oxford: Oxford University Press, 2014.

Haydu, Jeffrey. *Citizen Employers: Business Communities and Labor in Cincinnati and San Francisco, 1870-1916*. Ithaca, NY: Cornell University Press, 2008.

Heap, Chad. *Slumming: Sexual and Racial Encounters in American Nightlife, 1885-1940*. Chicago: University of Chicago Press, 2008.

Hernández, Kelly Lytle. *City of Inmates: Conquest, Rebellion, and the Rise of Human Caging in Los Angeles, 1771-1965*. Chapel Hill: University of North Carolina Press, 2017.

Hickey, Georgina. *Hope and Danger in the New South City: Working-Class Women and Urban Development in Atlanta, 1890-1940*. Athens: University of Georgia Press, 2003.

Higham, John. *Strangers in the Land: Patterns of American Nativism, 1860-1925*. New Brunswick, NJ: Rutgers University Press, 1994.

Hochschild, Arlie Russell. *Strangers in Their Own Land: Anger and Mourning on the American Right*. New York: New Press, 2016.

Hodes, Martha. "The Sexualization of Reconstruction Politics: White Women and Black Men in the South after the Civil War." *Journal of the History of Sexuality* 3, no. 3 (1993): 402–17.

Hoffnung-Garskof, Jesse. *Racial Migrations: New York City and the Revolutionary Politics of the Spanish Caribbean*. Princeton, NJ: Princeton University Press, 2019.

Hofstadter, Richard A. *The Age of Reform: From Bryan to F.D.R.* New York: Alfred A. Knopf, 1955.

Ives, Mike. "Overlooked No More: Yamei Kin, the Chinese Doctor Who Introduced Tofu to the West." *New York Times*, October 17, 2018. www.nytimes.com/2018/10/17/obituaries/yamei-kin-overlooked.html.

Jacobson, Matthew Frye. *Barbarian Virtues: The United States Encounters Foreign Peoples at Home and Abroad, 1876–1917*. New York: Hill and Wang, 2000.

———. *Whiteness of a Different Color: European Immigrants and the Alchemy of Race*. Cambridge, MA: Harvard University Press, 1999.

Janken, Kenneth Robert. *Walter White: Mr. NAACP*. Chapel Hill: University of North Carolina Press, 2003.

Jewell, Joseph O. "'An Injurious Effect on the Neighbourhood': Narratives of Neighbourhood Decline and Racialised Class Identities in Late Nineteenth-Century San Francisco." *Immigrants and Minorities* 36, no. 1 (2018): 1–19.

———. *Race, Social Reform, and the Making of a Middle Class: The American Missionary Association and Black Atlanta, 1870–1910*. Lanham, MD: Rowman and Littlefield, 2007.

Johnson, David R. "Frugal and Sparing: Interest Groups, Politics, and City Building in San Antonio, 1870–85." In *Urban Texas: Politics and Development*, edited by Char Miller and Heywood Sanders, 33–57. College Station: Texas A&M University Press, 1990.

———. *In the Loop: A Political and Economic History of San Antonio*. San Antonio, TX: Trinity University Press, 2020.

Jones, Mack H. "Black Political Empowerment in Atlanta: Myth and Reality." *Annals of the American Academy of Political and Social Science* 439, no. 1 (1978): 90–117.

Jung, Moon-Kie. *Beneath the Surface of White Supremacy: Denaturalizing U.S. Racisms Past and Present*. Palo Alto, CA: Stanford University Press, 2015.

Kelley, Blair Murphy. *Right to Ride: Streetcar Boycotts and African American Citizenship in the Era of "Plessy v. Ferguson."* Chapel Hill: University of North Carolina Press, 2010.

Kelley, Robin D. G. "'We Are Not What We Seem': Rethinking Black Working-Class Opposition in the Jim Crow South." *Journal of American History* 80, no. 1 (1993): 75–112.

Kibler, M. Alison. *Censoring Racial Ridicule: Irish, Jewish, and African American Struggles over Race and Representation, 1890–1930*. Chapel Hill: University of North Carolina Press, 2015.

Kitch, Sally. *The Specter of Sex: Gendered Foundations of Racial Formation in the United States* Albany: State University of New York Press, 2009.

Knight, Larry. "The Cart War: Defining American in San Antonio in the 1850s." *Southwestern Historical Quarterly* 109, no. 3 (2006): 318–35.

Kochhar, Rakesh. "The American Middle Class Is Stable in Size, but Losing Ground Financially to Upper-Income Families." Pew Research Center, September 6, 2018. www.pewresearch.org/fact-tank/2018/09/06/the-american-middle-class-is-stable-in-size-but-losing-ground-financially-to-upper-income-families/.

Kurashige, Scott. *The Shifting Grounds of Race: Black and Japanese Americans in the Making of Multiethnic Los Angeles*. Princeton, NJ: Princeton University Press, 2010.

Lacy, Karyn. *Blue-Chip Black: Race, Class, and Status in the New Black Middle Class*. Berkeley: University of California Press, 2007.

Lamont, Michèle. *The Dignity of Working Men*. Cambridge, MA: Harvard University Press, 2000.

Lamont, Michèle, and Virág Molnár. "The Study of Boundaries in the Social Sciences." *Annual Review of Sociology* 28 (2002): 167–95.

Lands, LeeAnn. *The Culture of Property: Race, Class, and Housing Landscapes in Atlanta, 1880-1950*. Athens: University of Georgia Press, 2011.

Lee, Erika. *At America's Gates: Chinese Immigration during the Exclusion Era, 1882-1943*. Chapel Hill: University of North Carolina Press, 2003.

Lewis, Amanda E. "'What Group?': Studying Whites and Whiteness in the Era of 'Color-Blindness.'" *Sociological Theory* 22, no. 4 (2004): 623–46.

Lew-Williams, Beth. *The Chinese Must Go: Violence, Exclusion, and the Making of the Alien in America*. Cambridge, MA: Harvard University Press, 2018.

Lim, Julian. *Porous Borders: Multiracial Migrations and the Law in the U.S.-Mexico Borderlands*. Chapel Hill: University of North Carolina Press, 2017.

Ling, Huping. *Chinese Chicago: Race, Transnational Migration, and Community since 1870*. Stanford, CA: Stanford University Press, 2012.

Litwack, Leon. *Trouble in Mind: Black Southerners in the Age of Jim Crow*. New York: Vintage Books, 1997.

Lott, Eric. *Love and Theft: Blackface Minstrelsy and the American Working Class*. Oxford University Press, 2013.

Loveman, Mara. *National Colors: Racial Classification and the State in Latin America*. Oxford University Press, 2014.

Lui, Mary Ting Yi. *The Chinatown Trunk Mystery: Murder, Miscegenation, and Other Dangerous Encounters in Turn-of-the-Century New York City*. Princeton, NJ: Princeton University Press, 2005.

MacLean, Nancy. *Behind the Mask of Chivalry: The Making of the Second Ku Klux Klan*. New York: Oxford University Press, 1994.

Maddox, Lucy. *Citizen Indians: Native American Intellectuals, Race, and Reform*. Ithaca, NY: Cornell University Press, 2006.

Maggor, Norman. "American Capitalism: From the Atlantic Economy to Domestic Industrialization." In *A Companion to the Gilded Age and Progressive Era*, edited by Christopher McKnight Nichols and Nancy C. Unger, 205-14. New York: John Wiley and Sons, 2017.

Marcus, Kenneth H., and Yong Chen. "Inside and outside Chinatown: Chinese Elites in Exclusion Era California." *Pacific Historical Review* 80, no. 3 (2011): 369-400.

Martinez, Monica Muñoz. *The Injustice Never Leaves You: Anti-Mexican Violence in Texas*. Cambridge, MA: Harvard University Press, 2018.

Martinez-Catsam, Ana Luisa. "'Los Precios Mas Baratos': The Role of Spanish-Language Newspaper Advertisements and the Biculturalization of Tejanos in San Antonio and Laredo, Texas." *New Mexico Historical Review* 86, no. 1 (Winter 2011): 83-105.

Martinez-Cola, Marisela. *The Bricks before Brown: The Chinese American, Native American, and Mexican Americans' Struggle for Educational Equality*. Athens: University of Georgia Press, 2022.

Mason, Kenneth. *African Americans and Race Relations in San Antonio, Texas, 1867–1937*. New York: Garland, 1998.

Mason, Nicholas W. "Anti-Chinese Mob Violence and the Legacy of Lynching Studies." *Journal of the Gilded Age and Progressive Era* 20, no. 1 (2021): 157–64.

Matovina, Timothy M. "Between Two Worlds." In *Tejano Journey, 1770–1850*, edited by Gerald E. Poyo, 73–88. Austin: University of Texas Press, 1996.

McClain, Charles J. *In Search of Equality: The Chinese Struggle against Discrimination in Nineteenth-Century America*. Berkeley: University of California Press, 1994.

McDonald, David R. *José Antonio Navarro: In Search of the American Dream in Nineteenth-Century Texas*. Austin: Texas State Historical Association, 2013.

McGovern, James R. "The American Woman's Pre-World War I Freedom in Manners and Morals." *Journal of American History* 55, no. 2 (1968): 315–33.

McMath, Robert C., Jr. *American Populism: A Social History*. New York: Hill and Wang, 1993.

McVeigh, Rory. "Structural Incentives for Conservative Mobilization: Power Devaluation and the Rise of the Ku Klux Klan, 1915–1925." *Social Forces* 77, no. 4 (1999): 1461–96.

Mei, June. "Socioeconomic Developments among the Chinese in San Francisco, 1848–1906." In *Labor Immigration under Capitalism: Asian Workers in the United States before World War II*, edited by Lucie Cheng and Edna Bonacich, 370–401. Berkeley: University of California Press, 1984.

Menchaca, Martha. *Naturalizing Mexican Immigrants: A Texas History*. Austin: University of Texas Press, 2011.

———. *Recovering History, Constructing Race: The Indian, Black, and White Roots of Mexican Americans*. Austin: University of Texas Press, 2001.

Mendoza, Alexander. "'For Our Own Best Interests': Nineteenth-Century Laredo Tejanos, Military Service, and the Development of American Nationalism." *Southwestern Historical Quarterly* 115, no. 2 (2011): 125–52.

Mikusko, M. Brady, and F. John Miller. *Carriers in a Common Cause: A History of Letter Carriers and the NALC*. Washington, DC: National Association of Letter Carriers, 2014.

Mixon, Gregory. *The Atlanta Riot: Race, Class, and Violence in a New South City*. Gainesville: University Press of Florida, 2005.

Molina, Natalia. *How Race Is Made in America: Immigration, Citizenship, and the Historical Power of Racial Scripts*. Berkeley: University of California Press, 2014.

Molina, Natalia, Daniel HoSang, and Ramón A. Gutiérrez, eds. *Relational Formations of Race: Theory, Method, and Practice*. Berkeley: University of California Press, 2019.

Montalto de Jesus, Carlos Augusto. *Historic Macao*. Hong Kong: Kelly and Walsh, 1902. www.google.com/books/edition/_/tMsNAAAAIAAJ?hl=en&gbpv=1.

Montejano, David. *Anglos and Mexicans in the Making of Texas, 1836–1986*. Austin: University of Texas Press, 1987.

Moore, John Hammond. "Jim Crow in Georgia." *South Atlantic Quarterly* 66 (1967): 554–65.

Mora, Anthony P. *Border Dilemmas: Racial and National Uncertainties in New Mexico, 1848–1912*. Durham, NC: Duke University Press, 2011.

Muhammad, Khalil Gibran. *The Condemnation of Blackness: Race, Crime, and the Making of Modern Urban America*. Cambridge, MA: Harvard University Press, 2011.

Neckerman, Kathryn M., Prudence Carter, and Jennifer Lee. "Segmented Assimilation and Minority Cultures of Mobility." *Ethnic and Racial Studies* 22, no. 6 (1999): 945–65.

Nelson, Megan Kate. *The Three-Cornered War: The Union, the Confederacy, and Native Peoples in the Fight for the West*. New York: Simon and Schuster, 2020.

Ngai, Mae M. "History as Law and Life: *Tape v. Hurley* and the Origins of the Chinese American Middle Class." In *Chinese Americans and the Politics of Race and Culture*, edited by Madeline Y. Hsu and Sucheng Chan, 62–90. Philadelphia: Temple University Press, 2008.

———. *The Lucky Ones: One Family and the Extraordinary Invention of Chinese America*. New York: Houghton Mifflin Harcourt, 2010.

———. "'A Slight Knowledge of the Barbarian Language': Chinese Interpreters in Late-Nineteenth and Early-Twentieth-Century America." *Journal of American Ethnic History* 30, no. 2 (2011): 5–32.

Omi, Michael, and Howard Winant. "Once More, with Feeling: Reflections on Racial Formation." *PMLA* 123, no. 5 (2008): 1565–72.

———. *Racial Formation in the United States*. 3rd ed. London: Routledge, 2014.

Orozco, Cynthia E. *Agent of Change: Adela Sloss-Vento*. Austin: University of Texas Press, 2020.

Orsi, Robert. "The Religious Boundaries of an Inbetween People: Street Feste and the Problem of the Dark-Skinned Other in Italian Harlem, 1920–1990." *American Quarterly* 44, no. 3 (1992): 313–47.

Pachucki, Mark A., Sabrina Pendergrass, and Michele Lamont. "Boundary Processes: Recent Theoretical Developments and New Contributions." *Poetics* 35, no. 6 (2007): 331–51.

Painter, Nell Irvin. *The History of White People*. New York: W. W. Norton, 2010.

———. *Standing at Armageddon: The United States, 1877–1919*. New York: W. W. Norton, 1989.

Pape, Robert A. "The Jan. 6 Insurrectionists Aren't Who You Think They Are." *Foreign Policy*, January 6, 2022. https://foreignpolicy.com/2022/01/06/trump-capitol-insurrection-january-6-insurrectionists-great-replacement-white-nationalism/.

Pascoe, Peggy. "Gender Systems in Conflict: The Marriages of Mission-Educated Chinese American Women, 1874–1939." *Journal of Social History* 22, no. 4 (1989): 631–52.

Peffer, George Anthony. *If They Don't Bring Their Women Here: Chinese Female Immigration before Exclusion*. Urbana: University of Illinois Press, 1999.

Pegram, Thomas R. *One Hundred Percent American: The Rebirth and Decline of the Ku Klux Klan in the 1920s*. London: Rowman and Littlefield, 2011.

Perkins, Clifford A. "Reminiscences of a Chinese Inspector." *Journal of Arizona History* 17, no. 2 (Summer 1976): 181–200.

Pfaelzer, Jean. *Driven Out: The Forgotten War against Chinese Americans*. Berkeley: University of California Press, 2008.

Pierce, Jason E. *Making the White Man's West: Whiteness and the Creation of the American West*. Boulder: University Press of Colorado, 2016.

Pilcher, Jeffrey M. "Who Chased Out the 'Chili Queens'?: Gender, Race, and Urban Reform in San Antonio, Texas, 1880–1943." *Food and Foodways* 16, no. 3 (2008): 173–200.

Polletta, Francesca, and Jessica Callahan. "Deep Stories, Nostalgia Narratives, and Fake News: Storytelling in the Trump Era." In *Politics of Meaning / Meaning of Politics: Cultural Sociology of the 2016 U.S. Presidential Election*, edited by Jason L. Mast and Jeffrey C. Alexander, 55–73. London: Palgrave Macmillan, 2019.

powell, john a. "The Race and Class Nexus: An Intersectional Perspective." *Law and Inequality* 25 (2007): 355–428.

Prince, Carl E., and Mollie Keller. *The U.S. Customs Service: A Bicentennial History*. Washington, DC: US Customs Service, Department of the Treasury, 1989.

Pulido, Laura. *Black, Brown, Yellow, and Left: Radical Activism in Los Angeles*. Berkeley: University of California Press, 2006.

Pulliam, Christopher, Richard V. Reeves, and Ariel Gelrud Shiro. "The Middle Class Is Already Racially Diverse." Brookings Institution, October 30, 2020. www.brookings .edu/blog/up-front/2020/10/30/the-middle-class-is-already-racially-diverse/.

Rabinowitz, Howard N. *Race Relations in the Urban South, 1865–1890*. New York: Oxford University Press, 1978.

Rable, George C. *But There Was No Peace: The Role of Violence in the Politics of Reconstruction*. Athens: University of Georgia Press, 1984.

Ramos, Raúl A. *Beyond the Alamo: Forging Mexican Ethnicity in San Antonio, 1821–1861*. Chapel Hill: University of North Carolina Press, 2009.

Ray, Victor. "A Theory of Racialized Organizations." *American Sociological Review* 84, no. 1 (2019): 26–53.

Reeves, Richard V., and Camille Busette. "The Middle Class Is Becoming Race-Plural, Just like the Rest of America." Brookings Institution, February 27, 2018. www.brookings.edu/blog/social-mobility-memos/2018/02/27/the-middle-class -is-becoming-race-plural-just-like-the-rest-of-america/.

Rhomberg, Chris. "Class, Race, and Urban Politics: The 1920s Ku Klux Klan Movement in the United States." *Political Power and Social Theory*, 17 (2005): 3–34.

Richard, Mark Paul. *Not a Catholic Nation: The Ku Klux Klan Confronts New England in the 1920s*. Amherst: University of Massachusetts Press, 2015.

Richardson, Joe M. *Christian Reconstruction: The American Missionary Association and Southern Blacks, 1861–1890*. Athens: University of Georgia Press, 1986.

Riis, Jacob August. *How the Other Half Lives: Studies among the Tenements of New York*. 1890; New York: Charles Scribner's Sons, 1914.

Robinson, Cedric J. *Black Marxism: The Making of the Black Radical Tradition*. Chapel Hill: University of North Carolina Press, 2000.

Roediger, David R. *The Sinking Middle Class: A Political History of Debt, Misery, and the Drift to the Right*. New York: Haymarket Books, 2022.

———. *Towards the Abolition of Whiteness: Essays on Race, Politics, and Working Class History*. New York: Verso, 1994.

———. *The Wages of Whiteness: Race and the Making of the American Working Class*. New York: Verso, 1991.

———. *Working toward Whiteness: How America's Immigrants Became White: The Strange Journey from Ellis Island to the Suburbs*. New York: Basic Books, 2006.

Román, Elda María. *Race and Upward Mobility: Seeking, Gatekeeping, and Other Class Strategies in Postwar America*. Palo Alto, CA: Stanford University Press, 2017.

Rubio, Philip F. *There's Always Work at the Post Office: African American Postal Workers and the Fight for Jobs, Justice, and Equality*. Chapel Hill: University of North Carolina Press, 2010.

Ruef, Martin. *Between Slavery and Capitalism: The Legacy of Emancipation in the American South*. Princeton, NJ: Princeton University Press, 2014.

Rutenbeck, Jeffrey B. "Newspapers Trends in the 1870s: Proliferation, Popularization, and Political Independence." *Journalism and Media Communication Quarterly* 72, no. 2 (Summer 1995): 361–75.

Salyer, Lucy E. *Laws as Harsh as Tigers: Chinese Immigrants and the Shaping of Modern Immigration Law*. Chapel Hill: University of North Carolina Press, 1995.

Sandmeyer, Elmer Clarence. *The Anti-Chinese Movement in California*. Urbana: University of Illinois Press, 1991.

San Miguel, Guadalupe, Jr. "From a Dual to a Tri-partite School System: The Origins and Development of Educational Segregation in Corpus Christi, Texas." *Integrated Education* 17, no. 5–6 (1979): 27–38.

Saperstein, Aliya, and Aaron Gullickson. "A 'Mulatto Escape Hatch' in the United States? Examining Evidence of Racial and Social Mobility during the Jim Crow Era." *Demography* 50, no. 5 (2013): 1921–42.

Saxton, Alexander. *The Indispensable Enemy: Labor and the Anti-Chinese Movement in California*. Berkeley: University of California Press, 1971.

———. *The Rise and Fall of the White Republic: Class Politics and Mass Culture in Nineteenth-Century America*. New York: Verso, 2003.

Sennett, Richard. *Families against the City: Middle Class Homes of Industrial Chicago, 1872–1890*. Cambridge, MA: Harvard University Press, 1984.

Sewell, William H., Jr. "Historical Events as Transformations of Structures: Inventing Revolution at the Bastille." *Theory and Society* 25, no. 6 (1996): 841–81.

———. "A Theory of Structure: Duality, Agency, and Transformation." *American Journal of Sociology* 98, no. 1 (1992): 1–29.

Shah, Nyan. *Contagious Divides: Epidemics and Race in San Francisco's Chinatown*. Berkeley: University of California Press, 2001.

Shefter, Martin. "Trade Unions and Political Machines: The Organization and Disorganization of the American Working Class in the Late Nineteenth Century." In *Working-Class Formation: Nineteenth-Century Patterns in Western Europe and the United States*, edited by Ira Katznelson and Aristide R. Zolberg, 197–276. Princeton, NJ: Princeton University Press, 1986.

Sheridan, Thomas E. *Los Tucsonenses: The Mexican Community in Tucson, 1854–1941*. Tucson: University of Arizona Press, 1992.

Smith-Rosenberg, Carroll. *Disorderly Conduct: Visions of Gender in Victorian America*. New York: Oxford University Press, 1987.

Sobek, Matthew. "Occupations." In *Historical Statistics of the United States, Millennial Edition* (online), edited by Susan B. Carter, Scott Sigmund Gartner, Michael R. Haines, Alan L. Olmstead, Richard Sutch, and Gavin Wright, 2-35–2-40. Cambridge: Cambridge University Press, 2006.

Somers, Margaret R. "The Narrative Constitution of Identity: A Relational and Network Approach." *Theory and Society* 23, no. 5 (1994): 605–49.

———. "Narrativity, Narrative Identity, and Social Action." *Social Science History* 16, no. 4 (1992): 591–630.

Stampp, Kenneth M. *The Era of Reconstruction, 1865–1877*. New York: Vintage Books, 1965.

Steinmetz, George. "Reflections on the Role of Social Narratives in Working-Class Formation: Narrative Theory in the Social Sciences." *Social Science History* 16, no. 3 (1992): 489–516.

Stewart, Kenneth L., and Arnoldo De León. *Not Room Enough: Mexicans, Anglos, and Socio-economic Change in Texas, 1850–1900*. Albuquerque: University of New Mexico Press, 1993.

Sueyoshi, Amy. *Discriminating Sex: White Leisure and the Making of the American "Oriental."* Urbana: University of Illinois Press, 2018.

Sullivan, Shannon. *Good White People: The Problem with Middle-Class White Anti-racism*. Albany: State University of New York Press, 2014.

Sullivan, Teresa A., Elizabeth Warren, and Jay Lawrence Westbrook. *The Fragile Middle Class: Americans in Debt*. New Haven, CT: Yale University Press, 2020.

Teng, Emma. *Eurasian: Mixed Identities in the United States, China, and Hong Kong, 1842–1943*. Berkeley: University of California Press, 2013.

Thompson, Jerry. *Tejanos in Gray: Civil War Letters of Captains Joseph Rafael de la Garza and Manuel Yturri*. College Station: Texas A&M University Press, 2011.

Tijerina, Andres. "Foreigners in Their Native Land: The Violent Struggle between Anglos and Tejanos for Land Titles in South Texas during Reconstruction." In *Still the Arena of Civil War: Violence and Turmoil in Reconstruction Texas, 1865–1874*, edited by Kenneth Wayne Howell, 305–25. Denton: University of North Texas Press, 2012.

Trauner, Joan B. "The Chinese as Medical Scapegoats in San Francisco, 1870–1905." *California History* 57, no. 1 (1978): 70–87.

Trotter, Joe W. *Workers on Arrival: Black Labor in the Making of America*. Berkeley: University of California Press, 2019.

US Bureau of the Census. *Historical Statistics of the United States: Colonial Times to 1970*. Vol. 1. Washington, DC: Government Printing Office, 1975.

Valerio-Jiménez, Omar. *River of Hope: Forging Identity and Nation in the Rio Grande Borderlands*. Durham, NC: Duke University Press, 2013.

Vallejo, Jody Agius. *Barrios to 'Burbs: The Making of the Mexican American Middle Class*. Stanford, CA: Stanford University Press, 2012.

Van Riper, Paul P. *History of the United States Civil Service.* New York: Row and Peterson, 1958.

Varon, Alberto. *Before Chicano: Citizenship and the Making of Mexican American Manhood, 1848-1959.* New York: New York University Press, 2018.

Verboven, Koenraad, Myriam Carlier, and Jan Dumolyn. "A Short Manual to the Art of Prosopography." In *Prosopography Approaches and Applications: A Handbook,* edited by Katharine S. B. Keats-Rohan, 36-69. Oxford: Unit for Prosopographical Research, Linacre College, Oxford University, 2007.

Walker, Thomas R. "Economic Opportunity on the Urban Frontier: Wealth and Nativity in Early San Francisco." *Explorations in Economic History* 37, no. 3 (2000): 258-77.

Walton, W. M. *Life and Adventures of Ben Thompson the Famous Texan: Including a Detailed and Authentic Statement of His Birth, History and Adventures, by One Who Has Known Him since a Child.* Facsimile ed. Austin, TX: Steck, 1956.

Warner, Sam Bass. *Streetcar Suburbs: The Process of Growth in Boston, 1870-1900.* Cambridge, MA: Harvard University Press, 1978.

Watts, Eugene J. "Black Political Progress in Atlanta: 1868-1895." *Journal of Negro History* 59, no. 3 (1974): 268-86.

Weatherwax, Sarah J. "Mocking the 'Other': The Irish American Experience." Library Company of Philadelphia. Accessed January 19, 2023. https://librarycompany.org/2019/09/06/mocking-the-other/.

Weber, David J., ed. *Foreigners in Their Native Land: Historical Roots of the Mexican Americans.* Albuquerque: University of New Mexico Press, 1992.

Weber, John. *From South Texas to the Nation: The Exploitation of Mexican Labor in the Twentieth Century.* Chapel Hill: University of North Carolina Press, 2015.

White, Walter F. *A Man Called White.* New York: Viking, 1948.

Wiebe, Robert H. *The Search for Order, 1877-1920.* New York: Macmillan, 1967.

Wimmer, Andreas. *Ethnic Boundary Making: Institutions, Power, Networks.* New York: Oxford University Press, 2013.

Winant, Howard. *Racial Conditions: Politics, Theory, Comparisons.* Minneapolis: University of Minnesota Press, 1994.

Wingfield, Adia Harvey. *No More Invisible Man: Race and Gender in Men's Work.* Philadelphia: Temple University Press, 2013.

Wong, K. Scott. "Cultural Defenders and Brokers: Chinese Responses to the Anti-Chinese Movement." In *Claiming America: Constructing Chinese American Identities during the Exclusion Era,* edited by K. Scott Wong and Sucheng Chan, 3-40. Philadelphia: Temple University Press, 1998.

Wong, K. Scott, and Sucheng Chan, eds. *Claiming America: Constructing Chinese American Identities during the Exclusion Era.* Philadelphia: Temple University Press, 1998.

Woo, Wesley. "Chinese Protestants in the San Francisco Bay Area." In *Entry Denied: Exclusion and the Chinese Community in America, 1882-1943,* edited by Sucheng Chan, 213-45. Philadelphia: Temple University Press, 1991.

Wood, Amy Louise. "Lynching Photography and the Visual Reproduction of White Supremacy." *American Nineteenth Century History* 6, no. 3 (2005): 373-99.

Yellin, Eric S. *Racism in the Nation's Service: Government Workers and the Color Line in Woodrow Wilson's America*. Chapel Hill: University of North Carolina Press, 2013.

Yu, Helen H. "Revisiting the Bamboo Ceiling: Perceptions from Asian Americans on Experiencing Workplace Discrimination." *Asian American Journal of Psychology* 11, no. 3 (2020): 158–67.

Zolberg, Aristide, and Long Litt Woon. "Why Islam Is like Spanish: Cultural Incorporation in Europe and the United States." *Politics and Society* 27, no. 1 (1999): 5–38.

Zunz, Olivier. *Making America Corporate, 1870–1920*. Chicago: University of Chicago Press, 1990.

Unpublished Dissertations and Theses

Chen, Wen-Hsien. "Chinese under Both Exclusion and Immigration Laws." PhD diss., University of Chicago, 1940.

Edelen, Mary B. "Bryan Callaghan II: His Early Political Career, 1885–1899." PhD diss., Trinity University, San Antonio, TX, 1971.

Li, Xiao. "'A New Woman': Yamei Kin's Contributions to Medicine and Women's Rights in China and the United States, 1864–1934." PhD diss., Southern Illinois University at Carbondale, 2020.

Maclachlan, Gretchen E. "Women's Work: Atlanta's Industrialization and Urbanization, 1879–1929." PhD diss., Emory University, 1992.

Martinez, Ana Luisa R. "Voice of the People: Pablo Cruz and *El Regidor*." PhD diss., Texas Tech University, 2003.

Morales, Ralph Edward, III. "The Tejano-Anglo Alliance: Tejanos, Ethnicity, and Politics in Texas, 1832–1865." PhD diss., Texas A&M University, 2010.

Perrin, Teresa Thomas. "Crime and Order in San Antonio during the Civil War and Reconstruction." PhD diss., University of Texas at Austin, 2001.

Waller, Lionel Randall. "The Callaghan Machine and San Antonio Politics, 1885–1912." PhD diss., Texas Tech University, 1973.

Walraven, Edward L. "Ambivalent Americans: Selected Spanish-Language Newspapers' Response to Anglo Domination in Texas, 1830–1910." PhD diss., Texas A&M University, 1999.

Index

abolition, 2, 17, 19

African Americans: as Atlanta postal workers, 7–8, 14, 32–61, 130; criminality and corruption attributed to, 48–53, 59, 61, 72, 77; in federal civil service, 35, 58, 130, 131; in San Antonio, 65, 68, 71; segregation of, 7, 19–20, 26–28, 30, 34, 37–39, 43, 58, 64, 66, 130, 136; sexual predation attributed to, 34–35, 39, 41, 42, 53–55, 61, 130–31, 132, 133; social mobility of, 1, 5–10, 13, 30, 34–35, 37–38, 44, 45, 47, 48–49, 58, 61; as unskilled and semiskilled laborers, 26, 34, 130

Alba, Richard, 24

Allgood, John, 55

American Surety Company, 47

Anderson, M. G., 84

Arnesen, Richard, 24

Arnett, Benjamin W., 53

Athens, Ga., 35

Atlanta, 26; Black homeowners in, 1; Black postal workers in, 7–8, 14, 32–61, 130; growth of, 26–27, 130; mob violence in, 32, 61; progressive reputation of, 26, 27, 32, 61; unskilled Black labor in, 34, 58; White backlash in, 7–8, 10, 14; White working women in, 41, 43

Atlanta University, 40, 49

Aubrey, William J, 85

Back, Les, 25

Bacon, Augustus, 53

Ballantine, Robert L., 57–58

Barr, Alwyn, 65

Barrera, Juan E., 70, 80, 88

Bartlett, Charles, 53, 54

Bass, Elijah, 47

Battle of Valverde (1862), 76

Bexareños Democrátas, 76

Blodgett, Edwin F., 51

Blodgett, Foster, 50

Bonilla-Silva, Eduardo, 21

Brodkin, Karen, 23

Brooks, Charlotte, 28

Brownsville, Texas. 63

Broyles, John, 32, 51, 56–57

Bruce, Philip A., 59

Buck, Alfred E., 47

Burbank, Agnes, 115–16, 117–18, 125–26

Cadena, Celedonio, 69, 70

Callaghan, Bryan V., Jr., 67–68, 75, 79, 81, 85, 86

Cameron, Donaldina, 107

Capital City Club (Atlanta), 46, 60

Cardenas, Juan T., 1, 69, 73, 75–77, 85, 88, 128

Carlisle, John G., 90, 100, 112

Cart War (1857), 67

Cassiano, José, Jr., 86, 88

casta system, 29

Cater, Charles C., 38

Chandler, Silas L., 55–56

Charleston, S.C., 26

Charo, Celestino, 62, 75

Chavez, Ignacio, 69

Chinese Americans: boundary crossing by, 28–29; criminality and corruption attributed to, 10, 106, 112, 113, 123, 124, 125, 133; immigrant brokering and, 92, 95–97; immigration controls on, 14–15, 18, 28, 38, 90, 91, 93–94; as

Printed in the USA
CPSIA information can be obtained
at www.ICGtesting.com
LVHW041955171023
761387LV00005B/29

9 781469 673493